In a Dark
TIME

In a Dark
TIME

The Apocalyptic Temper in the American Novel of the Nuclear Age

by

Joseph Dewey

Purdue University Press
West Lafayette, Indiana

Book and jacket designed by David L. Sigman

Library of Congress Cataloging-in-Publication Data

Dewey, Joseph, 1957–
In a dark time: the apocalyptic temper in the American novel of
the nuclear age / Joseph Dewey.
p.   cm.
Includes bibliographical references.
ISBN 1-55753-001-7 :
1. American fiction—20th century—History and criticism.
2. Apocalyptic literature—History and criticism. 3. End of the
world in literature. I. Title.
PS374.A65D4 1990   89-35864
813′.5409353—dc20

The angel said to me:
"These words are trustworthy and true;
the Lord, the God of prophetic spirits,
has sent his angel to show his servants
what must happen very soon."

"Remember, I am coming soon!
Happy the man who heeds
the prophetic message of this book!"

Revelation

Table of Contents

Acknowledgments

In addition to acknowledging the tremendous assistance of Purdue University Press and Douglas Robinson, Kenneth Roemer, and W. Warren Wagar, who provided critical guidance early in the project, I would like to tender particular thanks for the ceaseless encouragement and gentle direction of William T. Stafford. By example, he taught me the timeless virtue of literary criticism—the wisdom to relish the time spent with books. I would also like to express my thanks and love to my wife, Julie, whose assistance throughout the project was fueled by indomitable optimism.

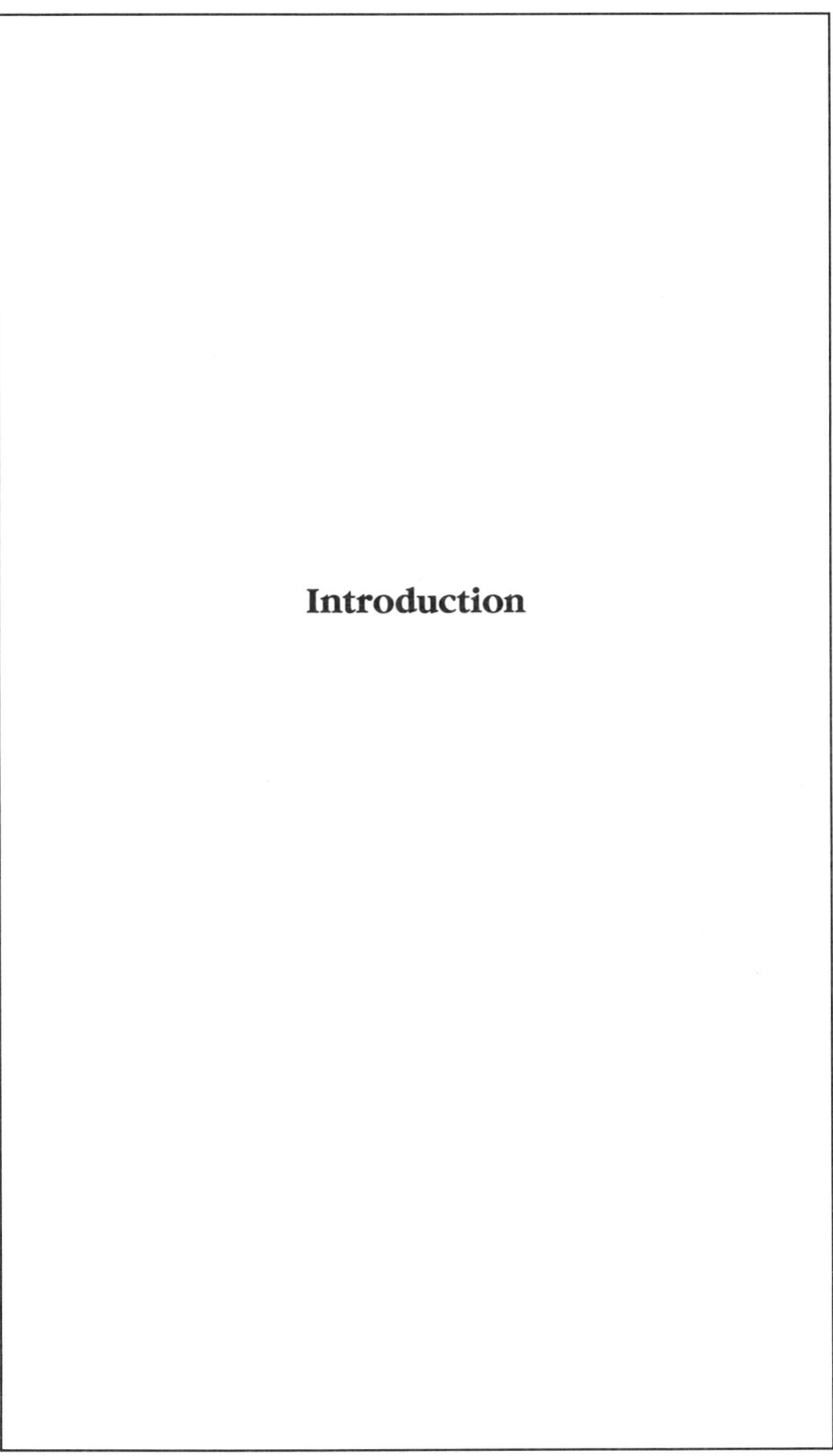

Introduction

The Shatterer of Worlds
The Apocalyptic Temper
in the American Tradition

This was the nearest to doomsday one can possibly imagine. I am sure that at the end of the world—in the last millisecond of the earth's existence—the last man will see something very similar to what we have seen.

George Kistiakowsky, chemist and explosives expert,
after the Alamogordo test blast

What was gunpowder? Trivial. What was electricity? Meaningless. This atomic bomb is the Second Coming in wrath.

Winston Churchill

We have discovered the most terrible weapon in the history of the world. It may be the fire of destruction prophesied in the Euphrates Valley era, after Noah and his fabulous ark.

Harry Truman

*All autumn, the chafe and jar
of nuclear war;
We have talked our extinction to death.
I swim like a minnow
behind my studio window.*

*Our end drifts nearer,
The moon lifts
radiant with terror.
The state
is a diver under a glass bell.*

> *A father's no shield*
> *for his child.*
> *We are like a lot of wild*
> *spiders crying together,*
> *but without tears . . .*
> **Robert Lowell, "Fall 1961"**

In *Black Rain*, Masuji Ibuse's powerful 1969 documentary-novel about the Hiroshima blast, the narrator, a businessman in Hiroshima, is stunned by the force of the early morning detonation. But he is more puzzled by the nature of the giant, swirling, mushroomlike cloud that pushes up defiantly from the heart of his shattered city:

> In its texture, it reminded [him] of cumulo-nimbus clouds [he] had seen in photographs taken after the Great Kanto Earthquake. But this one trailed a single, thick leg beneath it, and reached up high into the heavens. Flattening out at its peak, it swelled out fatter and fatter like an opening mushroom. . . . Although the cloud seemed at first glance to be motionless, it was by no means so. The head of the mushroom would billow out . . . again; each time, some part or other of its body would emit a fierce light. . . . And all the time it went on boiling out unceasingly from within. Its stalk, like a twisted veil of fine cloth, went on swelling busily too. The cloud loomed over the city as though waiting to pounce. (Ibuse, 53)

On that humid, late-summer morning, an awesome image entered the cultural mythos: the stout, churning column of the atomic mushroom cloud. Like the dazed citizenry of Hiroshima, Americans (as the first developers of the weaponry and the only culture to use it against another) have been puzzling just what such a terrifying image implies. We have become certain of only one premise: this force demands not only an entirely new vocabulary, but a new way of thinking. As W. H. Auden prophetically wrote in *For the Time Being*, it was as if before the introduction of "this Horror," this "outrageous novelty," we were just "children." It seemed, Auden wrote, merely "a moment ago." Now,

> nothing
> We learnt before It was there is now of the slightest use,
> For nothing like it has happened before. It's as if
> We had left our house for five minutes to mail a letter
> And during that time the living room had changed places
> With the room behind the mirror over the fireplace;
> It's as if, waking up with a start, we discovered
> Ourselves stretched out flat on the floor, watching
>   our shadow
> Sleepily stretching itself at the window. (ll. 64–65)

The careful government secrecy that insulated the work at Los Alamos guaranteed that the atomic age would be born quite suddenly—indeed, William L. Laurence, the *New York Times* science reporter handpicked by the government to cover the Manhattan Project, wrote that the thundering reverberation that quite literally shook the New Mexico desert floor the July morning of the Alamogordo test blast was nothing less than "the first cry of a newborn world" (Browne and Munro, 37). Never before had the world entered a new age so dramatically, so self-consciously. Unlike the introduction of gunpowder, the incandescent light bulb, the telephone, or even the airplane—in which the implications emerged over considerable time—the Hiroshima blast immediately ushered in a new age that was announced in world headlines, analyzed in political columns of every stripe, splashed across covers of news magazines. As E. B. White recorded in his *New Yorker* column on 18 August 1945, "For the first time in our lives, we can feel the disturbing vibrations of complete human readjustment. Usually the vibrations are so faint as to go unnoticed. This time they are so strong that even the ending of a war is overshadowed" (108).

Pitched headfirst into something called the atomic age, Americans were confronted with a mystery, a power that defied the military and political vocabulary that first tried to encompass it. The boiling columns of the Hiroshima and Nagasaki blasts raised questions that could not be answered by either the reassuring certainties of the new physics or the nerveless, calm necessities of geopolitics. There seemed born into the world a most supernatural presence, one that commanded a religious response. Indeed, Robert Oppenheimer—the principal architect of what he termed the atomic "gadget"—upon witnessing the mushroom cloud ascend in a single, bright, defiant sweep above Alamogordo, was moved to quote from the Bhagavad Gita: "I am become Death, the shatterer of worlds" (Wyden, 212). Initial reactions to the Hiroshima and Nagasaki blasts mingled the emotional language of religious awe with the curt jargon of political and military strategy. Searching for words able to capture the implications of the mushroom cloud, journalists, military leaders, politicians (most prominently, Truman and Churchill), and even the atomic scientists themselves found sufficient language in the radical vocabulary of religion.

In the celebratory rush that marked the rapid close of World War II, the atomic age itself commenced with a flurry of optimistic, confident predictions for life in a new world. Before the full implications of the atomic weapon were appreciated, the armistice celebrations hailed the bomb as proper response to Japanese atrocities and savagery, from the sneak attack on Pearl Harbor to the grueling death march at Bataan to the fanatical campaigns of the desperate kamikazes to the genocidal campaigns in China.¹ And the promise of the new age seemed inexhaustible. As Truman intoned, humanity had now harnessed the "basic power of the universe. . . . the force from which the sun draws its power" (Zuckerman, 111). Much like the first European explorers of the North American continent who entertained the tantalizing notion of a return to Eden, post-Hiroshima America, poised to take its own first hesitant steps into a radically new world, dreamed of a paradise. The atom would accomplish miracles in the medical field; it would virtually eliminate physical labor as cities and industries converted to the cheap, inexhaustible fuel supply; and it would certainly bring genuine international security. Powers around the world would be forced to renounce traditional war, for, as the title of a collection of essays published shortly after 1945 intoned, it was now either *One World or None*. It was an unfortunate accident of history, the argument followed, that the world at large was introduced to atomic energy as a tool of mass destruction.

Along with such potent idealism, however, grew fears that the laboratories at Los Alamos had unleashed a frightening power, a genie that would never return to its bottle. Disturbing thoughts dampened the euphoric response to a world suddenly at peace: questions about the ethics of Truman's decision to use the bomb twice; confusion about the lingering effects of radiation sickness; horror at the grim evidence of the absolute leveling of two major Japanese cities; and certainty that the technoscientific expertise that had assembled the bomb could never be kept solely in American hands. More profound was the revival of the Frankenstein complex, the fear, which Warren Wagar has identified, that has haunted Westerners since the age of the machine commenced— that our own technologies can not only dehumanize and enslave us but finally destroy us as well (Wagar, 25). Commentators marked the similarities between the blasts that decimated Hiroshima and Nagasaki and the images associated with the traditional Christian apocalypse: the suddenness, the all-engulfing fire, the disturbing completeness of obliteration. The firestorm that erupted in the heart of Hiroshima recalled God's promise to Noah—no more rain, the fire next time. The squat, cumbersome payload delivered by the reeling Enola Gay suggested eerily what Rev. 20:9 promised: the fire that "came down from God out of heaven and devoured them." The scientists who had worked so tirelessly to complete the Manhattan Project moved uncertainly between roles as new-age Promethean gods and latter-day Doctor Frankensteins or Fausts who had tinkered with knowledge forbidden humans. By 1956, Oppenheimer himself confessed, "We did the Devil's work" (Wyden, 351).

If the world had been ushered toward the gates of a new Eden, the language of the nuclear age intoned as well a darker vocabulary borrowed from Revelation. The billowing mushroom cloud represented the last crisis in human history. War was now genocide, civilians mere targets, and strategy now extermination. What had been visited upon the Japanese, any technologically advanced civilization—even Japan itself—could someday visit upon the United States. Like the first-generation Puritans, Americans now faced the very real belief in the imminent, very real end of the very real world. Once again, a generation pondered the possibility that it would be the world's last. The fiery sweep of the mushroom cloud would precede the world's consummation like John's thundering horsemen. As the German philosopher Karl Jaspers passionately argued in his 1959 treatise on living in the nuclear age, "The possible reality which we must henceforth reckon with . . . is no longer a fictitious end of the world. It is no world's end at all, but the extinction of life on the surface of the planet" (4).

That the trigger for this new apocalypse would be humanity rather than God added to the urgency—humans, it would seem, would plot, construct, and then execute their own demise. In the convoluted logic that would come more and more to define "reasonable" nuclear strategy, any nation in the vicious spiraling race to protect itself could destroy itself for its own good. As a worried Albert Einstein, whose explorations of the new physics had laid much of the groundwork for the formulation of both the fission and fusion bombs, cautioned, "the unleashed power of the atom has changed everything, save our modes of thinking, and thus we drift toward unparalleled disaster" (Schley, 451). What so violently shook the generation coming to terms with the smoke and fire of Hiroshima was that this mysterious power undermined a certainty as old as Ecclesiastes: suddenly, the earth would not necessarily abide forever. For all its technological wizardry, the nuclear age had returned people to a most medieval mindset. But without a reliable God figure who would incinerate the planet only as prelude to glorious eternity, humanity had only the grim act of what Raymond Aron termed "technological surprise," when humanity the creator would be humanity the destroyer.

The implications of the nuclear age demanded a sublime response, a willingness to face the big question. The bomb demanded an awareness, an engagement with the human community and with human history long out of fashion during the aesthetics and word explorations of the early century's literature. Gertrude Stein, a remnant of the ennui and convoluted, self-exhausting aestheticism that so characterized the Lost Generation, commented wearily in 1946:

> They asked me what I thought of the atomic bomb. I said I had not been
> able to take any interest in it. . . . What is the use, if they are really as

> destructive as all that there is nothing left and if there is nothing there [is]
> nobody to be interested and nothing to be interested about. . . . So you
> see the atomic [bomb] is not at all interesting, not any more interesting
> than any other machine. (3)

The bored response of the Lost Generation seemed radically out of place
as history had spontaneously created the Last Generation. Despite the
measured response of the government and the military that an actual
atomic cataclysm sufficient to destroy civilization (the so-called Armageddon Syndrome) was militarily infeasible, politically impractical, and
geographically impossible, what humanity glimpsed in the noiseless
flash over Hiroshima was the possibility of its own final, consummation.

Yet the response from the American literary community to the mushroom cloud would be slow in coming. As Paul Boyer has so thoroughly
sketched, the literary conscience of America did not seem ready in the
1940s and even in the 1950s to engage the menace of the mushroom
cloud. There were, of course, isolated responses: John Hersey's *Hiroshima* (1946), a documentary novel whose flat, reportorial voice suggested bare restraint before the magnitude of the bomb's fury, sought
by its unemotional narrative honesty to bring the reader into the experience; and Laurence's emotive newspaper panegyrics to the atomic age,
published in the collection *Dawn of Zero* (1946), which now prove to
be an uneven hodgepodge of the mystic and the journalistic. The bomb,
perhaps in its very apocalyptic suggestiveness, seemed a power beyond
the imagination. Indeed, Robert Jay Lifton and Lawrence Langer have
both sought to define this modern experience with the implications of
species-wide death, Lifton most prominently with his studies on Hiroshima and its victims, and Langer with his work on literature of the
Jewish Holocaust. They have both hypothesized about how the contemporary mind shuts down in the face of such catastrophe. Lifton has
explored what he calls the psychic numbing, the closing off of the mind
before such simple totality; and Langer, using the experience of the
concentration camps, argues the impotence of the human imagination,
the impossibility of contending with the implications of "nuclear-
induced extinction" (61).

But as Lewis Mumford, an early and vocal critic of atomic weaponry,
cautioned, "If our civilization is not to produce greater holocausts, our
writers will have to become something more than merely mirrors of its
violence and disintegration; they. . .will have to regain the initiative
for. . .the force of life, chaining up the demons we have allowed to run
loose" (109). Yet, save for a glut of forgettable speculative fiction that
embraced atomic devastation early, the American literary community
pondered the bomb only in tentative ways.[2]

With the unleashing of the hydrogen bomb in the early 1950s and the apocalyptic rhetoric of national paranoia that ensued in the formulative days of the cold war when the world divided—like John's vision—into the forces of light and darkness, the American public began its most curious acquiescence to living with imminent destruction. The government launched a campaign to improve the image of the bomb (Boyer, 291–302) even as it stockpiled nuclear weapons and withheld disturbing information about the frightening long-term effects of radiation. A nation began to accept the apocalypse, to dig backyard bomb shelters, to run air-raid drills in public schools, and to indulge the elaborate fantasy of civil defense. The bomb was simply the sole measure able to counter the menace of encroaching Soviet totalitarianism.

This collective act of willed blindness was enhanced once nuclear testing went underground following the Test Ban Treaty of 1963. As the awesome image of the mushroom cloud disappeared from newspapers and magazines, as it moved underground, so also did America submerge its atomic fears. And in the early 1960s, as the American novel began to work with the implications of the nuclear age, it addressed just this community willing to indulge the illusion of diminished risk.

This collective decision is not surprising. Jimmy Carter, in his Farewell Address in 1981, warned that the present nuclear arsenal would unleash "more destructive power than in all of the Second World War every second for the long afternoon that it would take for all the missiles and bombs to fall" (Humphrey, 195). If the atomic age was conceived as the human mind tried to comprehend how a single bomb carried by a single plane could in a single stroke incinerate a city and 130,000 civilians, how much more difficult is our job: to grapple with such power detonating every second. To complicate further the process of articulating a response to the nuclear age, the most direct treatments of the day of nuclear wrath itself come off as labored and as artificial as Michael Wigglesworth's 1662 attempt to create the Christian day of judgment. These fictions—*On the Beach* and *Alas, Babylon* come to mind—seem unconvincing, didactic to the point of accusative, and oddly (even serenely) cinematic.

Here, then, was a mystery, the product of unfathomable physics, an energy tapped in desert wastes, an energy able to exterminate in a single long afternoon the triad upon which Western civilization rested: Nature, God, and Art. Commencing earnestly in the 1960s, triggered at least partly by the nuclear High Noon over Cuba, the American novel began its exploration into how people could adjust to life in the thick penumbra of the mushroom cloud, how we could begin to think about the unthinkable. Like Jonathan Edwards, who harnessed the radical vocabulary of

Newtonian physics, these American writers faced squarely the age birthed by nuclear physics and found in its very darkness, difficult avenues to hope by rediscovering (as Edwards) that most potent, traditional response to a history in crisis: the apocalyptic temper.

Long before the mushroom cloud curled up into the leaden morning skies of Hiroshima, American literature had been most fascinated by the power and the myth of the apocalypse. Indeed, since its very beginnings, America has been curiously fascinated by visions of the end. The first-generation Puritans accepted and even celebrated the sobering paradox of a New World poised, nevertheless, on the very eve of the latter days of history. As David Ketterer has rightly observed, the apocalyptic temper thrives in periods of change; and in its two centuries America has seldom been at rest. America has flourished despite apocalyptic seers in every generation who have restlessly decoded the breakneck pace of America's unfolding history into a pattern that points toward an imminent end to that very history. Forsaking comfort in the obvious material success of the American experiment, these apocalyptics have proclaimed, often enthusiastically, the approaching end.

The apocalyptic temper, however, is one easily caricatured (and simplified): The End is Near in grim, black lettering on placards hoisted by bearded, robed, unnervingly calm disciples of some lunatic fringe. But restricting the apocalyptic temper to such warnings about impending universal holocaust or even to the more familiar notions of swirling visions of great horned beasts clashing with bands of militant angels robs the myth of the apocalypse of its most vital power: to reassure in times of widespread crisis.[3] Supremely, the apocalyptic temper, as Bernard McGinn defined it in talking about medieval apocalypticism, is a response, voiced often by a highly literate, imaginative minority, to a culture suddenly convulsed by evidence of a radical discontinuity in its history (31). History, the reassuring flow of events that contributes to a benevolent sense of pattern, is disturbed by a crisis or an event radically out of step with that history. The apocalyptic temper is an attempt by a culture that is genuinely puzzled and deeply disturbed to understand itself and its own time. In a culture caught by a crisis that challenges the very undergirdings of its makeup—its people suspended in graceless poses of helplessness, uncertainty, and fear—visionaries puzzle out a way of setting the present crisis within a larger context, a pattern greater than ever suspected, and judge that the crisis at hand is certainly of considerable dimension but is nevertheless part of an order as wide as the cosmos itself, an order that points humanity toward nothing less than the finale of its history.

Clearly, such self-appointment smacks of grandiloquent self-indulgence, the satisfaction from the romantic notion that *this* generation will be the one to send humanity finally over the threshold. Every culture, every age in the Hebraic-Christian tradition has formulated a considerable canon of apocalyptic literature, a genre that developed during the time of the Jewish oppressions and the first hundred years after Christ, culminating in perhaps the most recognized Christian apocalyptic tract, the Revelation of John of Patmos. It is surmised that Revelation was composed during the reign of Antiochus Domitian roughly seventy-five years after the death of Christ as support literature for Christians who needed inspiration to maintain faith during a period of harsh political, social, and religious sanctions and who needed reassurances that God had not forgotten the faithful, despite the failure of the Parousia to occur as Christ's message had again and again implied it would. The conditions that gave rise to this apocalyptic expression are familiar and central to our present concerns: a generation, caught by the surprise of history, striving to create a workable if radical method to respond to the intolerable evidence of its own history—a culture asserting, despite the considerable evidence of experience, a reason and a way to hope.

The apocalyptic temper, then, suggests that such challenges to rooted beliefs or to traditional institutions spark an outpouring of literature that refuses despair, resists surrender to an uncooperative history implied by the grim legend The End Is Near. In the face of apparent anomie, the apocalyptic temper resists the extremes of passivity and panic by speaking of continuity, by offering direction to a people overwhelmed by sheer process. It resists the crisis of change by inculcating change into its very vocabulary. It speaks most eloquently and most directly to a community of the frightened, the despairing, the uncertain and assures it that the apparent disorder of history will finally affirm order, will finally give heart. Refusing the fantasy of simple optimism, the apocalyptic temper resolves to face squarely the staggering implications of history gone suddenly awry by suggesting that the present can be understood compassionately only by imagining the end itself. In all its sacred and secular forms, the apocalyptic temper is a vital effort of the imagination—a contrivance—whether voiced with the authority of religious vision or published as a confection of speculative fiction. As Frank Kermode forcefully argued in his indispensable book *The Sense of an Ending* (1967), seen in an unflattering angle the apocalyptic temper is tyrannical, a fascistic attempt by people caught in the vast uncertain present (what Kermode calls the "middest") to impress time into rigid pattern. But the apocalyptic temper is finally not about that pattern or even about the end itself, where all mystery is resolved, all questions answered, all troubles calmed. The apocalyptic temper, as Otto Friedrich has carefully detailed in his absorbing historic study of the urge toward the apocalypse, is inspired by singular acts of history; Friedrich cites a scant seven such events since the rise of Rome. In its finest expression, the apocalyptic temper measures the effects of living at the very epicenter of one of history's truly altering events—the birth of Christ, the dismantling of Catholic hegemony, the discovery of the New World, the introduction of atomic weaponry. Confronted by the evidence of the historical discontinuity, the apocalyptic temper offers what Jacques Ellul defined as a counterreality, one hidden in the present chaos, a positive presence that counters the evidence of absence and gives heart to those still living within history's experience.

On the surface, the apocalyptic temper can be indicted as a deliberate withdrawal from history, an abandonment that seeks in visions of consummation a simple, quick way out of history. This charge is argued most forcefully by Martin Buber and Robert Alter and most emotionally by D. H. Lawrence. Putting aside the question raised by these men, that the idea of the end is a sort of collective paranoia, and assuming for a moment, as its literature does, that the end is, indeed, near, a response to the charge might begin in a quick classification scheme of the different approaches to the end. At the risk of simplification, the literature of endtimes can be separated into three broad types: the cataclysmic imagination, the millennialist spirit, and the apocalyptic temper. Each discipline, of course, shares basic tenets: a belief in the incessant linearity of history; an unashamed sense of cosmic scale; a sobering belief that history is best understood as a cooperative structure of beginning, middle, and end; the strong possibility of a fast-approaching end; a general dissatisfaction with the moral life of the present culture; a strong awareness of contemporary crisis that draws a definite line between good and evil; an inherently dramatic approach to history that is as riveting as any drama rushing toward a shuddering climax. But significant differences exist.

Largely (though not wholly) the province of speculative fiction (as the later treatment of Nathanael West will indicate), the cataclysmic imagination is the most unsettling, the most (perhaps unintentionally) cinematic, the most forceful and, finally, the most defiantly despairing. Drawn to the big event itself, the cataclysmic imagination ranges over methodology—how-to manuals for species extermination, from traditional natural disasters (earthquakes, floods, colliding comets, exploding stars, misaligned planets) to synthetic cataclysms (ecological, technological, nuclear) to the most inventive scenarios of extraterrestrial or even divine interventions. Relentlessly end-oriented, by its very nature harrowing, the cataclysmic imagination savors the radical violence of imminent planetary alteration: the buildup and climax of the apocalyptic event itself. Although inventive at times in devising the means of species extermination, the cataclysmic imagination offers little more than a raging polemic against humanity's moral confusions and shortcomings. Reading widely in the cataclysmic tradition is a rather numbing experience—like watching a succession of brakeless automobiles slowly heading up a long incline.

Far from such a notion of humanity's helplessness, the millennialist spirit accepts endings most cheerfully because of the fanatic commitment to better worlds emerging from the ruins. Possessing studied and insistent optimism, the millennialist spirit can both accept history and refute its evidence with an unflagging commitment to humanity—one fueled either by religious faith or, in the case of an Enlightenment perspective, in humanity itself. If the cataclysmic imagination dwells purposefully on the apocalyptic event itself, the millennialist spirit merely begins at such a moment and then builds, steadily and with pioneering determination, the new earth and the new heavens. Contemporary upheavals, the sudden sense of discontinuity, meld into a pattern that promises, once certain drastic measures are achieved (by an act of divine intervention for traditional fundamentalists or by the sheer will of history itself as, for instance, the Marxist vision suggests), humanity can step collectively into a new age. The cataclysmic imagination drives headlong toward the horizon; the millennialist spirit maintains itself only by keeping the horizon forever receding.

Both approaches to the endtimes have merit. The cataclysmic imagination seethes with a passion, a vision, and an accompanying rhetoric that enthralls. The rush to final crisis reduces the apparent tremblings of contemporary history into mere mild disturbances, a sort of "you ain't seen nothin' yet" effect. And the millennialist spirit offers a resilient confidence, an ever-expanding tomorrow. But both fail at critical points. The cataclysmic imagination reduces humanity to the huddled masses waiting for judgment or for simple execution. The millennialist spirit staves off the periodic threats of history but imposes on humanity an interminable sentence of waiting, of perpetual transition until, as Kermode cautions, the transition itself becomes an age. The choices, then, are default or deferment. Neither copes with history; neither faces history; neither can offer a message of hope or a strategy for living in endtimes. If, as Nathan Scott has rightfully observed, the idea of the apocalypse involves "expensive emotions" ("'New Heav'ns, New Earth'," 5)—after all, nothing less than a collapse of confidence in humanity—then certainly a finer sort of response must be tendered, finer than the unforgiving anger harbored by the cataclysmic imagination or the serene, detached assurances offered by the millennialist spirit. In either case, radical discontent forbids hope. For the present, humanity is left either to quake in fear or to tremble in anticipation. But the question persists, How are we to live in terminal times?

Between the certain destruction and the hopeful construction rests the steadying vision of the apocalyptic temper, a way of responding by a culture in crisis, a way of collective coping, a way of seeing history, and a way of understanding a contemporary world by accepting the very grimmest evidence of decline and professing nevertheless a healthy conviction that history need not be consigned to simple contingency because, for the moment, questions loom too large for adequate response. If humanity is indeed poised in the last stages of history, its people need a strategy for living without being offered the alternatives of waiting for the hammerfall or anticipating the hammerstrokes of a new earth being constructed. Consider a middle-aged patient in a hospital given irrefutable evidence of a catastrophic terminal illness. Reeling, stunned suddenly into an awareness of his own fragile mortality, he confronts the fact of death, each day now charged with urgency and importance because of that cold, quick glimpse of his own certain ending. Ministered by the cataclysmic imagination and by the millennialist spirit, the American experience, like that patient, is offered only a most dubious choice: the cold comfort of accuracy or the pleasant illusion of recovery.

Neither approach confronts the more fundamental need of such a confused and uncertain "patient"—how to get through the night, how to live carrying the awareness of the approaching end like a battered steamer trunk; how to accept that life indeed has proximate termination. The apocalyptic temper moves away from the impossible abstracts of life and death to recognize that living and dying are terms for the same process. Consider the Zen parable of a man chased by a hungry tiger. Trapped, he is driven over the edge of a sharp precipice and hangs there gripping only the slender branch of a tree. Dangling, he is suspended literally between life and death: between the hot, leathery breaths of the famished beast and the death drop into a deep chasm. At that very moment, he notices an ordinary berry bush sprouting wild among the crags of the cliffside. Hesitatingly, he plucks a single berry, tastes it, and finds it the very sweetest fruit imaginable.

That sweetness, distilled from the experience of the quotidian and charged by the awareness of momentary extinction, is what the apocalyptic temper seeks. Far from the simple, flashy pessimism of the cataclysmic imagination, far from the naive optimism of the millennialist spirit, the apocalyptic temper, as John R. May has argued, accepts the "agony of history" (*Toward a New Earth,* 227), refuses to indulge simply waiting for the end. The fact of the end, as D. S. Russell rightly observed, is of far more importance than the hour of the end (*Method,* 263). The apocalyptic temper, again in May's phrase, is the acceptance of the "full implication of living in history" (*Toward a New Earth,* 21)—within its shifts, contradictions, and sudden, volcanic changes.

The apocalyptic temper, then, brings more than what Kermode describes as the joy of plotting. It is more than a collective paranoia, a defensive strategy affected by the scared against the terrors of a history that seems to spin wildly out of control. It is more than a sugar pill for those who in the dark moments seem to see the very beast itself slouching toward Bethlehem. It is more than simply supplying form to time, a shape when it seems most defiantly shapeless. It is supremely an act of the moral imagination, a gesture of confidence and even defiance that challenges its own assumptions that history is itself tracked toward endings. The fact of the end serves only to create the urgency and the context for meaningful action in a suspenseful present. It is a singular, signal act of faith in humanity, giving us a way of living in a dark time. Far from a retreat from reality, it is—in the useful phrasing of Ketterer— the "radical reformulation of the nature of reality" (203). When history, then, goes critical; when God seems withdrawn, or silent or, even worse, casketed; when, as in this century, the finest instruments of our own technologies seem bent on destroying us; when night seems thickest and the earth itself an intricate absurdity, the apocalyptic temper refutes the bated breath of the cataclysmic imagination and the nonchalant breathlessness of the millennialist spirit. It refuses either simple annihilation or the simplistic spiral of inevitable progress to offer the oxymoron of humanity as a creature brave and timid: a refugee in a lifeboat from a distant, swamped ship, with back straight, bravely and purposefully rowing ahead. In its finest expression, it is a stirring assertion of dignity and the reassurance that a dangerous present is fraught as much with hope as it is with danger.

The apocalyptic temper has proven a most capable strategy for American writers, who have projected events of the nation's history into a cosmic design that has reassured even during the most uncertain times that America is possessed of a destiny greater than the disturbances of its own history. In every upheaval, apocalyptics were heard. When the first-generation Puritans faced the hostile wastes of coastal Massachusetts, they were convinced that this inhabitable wilderness was God's New World, His assurance that the work of the Protestant Reformation would continue on schedule to the final consummation. During the American Revolution, apocalyptics assured the colonists—pitted against the British Empire—that this America was an invention destined for liberty and was certain, once freed of British interests, to become the focal point of the coming reign of the saints on earth. When the Civil War split that nation, apocalyptics North and South valiantly recreated the bloody war of attrition played out in daily headlines as nothing less than the long-promised showdown between the forces of light and darkness, a biblical crusade in blue and grey whose outcome would be part of the ongoing destiny God had planned for the New World. During the labor unrest that threatened the self-satisfactions of the Gilded Age, the apocalyptic voice, appropriated now by the dissatisfied and the oppressed, warned of a coming workers' revolt, a sociopolitical Dies Irae that would lead to the creation of a workers' utopia more in line with God's promised New World than the decadent luxury of the capitalist state. When America faced the holocaust of World War I, apocalyptics sorted through the difficult fragments of their history and, tortured by disbelief, tried nevertheless to fashion from them a pattern sufficient to explain the horrors of the Great War.

It would, of course, be a simplification to suggest that the apocalyptic temper, so constant in American letters, has undergone no significant change. Once potent and reassuring in its vision of a directed time, it has undergone a steady decline into exhaustion that parallels a wider, more complicated cultural drift from God. The key to understanding this emerging impotence is the growing sense, during the last two centuries, that the end of the world is a fiction. That awareness followed the steady exhaustion of a sense of a core energy able to generate a believable vision of a world coming to an end. For Puritan apocalyptics, that core energy was clear: the benevolent might of God the Creator controlling every spin of His planet; every action, every achievement, every setback was part of His will. When the Enlightenment recast God into the diligent watchmaker, absenting Him from the day-to-day affairs of humans, the consolation of an approaching end to the cosmos seemed most impractical. Newton coaxed the Christian cosmos into a neat universe governed by meticulous laws of motion that seemed to resist the deus-ex-machina climax of the apocalypse and, indeed, rendered it something of an embarrassment. What emerged instead was an emphasis on the millennialist spirit, a secular, political faith in the thousand-year reign of the saints on earth, a utopian society of human cooperation. But this vision of a secular utopia, which so animated social and political discourse of the eighteenth and nineteenth centuries, eluded historical realization. As America drifted into a world deprived of the rich omnipotence of God, its writers, confronted by the puzzling inability of humanity to achieve the full promise of its own progress, faced the dubious possibility of time as mere mutability that mocked apocalyptic endings. They were left more and more with pieces and less and less with design.

There emerged, however, a faith in the creative energy of people—not in the political collective, but in the creative individual. Influenced by Continental theories of aesthetics that trumpeted a new resiliency of art, American writers in the early decades of this century (a generation that witnessed firsthand the cataclysm of world war) asserted that the apocalyptic energy able to create a pattern to the drift of time rested not with God and not with the political person, but with the artist. By creating graphic representations of the endtimes, these apocalyptics, most disturbingly fascinated by the cataclysmic imagination, bore not the traditional apocalyptic message of sublime finale, but the uncertain comfort of an artistically accurate rendering of the exhausted, final shuddering of a civilization rotten at its core. As God faded and as the political person proved powerless, America seemed propelled not toward glory, but toward an aesthetic catastrophe as the artist appropriated the roles of both creater and destroyer.

To assert with more completeness this scheme of the gradual exhaustion of the apocalyptic temper, this study will begin by highlighting Edwards, Herman Melville, and West. All three writers are traditionally associated with the apocalypse, and each, in turn, marks the shift in that temper from the hope in God to trust in the collective to faith in the artist-seer. To listen to the apocalyptic rhetoric that thunders in Edwards, that despairs in Melville, and that snickers in West is to sense the shifting away from passion and conviction toward bemusement and contempt. As the apocalyptic temper proved less and less effective against time, the menacing drift of history—as Melville first sensed—grew more and more apocalypse-proof.

When European adventurers first electrified the Continent with news that a New World had been found, both explorers and exploiters penned journals and promotional narratives rich in Edenic hyperbole. Finding the tractless wilderness of North America an irresistible parallel to the garden of Genesis, these writers looked back to Eden and, profoundly moved, sensed that God had allowed humanity to regain the paradise lost by Adam and Eve. This New World would be Europe's second chance, a return to the prelapsarian world that defied the evidence of European history, its decline and fall into sin since Eden. The ocean journey to the New World became, in its essence, an allegory for the miracle of Christian renewal, the journey from corruption to innocence.

The Puritans who crusaded to the New World shared this conviction of an unspoiled continent destined for a significant place in the unfolding of God's history. But far from being a return to the garden or a starting over, the New World represented to them the fulfillment of history, its culmination and completion. The Puritans translated the American wilderness not into the language of Genesis, but of Revelation, not of beginnings, but of glorious endings. The Commonwealth Era that fostered the Puritan sect in England felt keenly that history was actually entering into the final showdown between God and the Antichrist. The Cromwell Protectorate thrived amid militant apocalyptic urgency, the ongoing sense of crisis, and sobering preparation as it steered England toward the fast-approaching triumph of the forces of good. The Puritans in New England maintained in the New World the protectorate's crisis mentality and its sense of approaching endings. This continent, discovered at a providential moment in the inexorable process of the Reformation, would provide a suitable setting for an actual glorious millennium on earth, one that would usher in God's return. Far from fearing the certainty that humanity was pointed toward the final days of history, the Puritans, with the militant vigor of their spiritual conviction, faced the task of preparing themselves for the promised return of God.

Because they could accept fully the implications of living in the end-times, these Puritans generated a considerable body of literature firmly within the tradition of the apocalyptic temper. The first-generation Puritans voiced the steadying faith consistent with the apocalyptic temper. No crisis could shake its ongoing crusade in God's own wilderness. Certain that they understood history's larger pattern, secure within their religious commitment, they faced shipwrecks, Indian raids, stubborn or failed crops, even an earthquake (in 1638), and, much more profound, the steady, grinding isolation and terrifying sense of displacement—all with the resilient optimism that God sanctified their mission and that the day of glory was fast approaching. Even as they built the New World, they waited for its end.

Listen, for example, to John Cotton, who felt with unflappable assurance that New England would be the setting of Christ's kingdom on earth and who preached with compelling urgency that members of his own congregation would likely live to see its establishment, would live to experience the apocalypse itself. To understand history, Cotton studied the greatest artifact of the Christian apocalyptic temper. His sermons matched events of the decline of Rome (perceived by Protestant historians as the stronghold of the Antichrist) to the opening of the seven vials described cryptically in Rev. 16. Cotton concluded that six of the vials had already been broken. Further, though cautioning that he was no prophet, Cotton surmised nevertheless that the "forty and two month" time period given over to the Antichrist's reign in Rev. 12 stood not for 1,260 days, but 1,260 years. He then dated that reign from the year 395, when papal authority was consolidated. He marked 1655 as the probable date of the apocalypse. Using such arithmetical calculations, Cotton claimed—for instance, in his sermon "The Powring Out of the Seven Vialls" (1642)—that only the downfall of the papacy, already rife with corruption and ready to topple, remained before the dawn of Christ's day of glory. Cotton offered not a howling wilderness, but the final, great bastion against the rampaging antichristian forces that had already devoured Europe. He promised to a people often desperately surviving in a dark time that the elect among them "shall see Gods ancient people brought home, and the Lord shall be one over all the Earth, and his name which will prove a Resurrection unto all the churches of the Saints" (26).

The second-generation clergy, however, sensing its fading authority as this religious intensity waned, glimpsed a threat far more potent than the stretches of Massachusetts coastal wilds. This generation used the compassion of the apocalyptic temper to revile their congregations for eroded faith and to call them back to the faith of their fathers. They warned of the imminent end of history not as a day of glory, but as the day of wrath. Drifting from the intensity of its religious mission, more worldly, more contentious, more licentious, this new New England was one ripe for the midnight surprise of the day of judgment, when, as Urian Oakes warned in his trembling apocalyptic *New England Pleaded With* (1673), "the Earth should tremble and reel to and fro, the sea roar, the Mountains be cast into the midst of the Sea, and there be a Day of gloominess and thick Darkness. . ." (63). Visions of the rapture gave way to warnings about the terrors of judgment. In "The Day of Doom" (1662), Michael Wigglesworth worked this second-generation apocalyptic of passionate indictment into what has become its most anthologized form. Though annoyingly metrical and tediously long, the poem nevertheless recounts with hypnotic ferocity the cold logic of God's justified wrath. Although the poem highlights the Dies Irae itself, it more serves to warn that those who "sleep fast in their security" are doomed to be "surpriz'd. . .in such a snare as cometh suddenly" (stanza 4, lines 3–4).

When, in the 1690s, Cotton Mather surveyed this erosion of faith—confronted, in short, by a crisis of discontinuity—he grew convinced that, notwithstanding the eloquent sermons and treatises of his own family, the corporate fulfillment of the New England mission as the New Jerusalem promised in John's vision (and promulgated by preachers of the first-generation Great Migration) was unlikely. There was to his hypercritical eye abundant evidence of God's growing displeasure with New England. Political squabbling, mercantile obsessions, chronic starvation, relentless skirmishes with brutal Indian raiders, the corruption within the clergy itself—all seemed to deny New England's proud claim to be the setting of God's millennium.

Denied the solace of the promise of the millennium, Mather countered with visions of a cataclysmic apocalypse. In sermons such as "A Midnight Cry," he promoted the idea that only God's divine (and terrifying) intervention into history could initiate the return of Christ's elect on earth. Unlike Cotton, who looked to the return of Christ with radiant optimism as the copestone of the New World's effort toward a perfect Christian community, Mather saw the Parousia as a necessary purging before the millennium could commence. Before Cotton's golden age, Christ would first punish the wicked with a suddenness and a ferocity that Mather evoked with unseemly relish. The Parousia would come just as Christ had promised in His parables—like a thief in the night. It would be a terrifying thunderclap to awaken a morally dormant world mired in the depths of its corruption. Mather, a saint saddened by the evil of his age, pictured graphically and sensually the fire that would annihilate such wickedness. And only after the conflagration, with Satan securely bound for a thousand years, would there emerge the new earth. Until Christ's return to history, Mather could counsel the elect only on the wisdom of patience in a world lost to the Antichrist and the inner satisfaction of their being preserved from the impending explosion of Christ's rage.

The rekindling of spiritual energy that ignited the New England coast in the 1730s and 1740s not only dispersed the religious lassitude that had so enervated Mather's generation, but returned apocalyptic writing to Cotton's visionary optimism as well. Indeed, the millennial expectations engendered by the feverish religiosity of the Great Awakening embraced now the entire American continent, not merely Puritan New England, as the probable site for God's kingdom—an element significant in the process of uniting the colonies into a nation, as Alan Heimert and Ernest Tuveson, among others, have carefully argued. The intense emotionalism that spread along the preaching circuits of the touring evangelicals seemed a sure sign that God had not abandoned His kingdom on earth. Fanned by such zealous faith, apocalypticism would reach an intensity, a passion, a confidence during this period it would not achieve again until contemporary times. And Edwards, who "drank" most deeply from the apocalyptic tradition,[4] would become its keenest voice.

Pigeonholing Edwards's considerable writings on the apocalypse is virtually impossible. His abundant writings on Revelation, published in 1977 as part of the Yale Edwards series, testify to his consummate interest in the latter days. Indeed, Revelation is the only biblical book to which Edwards devoted a separate commentary. Granted, much of Edwards's painstaking commentary proves unimpressive reading in its passage-to-passage "decoding" of Revelation and may seem unpleasantly bigoted in its lengthy (if doctrinally sanctioned) diatribes against Catholicism, but it clearly reveals Edwards's lifelong fascination with endtimes. Stephen J. Stein, the editor of the notebooks, suggests in his introduction to that volume that Edwards based more than sixty sermons on themes offered by Revelation, themes tailored to fit a variety of pastoral moods from consolation over a parish death to indignant rage over religious indifference ("Notebook," 18). Edwards could engage mightily the flamethrowing rhetoric of imminent judgment as well as the gentler promises of the coming paradise on earth—the millennium that Edwards believed humanity itself would construct and maintain—a coming kingdom of harmony, knowledge, and virtue that would mark our final ascent to the sheer happiness of connecting, finally, with pure Being.

Although surely capable of such exercises in both the cataclysmic imagination and the millennialist spirit, the monumental achievement of Edwards's apocalyptic writings is finally its affirmation of the soaring compassion appropriate to the apocalyptic temper. Casting an unblinking eye on an age he perceived to be both pivotal and imperiled, Edwards found in the Christian pattern of endtimes the consolation that the approaching apocalypse only made vivid humanity's spare moment on God's stage. His was a vision, a way to sustain genuine hope in an age of spreading apostasy and the insistent heresies of the new science—a dark time that Edwards perceived as poised within the inexorable movement toward history's glorious finale.

And that is finally what makes Edwards's writings on the apocalypse so compelling today: despite his frequent disclaimers about determining with any precision the actual date of the Parousia, he never fully abandoned his faith that the very real end of the very real world was at hand. Like Cotton, he argued that six of the seven vials referred to in Revelation had already been broken. But Edwards rejected the fear made possible by such imminence. Even when he spoke directly of the cataclysm that must follow the reign of the saints and precede the commencement of eternity, his rhetoric never foamed in Matherian fury.

Indeed, Edwards argued quite dispassionately that the earth, after the conclusion of the reign of the saints, would be the most fitting place for the damned. He saw God lighting the earth ("some way or another") like a "great furnace" and then dispatching the damned there, not in righteous rage but, rather, like a caring, honest accountant balancing ledgers (*History*, 369).

If Edwards rejected Mather's premillennium cataclysm with its implicit denial of progress and its bald assertion that history simply deteriorated until God finally intervened (inconsistent as such ideas were with Edwards's assurance that God had designed the Creation to radiate His glory), Edwards instead posited humanity's gradual reformation through the steady infusion of grace, the inward fire of the Holy Spirit. A series of lengthy sermons preached in 1739 and published after Edwards's death as *History of the Work of Redemption* is his most systematic examination of the greater pattern of history itself. That volume charts with the meticulous care and confidence of an engineer the ages of God from the Creation to the incarnation to the judgment itself. Both prophecy and history promise humanity's evolution toward a golden age fiercely illuminated by divine guidance, he asserts. History, then, is a mesmerizing totality: God's works are "united, just as the several parts of one building." Edwards marvels at the edifice of history, with Christ and the cross as the cornerstone and the apocalyptic event as the "one top stone" (*History*, 382). Like a "large and long river, having innumerable branches, beginning in different regions, and a great distance one from another," time will gradually gather together more and more, until it finally will all connect, like tributaries discharging into the "same ocean" (382–83). Such a sense of design compelled Edwards to forsake Mather's counseled passivity before the apparent chaos of history. He induced the elect, despite their astounding indifference to their position in history's rapidly unfolding drama, to work for the reign of the saints, despite being bound in a history that seemed terminal. Even after the fever of the Great Awakening broke, he continued to pray for another general outpouring of faith by assuring himself and his congregation that God had historically chosen the darkest times just before allowing the break of divine light. Tribulation, apostasy, heresy could only help to propel them toward the endtime.

But the apocalyptic temper—which had given to both the confirmed doomsday prophet Mather and the more buoyant, visionary Edwards compelling evidence of a muscular God who designed every turn of the world—grew imperiled during the well-documented shift in the late eighteenth century from piety to moralism, from the sacred to the secular.[5] The rhetoric of the apocalyptic temper, with its radiant confidence in kingdoms-to-come, emerged not in the vocabulary of sermons, but in that of lawyers and politicians, the architects of the new American political entity. The growing opposition to evangelical emotionalism cautioned as early as midcentury—a full generation before America's revolution—that religion should be the highest expression of the mind, a considered faith tempered by reason and persuaded by evidence. Religious emotionalism typical of the height of the Great Awakening encouraged followers to expect the apocalypse momentarily. Indeed, to this generation of clergymen, the rhetoric of approaching judgment and restoration of paradise seemed at best amusing and imaginative, but at worst fanatical, extravagant, and counterproductive. The more practical virtues of this emerging age—material success as validation of worth, social reformation, political initiative—were keyed to a faith in the perfectability of humanity, independent of infusion of grace by the Holy Spirit. Such perfectability was a faith difficult to sustain and develop in a people trained only to listed for the hoofbeats of John's horsemen.

In two seminal works on American millennialism, Tuveson has charted the development of America's conception of itself as a chosen nation, its "racial mission" (*Redeemer Nation,* 115) in the unfolding drama of world redemption. Although it is clearly beyond the scope or purpose of the present study to rehearse the outline Tuveson sketches, what is germane is Tuveson's analysis of America's millennial role in history as product of the Enlightenment faith in the inevitable refinement and perfectablity of humanity, a secular faith in history not as sequence, but as plot moving toward glorious finale. What the American experiment would provide, Tuveson argues, was nothing less than the realization of this millennium, the playing out of humanity's finest instincts—the final, revolutionary triumph of the intellect and the moral sense over the primitive, the barbarian, the superstitious. As the millennial spirit emerged, the American Revolution became, in the stirring rhetoric of its prophets, a crusade of American Evolution.

Although it would be simplistic to suggest that in the bare generation between Edwards's death and the emergence of the American political entity God simply vanished (indeed, the revolution fostered a number of interpretations that relied on a sort of sacred secularism to suggest that America's fortunes were part of God's providential plan; see, for example, the sermons of Samuel Sherwood [Stein, "Apocalyptic," 211–13]), the spokesmen of the revolution portrayed the American political experiment as a journey toward a secular millennium in visionary prose that laundered out only the religious hyperbole of strict Calvinism.[6] Secular millennialists, ranging from the staid John Adams to the tempestuous Thomas Paine to the tempered Thomas Jefferson, offered in turn mesmerizing visions of a secular New World, a political state based upon civic virtue and its cooperative exercise. Very much in the millennialist spirit, these men used a troubled contemporary history to forge a dream of such an imperfect world moving toward very real perfection. But they were not given to religious ecstasies or prayerful vigilance and anticipation. They were consummate planners. They believed that people, guided by virtue and innate goodness, could create the millennial state. America would be the very empire of reason and virtue, the finest society that Christian people of the Enlightenment could assemble and maintain, a collective defiance of humanity's baser, brutal side. Blessed by geographical isolation, destined by its natural wealth, and guided by a covey of Enlightenment lawyer-philosophers (who so often approximated quasi prophets), America would be that most curious paradox—a synthetic miracle. And the New Jerusalem would be animated not by faith or grace, but by liberty. Although the new nation would be a society surely sanctioned by God, He would be a largely silent partner. The nation itself would be developed, established, and protected by its people.

When the great struggle closed in 1783, this new collective faced the responsibility of actually leading the world toward a new age of human perfection. Once again, a new world promised the completion of world reformation: we were the City on the Hill. Confirmed by the sweeping, apocalyptic revolution that rocked France in 1789, America—to read the potent millennial optimism of visionaries such as William Blake in *America: A Prophecy*—could inspire heady confidence indeed. In the new country itself, fledgling epic writers, among them Timothy Dwight and Joel Barlow, struggled to encompass what they saw as the importance of America in demanding Homeric paeans penned with the confidence that the long-awaited millennium was not only close but actually had begun. Quasi epics, such as Barlow's uneven *The Columbiad* (1807), hymned (at tedious length) reason, progress, and America as if the terms were synonymous. America's military triumph, its unashamed allegiance to France, its political aspirations and confidence transformed the Puritan vision of a sacred millennium engineered by God's elect into a secularized celebration of human possibilities and offered the rhetoric of a new faith in progress and a profound respect for every person as elect. Freed from the awesome hand of the all-directing Calvinist God, we, the people, now seemed poised to navigate our own way to corporate perfection.

The frenetic first half-century of the American experiment seemed to confirm the confidence of such expectations. The liberal faith in the political and social collective embraced with fervor the imported quasi religion of romanticism, which so adulated human creative potential. Intoxicated by such ideas, reassured by expanding industrialization and the power of the machine, and awed by the exponential expansion of the continent, the dynamic American seemed indeed poised on the very moment of the perfect state. It seemed quite possible. Not surprisingly, a fever of imminent millennial expectations shook America. By the 1830s, religious revivalists campaigned fiercely to scour America of its worst moral offenses—the blight of slavery, the taint of alcohol, the conscienceless rapacity of business. As Tuveson has argued, the national awareness of America as chosen nation brought with it the often difficult burden of having to succeed where civilizations from classic Greece to Reformation England had failed. In such a position, alcohol, slavery, greed were not merely wrongs, but more emphatically evils (*Redeemer Nation,* 168). Evangelists and abolitionists preached with equal millennial fervor to steer America toward a moral reformation that would not only validate ongoing material successes, but further its drive toward consummate spiritual perfection. Experimental utopian communities flourished. Charitable reform institutions sprang up. The rebellious gospel of transcendentalism hinted at the untapped spiritual energy in every person. In the 1830s, expectations ran high that the millennium was about to commence.

In 1833, William Miller, an obscure deist-turned-country-preacher living in New York State, revealed with scholarly sincerity that considerable biblical evidence, most prominently the Book of Daniel, indicated the return of Christ (and the subsequent commencement of the millennium) would occur sometime between 21 March 1843 and 21 March 1844. Far from trembling before such apocalyptic tidings, followers across America for ten years anticipated the moment, promoted by Miller's tireless preaching circuits and helped by sensationalized newspaper publicity. The Second Adventists, as Miller's considerable following was dubbed, circulated millions of pages of their own promotional literature. Camp meetings sponsored in 1843 drew nearly half a million. As the time neared, reports were published of a comet sighted at noon, of spectacular meteor showers, of rings around the sun—all of which seemed to validate the imminence of the end. Across New England, respectable Christians liquidated life savings, closed businesses, abandoned crops, sold off livestock. Newspapers suspended publication. Although the failure of the Parousia to commence on Miller's schedule (either an 1843 date or the "rescheduled" 1844 deadline, each set by Miller's more confident followers) dispatched the Second Adventists to the status of historical curiosity,[7] the conviction persisted nevertheless that America would indeed be the site for the inauguration of the millennium. It is heard in the zealous jingoism of Manifest Destiny, that quasi-religious boosterism that found in the furious pace of America's expansion a pattern that not only justified growth, but promised ascent as well. It is heard in the angry polemics of the abolitionist press, in the gently uplifting rhetoric of the Mormons headed west, and in the intoxicating hymns to the transcendental New Man.

But, as indicated earlier, the millennialist spirit, for all its energy and optimism, stays often curiously disconnected from the evidence of its own history. The America of the 1830s and 1840s was confident, certainly, but anxious as well over its potential, its direction. The deaths of Adams and Jefferson on the fiftieth anniversary of the Declaration of Independence proved a lurching moment (not unlike what a small child experiences at the death of both parents). It triggered questions of national identity within the first generation that had not known British rule, that was insistently American but lacked a clear definition of the term. Certainly there were American achievements, but at each hammerstroke of this new earth, anxieties emerged. After all, migration and continental expansion could be seen as simple rootlessness, success as the cannibalism of rapacity, exploration as exploitation, ambition as greed, individualism as rampant self-interest. It seemed that only the slimmest faith called such dizzying changes ameliorative. Institutions intrinsic to the American experiment seemed unduly imperiled: God emerged as a debatable proposition; agrarian virtues were dangerously eclipsed; the family felt every economic boom, every echoing bust.

And writers, foremost among them James Fenimore Cooper, Nathaniel Hawthorne, and Melville, gave voice to this cautious response. Against the optimism of secular millennialism, they thundered a most strident reminder that in such a gospel of self-sufficiency lurked the biblical sin of pride, the sort that goeth before destruction. Outraged by their generation's shallow optimism and stunned by its easy slide toward moral vacuity and relentless materialism, these writers, supremely Melville, dashed fictional worlds with apocalyptic fury.[8] Like the second-generation Puritan clergy who so often rose to their pulpits to warn that the Puritan mission had been betrayed into religious indifference and material obsessions, these apocalyptics voiced the belief that the American secular promise of an empire of reason and virtue had been betrayed, lost.

Cooper, for example, wrote from the conviction that America could have been the mythic redeemer nation. But he could not blink away the considerable evidence that America, slowly drifting toward the democratic mob, had steadily failed to live up to the promise of its own beginnings. In order to scrutinize the premise of a new earth made in

America, Cooper (who lived near the very epicenter of Miller's revival) used a labored allegory in *The Crater* (1847): a paradisiacal South Sea island-community mires down in mercantile obsessions and power struggles until a devastating apocalyptic earthquake leaves only an "extraordinary vacancy" (500). Then, in the reassuring voice of a Christian parable, Cooper responded: an Eden it cannot be.

Cooper sends his young hero, Mark Woolston, to reconnect humbly with the hand of the Creator, the hand that will at history's appointed moment fashion the new earth. Typically, Woolston moves quickly away from trust in the Father and toward a misplaced faith in his own invention and resourcefulness. As he coaxes a community from the unpromising ridge of reef where he is shipwrecked, he tries too earnestly to leave his mark on the island and comes to mistake Providence for something he can control and coerce, until the island becomes a place where the religious impulse becomes "jammed" (406). He makes the mistake as old as Babel and as contemporary as Cooper's America: he invests the illusion of permanence in something built by human hands.

For Cooper, the American experiment would someday confront limitations and recognize the law of dependency that centered the Christian cosmos much as gravity governed Newton's clockworklike universe. Living in a sort of self-imposed aristocratic exile within his own country, Cooper watched America emerge according to its own wonderland logic much as an old man watches an earnest child build intricate sand castles too close to the ocean's waves. In the face of the human comedy of limitations, Cooper offers as resolution the tempered optimism of a peroration that turns upward for its strength, that invokes the "invisible finger" that placed the earth in its orbit and would someday strike it out (504).

Hawthorne was also wary of the promotion of a millennial society in America, convinced as he was that the treacherous human heart stubbornly resisted reformation, precluding the corporate perfection envisioned by the millennium. Although he could never muster the traditional religious affirmations hymned in Cooper's closing words, Hawthorne nevertheless shared Cooper's profound discontent over America's brave assertion of independency and moral perfection, a communal illusion coaxed from the thinnest evidence. In "Earth's Holocaust" (written at the very height of Miller's Second Adventist hysteria in 1843), people begin to burn all the polluted trappings of civilization in a sort of cultural busking. Alcohol, weapons, money—all are tossed joyously into the fire. But as the conflagration grows more fierce and destructive (at one point zealots even toss the Bible into the fire), what remains unpurified, as a "dark-visaged stranger" watching the inferno intones, is that "foul cavern," the human heart (905). Millennial reformation in Hawthorne's work comes only to individuals in revelatory moments of intensity when private, rather than corporate, rejuvenation occurs.[9]

While Cooper feared with apocalyptic apprehension an America being handed over to the jackals of mob democracy and Hawthorne charted interior apocalypses, Melville possessed all the traditional earmarks of the apocalyptic temper—the swollen rhetoric, the unashamed cosmic scale, the awesome apprehension of history as the combat between good and evil, the relentless sense of moral indignation. In his later writings—*Moby-Dick* and *The Confidence-Man*, particularly[10]—Melville is drawn to powerful endscenes that reverberate with apocalyptic implications: the staving of the *Pequod*, the extinguishing of the solar lamp on the *Fidele*.

But Melville could not create a convincing, wholly successful apocalyptic vision.[11] Well versed in the Bible, both teased and tortured by the notion of God, Melville could not convert his questions into reassuring answers. Unlike Edwards, Melville possessed all the pieces of the cosmic puzzle but had merely an agonizing notion of the grand design that they fit. In a telling moment toward the close of *Moby-Dick*, Queequeg, after being "seized with a fever" that assures him that his death is near, orders his coffin made (606). But once recovered, he uses the coffin as a sea chest and carves on its lid "all manner of grotesque figures" that seem to mimic the elaborate hieroglyphs that decorate his tattooed body (612). Those tattooes, the work of an island prophet-seer, render "the complete theory of the heavens and the earth" (612), rather like the grand design so carefully argued by Edwards. But Queequeg's design, alien to the Christian Ishmael, is a riddle even to the pagan himself, who is uncertain of the meaning of his own tattooes.

As an apocalyptic, Melville, like Queequeg, is twice-disinherited. He is unable to participate in the solace offered by the traditional sacred apocalypse and unable to accept the confidence offered by the contemporary secular millennialist spirit. Not a Mather able to live in a rapacious age of moral indifference and still find comfort in the assurance that God would soon return to right the world, and not an Edwards able to fashion from even the darkest fragments of history a radiant scheme of human history, Melville shaped a distinct apocalyptic vision—one significant in charting its eventual exhaustion—that trembles not so much with rapture as with frustration.

No book in the Melville canon trembles quite like *Moby-Dick*. So much of the drama of the *Pequod*'s voyage seems deliberately foredoomed. Events anticipate the apocalyptic moment when the great whale will stave the ship with all the appropriate abruptness and omnipotence of what Ishmael calls "a speechlessly quick chaotic bundling of a man into Eternity" (66).

But despite a preoccupation with the *Pequod*'s annihilation, the apocalyptic temper here is one without the prop of faith, without which its clarifying cohesive vision and its compassion give way to disturbing questions and dark riddles. Edwards's sure and steady river of history has swelled into the "unshored, harborless immensities" (269) of Melville's ocean, a metaphor that promises not the compelling symmetry of heaven and hell, but merely the marginless void of time and space that mocks endings. Without a God to direct the world of the *Pequod*, its fate is placed only in the hands of men, and fulfillment gives way to mere destruction. The neat roles of Lamb of God and Antichrist forever shift in this world—Ahab as much the loosened Antichrist as a raging man-god; the whale itself that delivers the apocalyptic judgment not so much god or Antichrist as disturbingly indifferent. Ambiguity haunts the fate of the *Pequod*. Indeed, if *Moby-Dick* can be accepted as the journey toward the rejuvenation of Ishmael's Christian soul, that reformation comes at the expense of the *Pequod*, which meets a strangely foredoomed destruction that makes sense only to the mad Ahab.

This is not to underplay the compensating strength of the emergence of Ishmael. In a world of God's strange silence and Ahab's flaming exhortations, there is Ishmael, who feels the maiming madness of Ahab and who watches it take the *Pequod* toward collapse. Ishmael survives; he returns to confront in his narrative the savage unreality of a world gone critical, a cosmos shattered. Ishmael has been schooled in an urgent vision of life on the brink. And as the *Rachel* threads the spars of the staved *Pequod* to scoop up this survivor, Ishmael is there to thrust a slim but graceful bar of light in the dark time of Ahab's unrelenting night watch. This is far from the stuff of millennial hymns of humanity, but Melville turns finally to humanity itself—battered, tested, imperfect, stumbling toward identity and compassion, tapping unsuspected reservoirs of persistence. Not surprisingly, in the fictions of nuclear America, this Ishmael figure emerges, the survivor of a world destroyed by madness. What is important here, however, is that Melville's flickering faith in humanity could not be sustained even in the body of his own fiction. In *The Confidence-Man*, faith itself becomes a shadow show, a dodge, a well-played ploy, a sham.

Aboard the *Fidele*, the affidavit offered by Ishmael's resilient testimony turns ironic. Like Cooper and Hawthorne, Melville turns a cold eye on the pretentions and assumptions of his nation. Melville's scathing satire on American commercialism and superficial optimism ends, as R. W. B.

Lewis has argued, with a mock apocalypse, a punch line delivered to the masquerade-joke. *The Confidence-Man* is certainly a sustained attack on the preposterous faith in America that motivated midcentury confidence in an approaching secular millennium; indeed, at one point, the Confidence-Man sells shares in a bogus New Jerusalem settlement in Minnesota. Yet Melville's disenchantment with America's moral indifference and his troubled assessment of Christianity in decline is delivered in a most Gilbert-and-Sullivan atmosphere, one of successive dupings and outlandish wiles. And this comic tone not only satirizes the millennialist optimism, but calls into serious doubt the undergirdings of the apocalyptic temper itself. Melville renders an absurd world that is virtually apocalypse-proof, for what is disconcerting about the Confidence-Man's world is, of course, its resistance to ending. He is mere reflection, simple shadow. The apocalypse played out in the darkened stateroom at the apocalyptic stroke of midnight at the close of April Fool's Day has all the Barnumesque touches of a master manipulator, all part of a game of illusions and ambiguities that is frightening and compelling because it is so completely self-sustaining. It never necessarily ends. On the *Fidele*, Melville creates a drifting world, animated by the tense interaction of naivete and deceit, liberality and rapacity, and denies that world the supranatural energy of the apocalyptic moment that could, in the tradition of the apocalyptic temper, help to make some sense of it. There is no God to pass judgment; there is not even the awesome direction of fate that seems to drive the whale into the *Pequod*. There is only the enigmatic Confidence-Man, an Antichrist figure at once frightening and unnervingly attractive.[12] The world that the Confidence-Man inhabits is like a novelty candle on a child's birthday cake, one that playfully resists extinguishing. But, of course, the longer the frustrated child persists, the less playful and the more menacing the candle becomes.

Unavailable to the compassion of the traditional apocalyptic temper and moving toward an indictment of the rhetoric of the millennialist spirit, Melville countered the national preoccupation with optimistic evolution by suggesting darkly that such faith smacked of radical arrogance, that the human condition had always resisted perfection. Melville warned that the assumption that the American soul would somehow prove glorious exception to humanity's fallen nature bordered on willful blindness. But unlike Mather and Cooper, Melville could not turn toward God; there he found an odd, shadowy space. And he could not sustain his confidence in humanity; such hope bobs a thin and tiny figure in a swirling vortex as wide as the Pacific. A Jeremiah plagued by fierce discontent over his nation, Melville felt stirred to visions appropriate to the cataclysmic imagination—but finally he resisted such simple erasure. Unlike Edwards, whose pastoral message brought clarity and compassion to lapsed congregations, Melville could not offer a convincing strategy to make the end fitting, likely, or consoling. Thus, the apocalyptic temper in Melville—a prophet lost to God, lost to humanity, lost even to any real faith in endings—ended up strangely domesticated; in *The Confidence-Man* it became a literary effect, an aesthetic rather than historical urgency. At the moment Moby Dick with an indifferent eye drove a bleached, gnarled forehead into the hull of the helpless *Pequod,* battering it to splinters, the apocalyptic temper in American literature began its movement to exhaustion, its withdrawal from history, its movement toward the emphatic, frustrated anger of the cataclysmic imagination. And with *The Confidence-Man,* Melville devastated the millennialist spirit as well. In the agony over his own growing sense of time's resistance to pattern and history's indifference to meaning, Melville could not tap the apocalyptic temper and, so, reduced the millennialist spirit to the sham dealings of a consummate snake-oil huckster. In any promise of delivery into eternity, whether the apocalyptic end or the millennialist paradise regained, Melville could see only another con, leaving him with visions of destruction but forced to concede a real world able to withstand such visions.

It is important, however, to recall that Melville trembled his indignant dissatisfaction to a nation almost relentlessly upbeat, a nation that relegated him to minor writer of South Sea romances. In the euphoria that would follow the reunion of North and South and would be sustained by a steady succession of business-minded Republican administrations, the millennialist spirit was transfigured by the energetic confidence and get-ahead prosperity hailed by the Gilded Age. The transcendental optimism, that aggressive spirituality that had enhanced the earlier secular millennialism, was ruthlessly cashiered by the new pursuit of simple material satisfaction—a comprehensive faith in the age of science, energy, and technology that would provide ultimately a worldwide technological millennium, an Eden full of efficient gadgets and peopled by the neatly outfitted ladies and gentlemen of the newly leisured classes.

But the electrifying pace of this prosperity proved disconcerting to many. The closing decades of the century were riven by new confusions and frustrations as, by the mid-1880s, America seemed sharply divided between the indifferent haves and the anxious have-nots. Fueled by anxieties over the moral state of such a consummately materialistic America, the apocalyptic temper, that trembling sense of imminent change, countered the exorbitant claims of the new materialistic millennialism by pointing out social inequalities, the collapse of traditional religion, the dismantling of the family, the wholesale abandonment of the rural tradition of the American farmer. Historians, among them Frederic Jaher and Kenneth Roemer, have offered reasons for the revival of what Jaher labels "cataclysmic thought" in America during the fin de siècle: the unsettling effects of rapid urbanization, the xenophobic fears over mass immigration, the often-violent agitation of the new labor movement, the disappearance of rural America. It was a time of questioning by those suddenly decidedly not in power. The country seemed to be facing a moral vacuum as the millennium, with its redeeming implication of moral dimension, gave way to the notion of a coming utopia, the notion that this generation was suddenly perfecting humanity on a most basic level, readying a paradise for its grandchildren to inherit.

But there was a disturbing undertow of misgiving over the unflappable gospel of getting ahead. There was a foreboding, a sense of imminent endings, imminent change. The great American frontier, long a metaphor for space and vastness, for potential and possibility, was declared officially closed by the Census Bureau in the 1890s. With people proving so irredeemably feral, governments proving casually corrupt, and God so abruptly excused from the Darwinian cosmos, these fin de siècle apocalyptics faced a stubbornly concrete world. Unlike Melville, whose apocalypticism was a response to the flush of national optimism, these Gilded Age apocalyptics railed not so much at a national attitude as at the realities of a carnivorous world: industrial capitalism, materialism, and the hunger for luxury. The Antichrist evolved into a most allegorical figure of Greed. No longer did they believe that God would level this late-century Sodom. These apocalyptics, ultimately reform-minded, envisioned that without drastic reordering of priorities the shoddy construct of capitalism would inevitably collapse of its own dead weight, wearing itself out by its own amorality. Influenced by Marxist theories of history as impelled to inevitable change and awed by the implications of Darwin's survival thesis, which seemed to confirm a ruthless doctrine of the oppression of the weak, these apocalyptics were minority voices expressing a moral outrage over a blithely thriving America. Displaced, outraged, cheated, these apocalyptics became not vigorous, compassionate visionaries, but curiously enervated dreamers, nostalgics who found the ideal world not waiting in the future, but sleeping in the American past. One such apocalyptic, the part-time novelist and Populist social reformer Ignatius Donnelly, exemplifies this phase of the exhaustion of the apocalyptic temper.[13] He considered himself "swept aside," to use Jaher's phrasing, by the rising fortunes of capitalism, a system that he viewed as the new embodiment of the Antichrist. In reaction, he offered less the consolation of the apocalyptic temper than the cold, unforgiving anger of the cataclysmic imagination.

Donnelly, outraged by the moral horrors engendered by competitive capitalism, worked tirelessly to coax America back to its agrarian roots. His *Caesar's Column: A Story of the Twentieth Century* (1891) projects a grim picture of a 1988 New York City: a wasteland of predatory capitalism spawned by the relentless tensions between the haves and the have-nots. The Brotherhood of Destruction, a seething conspiracy of the oppressed led by the savage Caesar Lomellini, spectacularly levels the city; but the triumph of the poor brings only pillaging and violence, in short, anarchy, which is suggested by the grim column of stacked bodies—the victims of the revolution that sweeps the city. Donnelly's historical vision warns that American civilization, pursuing its present course, is doomed. Only a remnant survive the devastation of New York, establishing a utopian community in Uganda, far from the infectious taint of American capitalism. Donnelly simplifies Melville's ambiguities. He anticipates that without altering the fundamental structure of capitalism, the tense interplay of oppressor and oppressed, there will be a brutal uprising, a carnage where blood will literally flow in the streets. He targets not abstracts as the focus of evil, but the social and political system in America that has disconnected itself from the land, has revoked its ties to Christian compassion and humanity, and has drifted now without hope toward a cataclysmic moment when the inequalities and moral horrors casually practiced by its masters will finally destroy it. Rebirth can come only with violence—a fiery passage that marks the haves and the have-nots alike with the taint of infectious amorality.

Donnelly is far from interested in any compensating visions of the new earth once the have-nots revolt and the lumbering behemoth of American wealth has fallen. Unlike Ishmael's steadying testimony that balances the mad excesses of the destructive Ahab, the Ugandan coda offered by Donnelly hardly balances the extended nightmare of his New York, a workers' "paradise" ruled by a brutal cartel of rich foreigners that enslaves workers within the grim grind of inhumane poverty. But if Donnelly warns that his America is turned toward the last days, his is a voice in which the apocalyptic temper stills. In the closing decades of Donnelly's century, the national literature of living in the last days turned toward the chilling certainty of the cataclysmic imagination: the blunt, straightforward rehearsal of the energy of exploding and imploding worlds. The cataclysmic imagination serves Donnelly as social purgation; but the novel moves finally too far afield of compassion. As an exercise in the scare tactics of the cataclysmic imagination, the book confronts the reader much as a child who comes to the door waving a skeleton on Halloween night.

Donnelly forsakes the expansive vision of the apocalyptic temper to press hard the cataclysm; the battle for New York renders a civilization's shudder and fall graphically. It is meticulous, earnest, strident, and—as is the case in so much of the cataclysmic imagination—finally numbing and inaccessible. As such, it oddly anticipates the pseudoapocalypse played out forty years later in front of the Persian Palace Theatre in West's *The Day of the Locust*, save that by the time West had inherited the cataclysmic imagination, the social and political gravity so critical to Donnelly had given way to scornful irony, and Donnelly's resilient Populism had mutated into West's irrepressible, smirking aestheticism.

Donnelly, writing shortly after his cherished Populist Party had lost much of its clout, projected the destruction of New York City, certain that such a fate awaited America. The end would come as confirmation that the social ills diagnosed by his cataclysmic vision were indeed as profound and serious as he had claimed. The apocalyptic was now rather like a grim doctor triumphantly pointing at the dead patient who had refused to believe that his cold was really pneumonia. In a generation more pragmatic and less enthralled by the vitality of a spiritual dimension than they, these cataclysmics responded with visions of America's headlong rush toward social disintegration: Ishmael-less testaments of worlds destroyed by greed or forces labeled but uncontrolled by the new sciences.

Given such a bleak atmosphere of disenchantment over humanity's millennium, World War I proved an irresistible metaphor for that civilization's final collapse. The genocidal holocaust coupled with the political insanities that ignited the conflict and then sustained it for six ghastly years confirmed the darkest misgivings that American apocalyptics since Melville had voiced over humanity's ability to realize a perfect world. World War I became a powerful image of modern anomie. But the world that was lost was not the physical world, as Mather predicted, but a way of life, a sense of cosmic order that had undergirded Western civilization since the carefully argued optimism of the Enlightenment. What emerged was an eerie sense of living already in a postapocalypse world, a conviction on the part of these writers—particularly strong in those who had engaged the Great War firsthand—that they were like biblical survivors wandering in a world of ash. Humanity had refuted the faith in its own potential. What arose from the debris of Europe and from the shattered spirit of those who had watched it collapse was the wasteland malaise, a self-conscious paralysis affecting a generation convinced that the war had been a Dies Irae that had judged the corrupt capitalist millennium wanting and had damned it now to sterility, ugliness, and cheapness. The apocalyptic temper, with its compassionate faith in history and its vision of outcome, gave way to a new message: progress had become uncertain drift; direction, mere consequence; and outcome, exhausted inevitability. God was not there to pull a new heaven and a new earth from the rubble like a cosmic magician. Christianity itself had long been gelded into polite community ritual. And humanity could not be counted upon to build its own New Jerusalem. After all, we had beaten the plowshares into swords.

With the genuine apocalyptic event unavailable and the millennium itself a bad gesture of irony, these artists turned inward. As apocalyptics, certain of living at a pivotal moment in history and searching for coherence and a way to understand that certainty, they became, supremely, artists. To borrow from Scott, who has diagnosed at length in *The Broken Center* how literature came to terms with the loss of God, these artists, denied the sustaining community of beliefs typical of Christian civilizations (that world lay in rubble) worked instead to communicate private beliefs, private revelations. They constructed inner cosmos that obeyed the laws of their creators, unlike the cosmos at large, which seemed to drift helplessly between fate and chance. In that public cosmos, God had been silenced, and Western civilization was, to use Ezra Pound's phrase, "an old bitch gone in the teeth." Art, however, could provide alternatives to such insanity. A compelling faith in art as orderer came to influence a generation of American apocalyptics. The apocalyptic temper, which had traditionally provided to a troubled people a consoling vision of history that promised coherence to what seemed chaos, became, in the hands of these self-conscious artisans, the Joycean epiphany. Troubled, frustrated souls glimpse in overwhelming moments of sudden, clear sight patterns to their own fragmented lives. Abandoning the world at large to the pulls of centrifugal chaos and convinced of an atomistic world that could never cohere long enough for the apocalyptic bang, these artisans fashioned constructs disconnected from history. As Melville had feared, the actual world had grown decidedly apocalypse-proof.

By the 1930s, writers, themselves disconnected from the experience of the war firsthand but still under the powerful, narcotic sway of that generation's wasteland metaphor, concocted extravagant, often theatrical apocalypses.[14] The apocalypse was appropriated by the artist committed to it as a literary effect, a stunning metaphor, a beautiful artifact of sublime consummation. As a character in Jean Giraudoux's *Sodome et Gomorrhe* (1943) remarked with amusement, "C'est beau, n'est-ce pas, la fin de monde?" (act 2, sc. 2). Once the observable world could not be held subject to the apocalyptic structure of time, the apocalypse itself became merely good theater. The urgency of the approaching end became the drift toward cataclysm. There is no better summary of this exhausted apocalypticism than *The Day of the Locust.* West's southern California demands a biblical purging. But the characters of this modern Sodom are either strangely bored by the reign of the Antichrist, appallingly fascinated by it, or simply in full retreat from its implications. Forced to comprehend history from within an absurd cosmos, West cannot render the apocalyptic temper or the millennialist spirit believable, and his vision becomes an absurd celebration of the collapse of a diseased civilization whose lingering death has fostered an ugliness that, as Victor Comerchero has written, only violence could sponge clean. West cannot offer a convincing rationale able to place the apocalyptic holocaust into any genuine moral scheme, and he cannot resist smirking at any vision of rejuvenated worlds after the cataclysm.

West does, however, offer the artist and his artifact. Tod's painting—a static, cataclysmic tableau, unanimated by faith, unmoved by hope, generated only by unforgiving curiosity and a most sadistic fascination with the damned and the dead—is merely a private retreat for the artist, who is himself detached from history.[15] Unlike Ishmael, who learns to engage, Tod retreats into his mind. He concentrates on his ongoing project, *The Burning of Los Angeles,* whenever the barrenness or the absurdity of his life closes in on him, whenever Faye momentarily stimulates him with her sexual exudings, or when at the close of the novel the Hollywood mob traps him with its released rage. Tod (and West himself) is more craftsman than prophet: his reputation, the reader is told, will rest on the accomplishment of his painting of the imagined conflagration of Los Angeles (60). Like Tod, West respects the mob, works to capture its violence, its boredom, its perversions, its inner rages all as part of his ongoing metaphor of Hollywood-as-America. He is unconcerned with addressing questions of how to survive in such a doomed world or how to chart a rise out of its imminent collapse. The novel ends with the apocalypse in full swing and Tod doing what Tod does best—merely imitating. The apocalyptic temper, which voices a message of survival and endurance, cannot be summoned convincingly by Tod, whose very name suggests merely death. He is supremely an artist. Like the siren that he imitates, his is a warning that comes too late.

There persists about the eruption of West's cataclysm a deliberate unreality, an artificiality. The crowd seems not as intent on destruction as exhilarated by its released energy—like the wave, which Homer feels forever building, finally crashing. (An interesting apocalyptic metaphor:

how apocalyptic can a wave be, when so many come after it?) Caught up in the pleasure and pain of being roused from inertia and a lifetime of relishing mere wishes as if they were feelings, the crowd is drawn to the riot. Many of the rioters indulge grotesque acts that merge the sexual and the violent at the very height of the mob scene. But a book that so deliberately draws on the notion of America as a sort of Kafkaesque Disneyland full of frustrated and bored dreamers who are lost to the white-hot energy of feeling, cannot sustain a meaningful apocalyptic moment. Disneyland is, after all, apocalypse-proof; it merely closes for the night. When time is therefore reduced to meaningless stasis and the illusion of movement, its apocalyptic interruption becomes simply an extension of that stasis and meaninglessness. Without an operating, moral imperative behind it, the end of the world in Hollywood is just another "wrap."

Except, of course, to the artist. Tod (and West) observes from a dispassionate distance and retreats to an artifact, there to fashion an impressive, coherent prophecy of apocalyptic intensity. Surely the world that engulfs Tod seems destined for a violent, shuddering end. But it is Tod who imposes the apocalyptic overtones onto the Persian-Palace crowd. His art functions as a surrogate God able to render cohesion to the drift and fragmentation by bringing Los Angeles/Hollywood to cataclysmic conclusion. But art, West demonstrates, is the greatest cheat of them all, "the ultimate fantasy" (Widmer, 180). West exploits the offer of faith in art as a way out of the illusions. Art is itself an illusion. The pilgrim Tod wanders through Hollywood, the Sargasso Sea of dreams and illusions, suffers the painful theatricality of Faye's hooker-as-starlet routine, observes Hollywood sets that mimic the rise and fall of civilizations, and lives surrounded by Hollywood houses that copy all styles of architecture and Hollywood people twisted into decadent roles. This southern California wonderland, one rank with facade, artificiality, and theatricality, suggests how little comfort art can provide.

Disconnected from a meaningless history, indifferent to those caught within its webbing, robbed of its power against time, the apocalyptic temper corrupts into the cataclysmic imagination—a bizarre celebration of discontinuity, a break in the stultifying routine of life. The reader is caught up by the possibility of cataclysm like a small animal momentarily stunned by the slashing headlights of an approaching automobile. Divorced from the more difficult job of the apocalyptic temper, Tod can paint the end of the world with happiness. On his canvas, flames appear "flying like bright flags...from roofs more than a...holocaust" (118). Divorced from the implications of the apocalypse, Tod can find supreme satisfaction in his rendering of it. The street riot itself is merely another mock riot in the novel's series of mock riots: the fistfight that erupts at the whorehouse when the film projector breaks down (a fight from which Tod, characteristically, flees), the collapse of the movie set, the cockfight (again, with Tod on the periphery). They are all small-scale apocalypses, mock cataclysms without resolution, without direction, and without outcome. The artist is detached from reality, which West suggests not only by Tod's automatic retreat mechanism, but more tellingly by the odd moment during the street riot when, crushed between two sides of the mob, Tod is pushed up, his feet literally off the ground (181). Indeed, West eliminated the original closing pages in which Tod retreats to Claude's house after the riot and there rants, until medication calms him, about the possibility of the cheated all over the world rising up, a solution tuned (rather satirically) to the millennial effusions characteristic of the proletarian literature of the depression.[16] Clearly, West intended to end the novel focusing not on such a social and political millennialism, but on Tod the artist escaping from the churning absurdity of the street riot (and the very real pain in his pinned leg) by concentrating on the finest detail of his canvas—the tongue of flame licking up from the nutburger stand.

The clarity of vision so prized by the apocalyptic temper, the gift of being able to render order from the fragments of time, is now at best an escape device, at worst deliriums. If Tod is the book's apocalyptic, then his clarity of vision (he does, for example, notice immediately that the horse in Claude's pool is made of rubber [70]) brings with it only impotence, suggested strongly by Tod's drift through the novel and by his helplessness in the mob scene. Without the reassurance of purpose, history, when clearly seen, is a frightening prospect of violence, happenstance, and drift. Helpless before history, West's apocalyptic turns inward there to fashion a private Armageddon, which resolves all the anxiety and doubts by offering an aesthetically pleasing artifact. But like the characters running in panic in Tod's painting, Tod (and West) is in full flight from history.

In a letter to Jack Conroy, West characterized himself as "the fellow who yells fire and indicates where some of the smoke is coming from without actually dragging the hose to the spot" (Martin, 336). As a writer more comfortable with a neutrality that is not so much uncompassionate as it is dispassionately concerned to observe and record absurdity accurately, West indeed watches things burn.[17] Convinced that violence and illusion dictate the world, he concocts his succession of meaningless mock apocalypses—cataclysms that follow without progress, without direction, like frames of an endless movie reel. In a world where the dream dominates, there can be none of the intensity and visionary rapture of Edwards. The asbestos world of southern California is kept at a distance by West's jarringly figurative language, the deliberate artificiality of his characters' cliches and banal conversations, the succession of unlikeable characters, the limitless examples of sham and facade. And when the apocalypse finally comes—another meaningless gesture of violence, triggered by the repressed anger of a meaningless man—it is almost as if the reader can see Tod working furiously behind the scenes, pumping the thunder machine and stomping heavily on the stage boards to make his stage shake with appropriate apocalyptic effect. But the consummation is trivial. As Comerchero notes, the novel, for all its lurking sexuality, is really about frustration (148). Faye's sexual prowess is never developed beyond carnal fits, the crowd seethes with frustrated energy, and the long-promised apocalypse fizzles. It cannot work. History is a damp fuse. The consolation of consummation cannot be sustained. People are stuck in history, their only escape through the illusions of art.

Denied the apocalyptic temper if nevertheless drawn to its design and rhetoric, West offers a vivid image of the modern apocalyptic in the age of the cataclysmic imagination. In an interlude midway through the novel, Tod joins Earle Shoop and Faye on a camping trip in the California desert country to check Earle's quail traps. The campsite is in a clearing in a wooded canyon that, Tod notes, is thick with eucalyptus trees, a detail that mocks "apocalypse" (eucalyptus trees ring the Persian-Palace crowd). When Tod accompanies Earle to check the traps, he pauses to listen to the birds in the fields: a mockingbird (significant in a novel so full of shams), and then the quails. But he is arrested momentarily by the sound of one: "This one called from near the center of the field. It was a trapped bird, but the sound it made had no anxiety in it, only sadness, impersonal, and without hope" (114). Here is the traditional apocalyptic. In a creaking, lurching universe, he now sings in the trap of history, sadly, impersonally, unable to offer hope. It is now only the song itself that matters. In West, the apocalyptic temper becomes the cold eye cast, the impersonal artistic construct, the aesthetic achievement in which even West invests little faith. After all, Earle Shoop reaches into the trap and quickly, efficiently twists off the head of the trapped quail.

Ineffectual, Tod can only dream endings on his canvas. Like his offhand comment that the gaudy excesses of the Hollywood architectural mishmash need dynamite to set them right (61), his apocalypse is an assertion without urgency, or in the chilling words of Bob Dylan—a later generation's poet of the cataclysmic imagination—"The locusts sang . . . and it gave me a chill / Oh the locust sang such a sweet melody."

In West, the locusts do indeed sing a sweet melody. Gone is the urgent emotionalism, the intimate compassion that so animated Edwards's rhetoric. Just as Tod can escape the passion of the street riot, so the reader can shrug off its implications in Tod's vision. Hollywood, after all, will survive the riot and defy the painting. Hollywood is able to burn fiercely yet never be consumed, like "the filaments of an incandescent lamp" (102). In a world where all is sham, all is pretense, all is paper made to look like brick and steel, there is no urgency in its collapse. The reader can, like the half-naked Faye smiling in Tod's painting, merely enjoy the release, the "wild flight of pent-up energy" (108). Unable to master history, unable to decode the fury of the mob into a satisfactory pattern, humanity is robbed of the imaginative supranatural experience of the apocalyptic temper, which can widen its focus beyond the troubling chaos of the present. If the alternatives are Homer's studied inertia and Tod's calculated retreat, West is clearly dissatisfied with both strategies. West could bring the world of rampant vice and dehumanized violence to an appropriate biblical Sodom-and-Gomorrah finale, but he cannot be convincing about it. It will not stay dead, like the Hollywood stunt man who is shot and falls from his horse, only to stand up and dust himself off when the director yells "Cut!" Without the idea of God, history curves into endless repetition: the artist, in full retreat from history, creates Armageddon, and history, unaware of such significance, continues to grind away in chaotic, meaningless fashion.

Imaginative humanity, it seemed, awaited an experience—a crisis of discontinuity—sufficient to jar the advance of such historical ennui and return the sense of direction and urgent vision that had first engendered the apocalyptic temper. The angry fist of the flaming mushroom cloud that burst out of the heart of startled Hiroshima provided just that: a panicky glimpse of a very real end. Speaking in the mid-1960s, Kermode defined nuclear anxiety as part of a more general immemorial hunger for ends, that it is part of a greater "pattern of anxiety" (96). And other commentators, most prominently Ketterer, have suggested that the bomb and all its energy merely completed the secularization of the apocalyptic temper begun in earnest during the midnineteenth century, a view that offers little but the studied pessimism of waiting for the final absurd explosion and, thus, closes off the contemporary expression of the apocalyptic temper to the possibility of hope. It is the offering of a literature simply disconnected from the implications of living within a dangerous history—one excused from dealing with the existence of the bomb. Accepting the volume of data generated by the Hiroshima and Nagasaki blasts and paging through even briefly the impersonal findings and predictions published by the scientific community in the last ten years about the certain effects of actually triggering the present nuclear arsenals, it is easy to suggest, however, that certainly Kermode's reassurances might be a bit naive. The reality of living in the nuclear age implies that humanity is no longer spinning imaginary endings; the difficulty is in accepting this and still refusing the despair that Ketterer has diagnosed.

Turning away from the realities of our history by pretending that the world has not been altered by the secrets of Los Alamos, or even protesting in the streets the existence of the arsenals are both insufficient responses; each implies, if in different ways, that a complicated history can be made to go away. As Wolfgang Giegerich has suggested, humanity must accept that the implications of the bomb cannot be tamed, cannot be ignored, cannot be demonstrated against. The bomb, he observes, is our contemporary spiritual dimension, the troubling sense of terror and absoluteness that cannot be contained. We must, he concludes, reawaken fear and turn bravely to face the history our own generation has constructed.

This sense of reconnection is, in essence, the argument of the present study. The voices of American literature since roughly the mid-1950s have reawakened the apocalyptic temper, a vision that rejects the contention that to accept history is to abandon hope. In whatever its angle of vision, the apocalypse has become, in Earl Rovit's words, "the best model for viewing our contemporary human condition" (463). This model is found not merely in the fringe elements, such as speculative fiction and its offspring, the white-knuckle political thriller (often the stuff of the cataclysmic imagination, doomsday scenarios or alarmist tales about horrific destruction after intricate political intrigues collapse), and the brave tales of humble communities of determined survivors emerging from the rubble of a nuclear holocaust—tales very much in the millennialist spirit. As we have observed, the one offers the pyrotechnics of planetary explosion, the other the pleasant illusion that all will be well. Perhaps taking its signal from Hersey's *Hiroshima,* which focuses on survivors rather than destruction, the resurgence of the apocalyptic temper has again brought our literature to grapple with the question of how to live in a dark time. It has been an urgent search for hope, and in its finest manifestations—the early work of Kurt Vonnegut, Jr., and Robert Coover, the theological argument of Walker Percy, and the soaring affirmation that compels Thomas Pynchon's *Gravity's Rainbow*—it has performed the traditional function of a literary genre that first emerged in the dark time of religious oppression and uncertainty, that of bearing the sublime message of hope.

This study will examine the revival of the apocalyptic temper by engaging the works of six American novelists of the post-Hiroshima era, writers who reject the larger, more ominous capitulation to silence that has come to mark our cultural adjustment to living in the endtimes, an adjustment that is a most unnerving surrender to insanity. As in any period study of a national literature, the choices here seek to sample a variety of responses to the challenge of the endtimes, and each plays a variation on the theme of hope. It illuminates the desperate courage of Vonnegut's black comedy, the inventive energy of Coover's metafiction, the steady heart of Percy's theological argument, the encyclopedic reach of Pynchon's historical epic, the gripping claustrophobia of William Gaddis's political gothic, and the cohesive vitality of Don DeLillo's domestic comedy. The choices here could not begin to exhaust the contemporary revival of the apocalyptic temper; it is heard in Saul Bellow's resilient idealism; in John Barth's persistent, self-enclosing wordplaying; in Flannery O'Connor's sublime Catholicism; in Norman Mailer's angry posturings; in William S. Burroughs's hallucinogenic collages; in James Baldwin's smoldering rage—to name only a few. Indeed, it rings in the writing of Martin Luther King, Jr., perhaps the clearest voice within the traditional apocalyptic temper of the period surveyed by this study, although that voice is finally more appropriate to political or social histories, since he wrote no fiction. The nearest to such thunder in fiction is Baldwin's unflinching anger that so often invokes apocalyptic rhetoric to add urgency to and tap community response for a social agenda of long-delayed change and redress. And the apocalyptic temper, or at least the impulse toward the endtimes, has generated as well a body of work in the 1970s and early 1980s that could be loosely grouped as utopian fictions. Consider, for example, the work of Margaret Atwood (*The Handmaid's Tale*), Ursula LeGuin (*The Dispossessed*), or Marge Piercy (*Woman on the Edge of Time*). Such fictions surely share with the apocalyptic temper a sense of radical change, an appreciation of the global stage, and a sense of ministering to a community in crisis. These works, of course, do not concern specifically the end of history— by their very definitions, ending is not in the vocabulary. This genre, rather, imagines sweeping transformations—positive and negative— often projecting current dissatisfactions through the imaginative rendering of future civilizations. Such works often touch the rich vein of speculative fiction; LeGuin's work, for instance, pushes fantasy toward alternate star systems and elaborate allegories of distant planets and seeks answers there that the more traditional expressions of the apocalyptic temper would seek in the heart and soul of those caught within such an urgent history. That temper is finally hard edged, forsaking such speculations as elaborate maneuverings and dodges (consider, for example, Vonnegut's ruthless, emphatic rejection of his speculative fictionist John/Jonah). The apocalyptic temper stares straight at our history and finds there the stuff of hope and compassion. But clearly the literature of endtimes has shaped the fiction of this generation.

The writers selected here shape an argument that will begin a dialogue on this single most critical element in our national voice. These writers resist all but the compelling showdown with their own history and collectively rage against the coming of the light. They step forward to confront a most disturbing history. Confronting the mystery of the fusion of the atom like biblical prophets charged by an awareness of an energy far vaster than the sun itself, disturbed by a community of the helpless who elect to ignore the urgency of the times and, in turn, passively accept a terminal history, these writers move characters through a most treacherous post-Hiroshima landscape.

Their novels focus on characters certain of approaching ends, mock apocalyptics who indulge the cataclysmic imagination, who relish the coming destruction, who fail to fashion from such an awareness the traditional act of hope. The authors caricature, dismiss, and undercut these doomsayers, who can dream only of worlds following paths to death. These characters prove to be narrow of vision, to possess sour hearts, and to be unable to love and live; hence, they are defeated in the end. Each novel, however, offers a minor character, in some cases a presence on a scant handful of pages, who nevertheless asserts with conviction a way out of the darkness, a way to live, a way to see in a dark time.

Clearly, contemporary American literature is finding a way to encompass the meaning, if not the fact, of the nuclear threat.[18] It has found a way to guide its most authentic characters to positions where, despite the reconciliation to the menace of instant and, hence, meaningless death, there pulses the will to live and to love in a fragile world. These are not political statements. These are not the harsh, shrill voices of quasi prophets, although the rhetoric of their solutions is unabashedly religious in its tone. Like the first-generation Puritan sermons that evoked the sulphurous flames of judgment more to compel a radical faith, these novels are the forceful documents that in the tradition of the apocalyptic temper are intended as artifacts of hope for the community of the hopeless. They offer nothing less than what the awesome destruction of the nuclear age threatens most profoundly by salvaging human life with its dignity and passion in the face of evidence that human life has been reduced to the murderous calculus of species genocide.

On the cover of the *Bulletin of the Atomic Scientists* is one of the most disturbing images of the atomic age—the doomsday clock set since 1945 at ten minutes to midnight. By January 1987, the clock had advanced seven minutes. The times had, indeed, become perilous.

Despite a delayed period of adjustment, our literature has responded to the image of the mushroom cloud. When asked whether man could survive in the nuclear age, Carl Jung responded, "Only if man can contain the Opposites within his own mind" (Schley, 530). This is the difficult act of containment achieved by our finest apocalyptic writers in characters who courageously face the evidence of history and nevertheless resolve to live—absolute death balanced with the resilient will to cling to nothing less than absolute life. This is the achievement of American literature in the nuclear age. In accepting the National Medal for Literature, John Cheever (himself less than two months from death) closed with a brave word that can serve as appropriate summary of the apocalyptic temper of American literature in the age of Hiroshima a bare three minutes before midnight:

> Literature is the only consciousness we possess and...its role as consciousness must inform us of our ability to comprehend the hideous nature of nuclear power. Literature has been the salvation of the damned, literature has inspired and guided lovers, routed despair and can perhaps in this case save the world.

Notes

1. In the wake of the Hiroshima and Nagasaki bombings, some over-zealous responses suggested that the atomic fury was nothing less than God's wrath brought down upon the godless Japanese warrior-nation. Taking its cue from Revelation and the rhetoric of judgment day, this response placed America itself in the position of the judging deity. In "Atomic Power," a hit record released in August 1945 by cowboy singer Fred Kirby, this notion of the judgment day is suggested:

> Hiroshima, Nagasaki paid a big price for their
>   sin.
> When scorched from the face of the earth, their
>   battle they could not win.
> Take warning, my dear brother, be careful how you
>   plan,
> You're working with the power of God's own holy
>   hand. (Zuckerman, 72)

2. Exceptions ought to be made to this mass-market rush of doomsday novels: Walter M. Miller's *A Canticle for Leibowitz* (1959) and Ray Bradbury's collection *The Martian Chronicles* (1950).

3. The work done in this century toward a definition of the apocalyptic temper goes quite beyond the scope of a single note. Particular analyses, how-

ever, that were valuable in shaping the definition offered here include Adela Yarbro Collins's brief book *Crisis and Catharsis*; Paul D. Hanson's *The Dawn of Apocalyptic*, specifically pages 402–13; Walter Schmithals's *The Apocalyptic Movement*, pages 29–49; and Amos N. Wilder's "The Rhetoric of Ancient and Modern Apocalyptic."

4. The phrase is from Stephen J. Stein ("Notebook," 634), but Puritan scholars have long associated Edwards with the apocalyptic scheme. Although the recently published Yale series volume on Edwards's apocalyptic writing has corrected a number of the assertions, two early essays are still valuable to show how thoroughly grounded Edwards was in Revelation rhetoric—C. C. Goen's essay and Perry Miller's essay from the fifties. More recent studies are best covered by Stein, who worked with the Yale volume. Other critics, however, have linked Edwards to the apocalyptic temper without benefit of the Yale notebooks, most prominently Lakshmi Mani and James West Davidson, who have both worked closely with Edwards's *History of the Work of Redemption*.

5. See, for instance, Heimert and Joseph Haroutunian.

6. It would be difficult to summarize the many approaches that have argued the American revolution was prompted by millennialist writings. Sacvan Bercovitch draws a convincing continuum between Governor Winthrop and General Washington as redeemer figures; Tuveson uses the epic poetry of Timothy Dwight to illustrate the connection; in his essay, Davidson uses the heated political rhetoric exchanged during the rise of the Jeffersonian party in the 1790s; Walter Sutton uses the nationalistic verse of Joel Barlow; Stein follows the text of a sermon preached by Samuel Sherwood that outlined in point-by-point fashion how Revelation could be used to understand events unfolding in colonial New England; and Cecelia Tichi argues that it was Revelation that first encouraged the colonies to think in terms of the Continent.

7. For more thorough analysis of Miller's movement, see pertinent sections of J. F. C. Harrison and see Leon Festinger et al. (particularly pages 2–23), which examines the Adventists in light of Festinger's theories about group dynamics and religious belief.

8. Another of the darker romantics, Edgar Allan Poe, frequently worked with the image of worlds shattering. In narratives with apocalyptic endings, such as "The Masque of the Red Death," "The Fall of the House of Usher," and *The Narrative of Arthur Gordon Pym*, the implications of each apocalyptic moment—the ravaging of the costumed partiers, the splitting of the Usher castle, the stark bleached vortex of the Antarctic Ocean—are more deliberately suggestive of psychological destruction. Each is a case study of individuals whose interior worlds collapse, without direct reference to the ending of an actual, external world. Indeed, such a noisome event would, no doubt, be of little interest to Poe, who was absorbed by the countless apocalypses that shatter individual minds at every tick of the clock.

9. For a strong presentation of Hawthorne's use of apocalyptic imagery to suggest moments of inner revelation, see Mani's chapter on Hawthorne, which works primarily with Arthur Dimmesdale and Miles Coverdale.

10. Although Melville's two other major later writings—*Pierre* and *Billy Budd*—fall outside the specific interest of this survey, both novels culminate in suggestive day-of-judgment scenes. In both cases, however, the catastrophe is an individual one, the apocalypse (or "revelation") an intensely private epiphanic moment that illuminates private worlds ending. *Pierre*, with its melodramatic, deliberately overplayed multiple deaths and suicides, is less apocalyptic and more Melville's deliberate parody of romantic novels, which Melville satirizes by sending his innocent hero out into a world of ambiguous vice and virtue. Pierre's world collapses from the moment he is exposed to the darkly beautiful Isabel. In *Billy Budd*, Melville seems less drawn to Revelation and more toward Genesis. In apocalyptic fashion, however, the forces of good and evil seem to square off on board the *Bellipotent*, with the final judgment rendered by Captain Vere. The characters, however, pit the unspoiled innocence of natural man against the forces of civilization that can corrupt and destroy such innocence to preserve its order. It is the story of Adam or Christ, not of John of Patmos. It is a story of acceptance, not a vision of approaching change. The judgment toward which Billy inexorably moves marks the disturbing destruction only of his innocence.

11. Though *apocalypticism* and *apocalypses* are terms used widely (and abused unintentionally) by Melville critics trying to convey the depth of *Moby-Dick*'s passion, those critics more concerned with the apocalyptic as genre have tended to dispute whether Melville, so obviously alienated from the surety of faith, could construct a successful apocalyptic vision. Nathalia Wright, for instance, argues that the elemental energy of the apocalypse attracted Melville but that he wasn't systematic enough to be familiar with its theology; Lawrence Thompson argues Melville smashed his fictional world out of anger over God's miscontrived one; Mani argues the apocalyptic vision was more a way for Melville to demonstrate his growing misgivings over America; Zbigniew Lewicki argues that despite the destruction of the *Pequod*, the apocalyptic consolation is offered by the redeeming figure of Ishmael, who balances the heresy of Ahab and makes the novel, finally, optimistic.

12. Elizabeth Foster is the most thoughtful exponent of the Confidence-Man as a Satan figure, although convincing supporting arguments have been offered by John W. Shroeder, May (*Toward a New Earth*), and Mani; the latter two, in fact, draw specific parallels between the Confidence-Man and the Antichrist prophesied in Revelation. But other critics have found in the Confidence-Man Melville's supreme artist figure. Paul Brodtkorb, Jr., argues that the Confidence-Man is heroic in his mastery, humorous serenity, and willingness to lead the passengers of the *Fidele* toward the disturbing illumination of darkness. Perhaps Lewis strikes the compromise by arguing that the Confidence-Man is a "Satanic comedian," the comic king of chaos who foreshadows similar figures in Mark Twain, West, and Ralph Ellison.

13. Another figure often mentioned in connection with late-century apocalyptics is Twain, who turned against America in particular, but humanity in general with an apocalyptic vengeance at the end of his career. In the closing scene of *Connecticut Yankee*, for instance, the wizard of nineteenth-century technology leads medieval England toward a slaughter that numbs the imagination. In the enigmatic conclusion of *The Mysterious Stranger*, the Satan figure, who has relished constructing tiny play villages and then destroying them, sneers that all history is a dream and that humanity's desperate attempts to forge it are all for nothing. Twain, however, insists on a tone of private, unforgiving bitterness that narrows his compassion and stunts his vision. He makes a poor apocalyptic—more a muttering naysayer in the cataclysmic tradition—completely forsaking history to drift and humanity to carnivorous rapacity and folly. His only antidote to such a world is laughter, which sounds, finally, so hollow.

14. In an interesting reversal of situation, the millennial voice (so characteristically the majority voice during the American rush to prosperity during the nineteenth century and easily subsumed into all the patriotic gore of the Establishment rhetoric during the Great War) was battered into a resilient minority voice during the 1930s. The proletarian realists, particularly John Steinbeck, appropriated the biblical, quasi-mystical faith in inevitable progress to chart the way out of the depression, offering the traditional message of dignity and endurance to a generation blasted into indignity and poverty.

15. A follower of the dadaists and the symbolists, West saw in art a refuge and a solution to the inherited wasteland. Jay Martin, his biographer, argues that West, deeply influenced by T. S. Eliot's faith in art, offered Tod's painting as an artifact that had obviously survived the collapse of society and had remained long after the society itself was consumed. Comerchero also refers to Eliot in arguing that Tod is a Tiresias figure whose vision alone gives coherence to the fragmentation of the world. James F. Light argues convincingly that West, attracted perhaps by the rhetoric of the 1930s proletarian writers, nevertheless stayed detached and curious—more the artist than social commentator. Randall Reid most completely addresses this question by assessing West as supremely a parodist, one who imitates not life or the interior life, but art itself; in particular, West parodies the Eliot faith in art by exposing its artificiality and by using Greek drama techniques to enhance his own world's theatricality.

16. Martin provides a clear comentary on the deleted final pages (314–18) as well as the text itself in part of a photograph section.

17. Martin includes the full text of a poem (sixteen lines of which West published in 1933) called "Burn the Cities." It is a lengthy description of the burning of Jerusalem, Paris, and London, obviously capitals of some importance to Western civilization. What West offers is all the smoke and flame with little explanation—save rather indirect hints that the conflagration results from some sort of workers' uprising. The fascination rests with the exquisite beauty of the devouring flames.

18. In Boyer's exhaustive study of the years immediately following the atomic blast at Hiroshima, he concludes with a curt chapter summarizing the period from the Cuban missile crisis to the Reagan administration—the period roughly surveyed by this study—and concludes that the American cultural response to nuclear weaponry was largely silent. Indeed, he dismisses this period as the "Big Sleep," citing in part the Vietnam War as cause. Involved with a very real conflict that proved menacingly inert, the American people largely displaced the anxieties over the war-to-end-all-wars implied by the stockpiles of nuclear weapons. This study will take issue with such findings. The apocalyptic temper emerged strongest in the very period Boyer dismisses. As this study describes, however, the response did not undertake the direct treatment of doomsday scenarios, but instead dealt indirectly with how people adjust to life in perilous times.

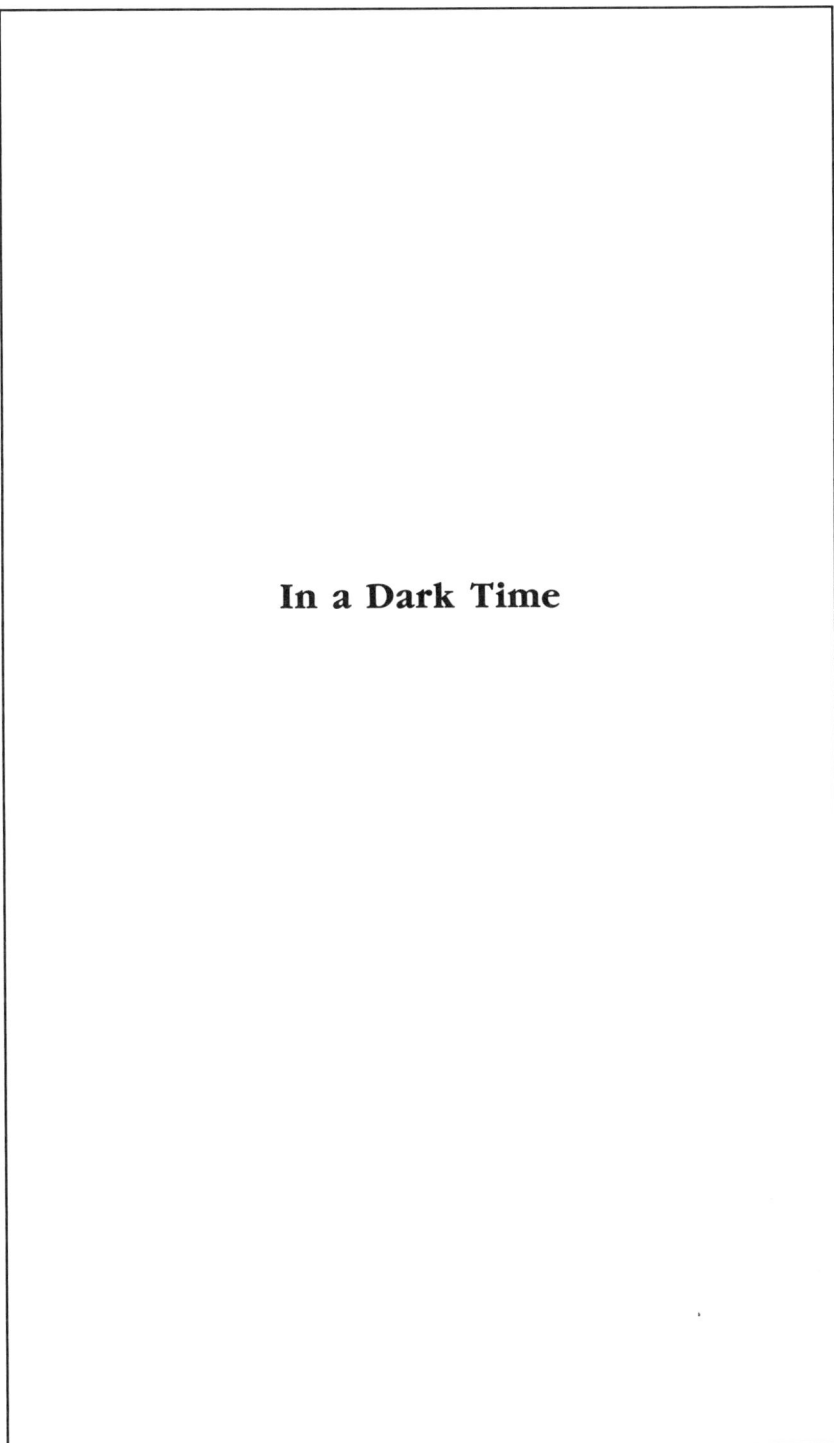

In a Dark Time

These are the days of miracle and wonder.
Don't cry, baby, don't cry.

Paul Simon, "The Boy in the Bubble"

Chapter 1

The Gladder You Will Be
to Stand the Pain
The Failure of the Apocalyptic
Temper in Kurt Vonnegut

up, up and see
The great doom's image!
Macbeth

We know how little of the deep new knowledge which has altered the
face of the world...resulted from the quest for practical ends or an
interest in exercising the power that knowledge gives. For most of us,
in most of those moments when we were most free of corruption, it
has been the beauty of the world of nature and the strange and com-
pelling harmony of its order, that has sustained, inspired, and led us.
Robert Oppenheimer

She smiled hopefully. "Is it a funny book?"
"I hope so..."
Cat's Cradle

When Philip Castle confronts John/Jonah, the narrator of Vonnegut's
Cat's Cradle, he tells him that his father, a doctor who runs a hospital
on the island of San Lorenzo called the House of Hope and Mercy in
the Jungle, needs "some kind of book to read to people who are dying
or in terrible pain" (106). The comparison that Philip develops between
books and aspirin and between writers and drug salespeople has haunted
and threatens to eclipse much of the best work in the Vonnegut canon.
In his books Vonnegut seems to man little outposts of mercy and hope
in the dark, tangled jungles of the twentieth century. And there, with
a grumpy (if avuncular) smirk, he calms his legions of readers, who are
terrified by the implications of contemporary history, by telling pop

fables spun from the stuff of science fiction and comic books. The argument follows that Vonnegut attracts not so much readers as fans who are charmed rather than challenged by his simplifications of history, which seem to reduce the implications of his profound awareness of twentieth-century atrocities to sentimental morals. Vonnegut prescribes bromides like aspirin tablets, telling us all to love more or to laugh more in order to keep us going.[1]

But the twentieth century of Vonnegut's vision is a dark time: an age of insensate greed, of all-too-regular genocidal rages, of continuing political insanities, and of unrestrained technology; an age, in short, in which humanity has pushed itself to the very brink of apocalyptic ending. Vonnegut's fiction works with the raw, ugly stuff of twentieth-century history—the emasculation of man by machine, the amorality of political corruption, the cataclysm of Hiroshima, the firestorm at Dresden, the horrors of the Jewish Holocaust. His is a world haunted by time running out, much like the Kilgore Trout plot of the planet Vicuna (detailed in *Jailbird*), where time is burned like fossil fuel, and finally, after generations of waste, the "fuel" runs out. The question that Vonnegut's best fiction poses is how to live in a world so dangerously close to biblical-scale extermination. Sidestepping or trying to excuse the deliberate editorializing central to Vonnegut's insistently moral fiction and concentrating on his "experimentations" with disjointed, elliptical (and hence, postmodern) style ignores an ethical message that has only grown more strident in his work.[2] He resolutely refuses to turn away from history. And what he has found there is pain, an awareness that in our century genocide has become as commonplace as hiccups, that the apocalypse has been appropriated into the banal patter of the evening news, and that human life itself seems robbed of purpose and dignity. In the best tradition of the apocalyptic temper, Vonnegut's imagination reclaims this pain, examines history without flinching, deals with its most profound implications, and still promises not cataclysm, but a complicated strategy toward hope. In an early Vonnegut science-fiction novel, *The Sirens of Titan* (1959), Malachi Constant, who has been kidnapped and brainwashed as part of a Martian force being assembled to invade the earth, is implanted with a device in his brain intended to insure obedience by inflicting horrendous pain whenever he questions authority or tries to recall his past. In a poignant letter that he writes to himself in a lucid moment, he says:

> Whenever I ask a question, and the pain comes, I know I have asked a really good question. . . . The more pain I train myself to stand, the more I learn. You are afraid of the pain now . . . but you won't learn anything if

you don't invite the pain. And the more you learn, the gladder you will be to stand the pain. (125)

This determined effort to examine the past, to question it, and to learn from the pain inevitable in such a process is the driving force behind Vonnegut's apocalyptic vision.

Unquestionably, Vonnegut has become the most consistent apocalyptic voice in contemporary American literature. His fictions are dominated by the urgent sense of history speeding toward an end.[3] Denied a reliable God to make sense of such endings (after all, a human finger rests on the button), Vonnegut concentrates instead on the secular Antichrist figure that relentlessly hounds humanity toward species destruction: a two-headed beast, government and science. He offers in his two most deliberately apocalyptic novels—*Cat's Cradle* (1963) and *Slaughterhouse-Five* (1969)[4]—messengers who see such a cataclysm as inevitable. Although his two apocalyptic messengers—John/Jonah in *Cat's Cradle* and Billy Pilgrim in *Slaughterhouse-Five*—are convinced that humanity now faces the end of time, Vonnegut himself refuses such a dark message. In these two novels, to accept the simple message that The End Is Near is to accept the easy way out of history, to refuse to come to terms with its implications, with its pain. The vision that points only to cataclysm is the aspirin in the Vonnegut apothecary, and it is prescribed not by Vonnegut, but by eccentric, oddly misogynistic characters. In the traditional act of apocalyptic consolation, Vonnegut, in these two early works, addresses a community in crisis, refuses to simplify history, fully suggests the possibility of the technological Götterdämmerung, and still holds out hope for avoiding such an endgame. In spite of his narrating voices, he delivers a message that holds out ways to sustain time in a century where technological might and political folly have joined in a macabre fandango to raise the possibility of time's own extinction. In his work of the last decade, Vonnegut has found difficulty sustaining the optimism of his earlier fiction, and this is a measure of how much his work has shifted from the larger concerns of the apocalyptic temper toward the narrower range of the cataclysmic imagination. This does not, however, qualify the achievement of these two seminal works in the contemporary apocalyptic rediscovery. I will, therefore, review in detail the strategy of *Cat's Cradle* and, to a lesser extent, *Slaughterhouse-Five* and then suggest only briefly the movement toward cataclysm that characterizes the more current, bleaker fictions of the Vonnegut imagination.

At first reading, *Cat's Cradle* might suggest less the apocalyptic temper and more the insistent movement toward endgame associated with the cataclysmic imagination. The novel, written by a modern-day Jonah, relates the actual end of the world. A compound called *ice-nine*, fashioned by Dr. Felix Hoenikker, a scientist also known as the Father of the Atom Bomb, is able to raise the melting point of water to 114.4 degrees. When a chip of it is dropped accidentally into the ocean, it sets off a chain reaction that insures within months the freezing of the earth's waterways and the eventual extinction of all life on the planet. Writing in the eerie interregnum before the end among the last survivors in a blue world of ice, Jonah delivers an invective against science and a caustic philippic denouncing the stupidity of people. From his vantage point, Jonah sees history only as a choreographed movement toward absurd finale. Indeed, his vision, his apocalyptic revelation, that history conforms to pattern comes to him while he visits a tombstone salesroom. As with the more elemental prophets of the cataclysmic imagination, Jonah looks back at history and decides that death is its central impulse. Death is everything.

Vonnegut uses his Jonah to deliver a clear warning, fashioning a latter-day drama between the amoral insanity of science (the forces of the Antichrist suggested by Felix Hoenikker) and the vestigial impulses of Christian love and compassion (the forces of the Lamb suggested by the ethereal Mona). But is the novel then an overwhelmingly pessimistic vision of the Good losing? Jonah does helplessly observe the folly of events that leads finally to the *ice-nine* compound tumbling (with Rube Goldberg absurdity) into the sea off San Lorenzo: the dying dictator of the island, "Papa" Monzano, kills himself on his deathbed by swallowing a vial of *ice-nine*, which freezes his body blue; a plane, out of control during a military review, plunges into a cliff below the presidential palace, destroying just enough of it to cause Papa to drop, bed and all, into the sea, his frozen body touching off the cataclysmic whirlwind of ice. As if to reenforce the idea of apocalypse, Vonnegut has Horlick Minton, the American ambassador to San Lorenzo, deliver a scathing, quasi-divine judgment against humanity just before the plane crashes. As he tosses a wreath into the San Lorenzo harbor to commemorate the deaths of San Lorenzans during World War II, Ambassador Minton reviles humanity for its indifference to life, its willful indulgence of war, and, in general, its "stupidity and viciousness" (170). Barely does he finish when the thunder and the flames (of the plane crash) commence, followed by the swift stroke of the apocalyptic judgment itself, the unleashing of *ice-nine*. For all the comic touches, then, Vonnegut's insistent message seems to move relentlessly toward the cataclysm that awaits twentieth-century humanity, the hapless victims of science and government. The force of evil is certainly Dr. Hoenikker himself: a childlike innocent whose laboratory may be scattered with cheap children's toys, but who nonetheless is the mind behind both the atomic bomb and *ice-nine*; a man-child curiously unfamiliar with concepts such as sin and God; a moral mutation who believes with Faustian pride that humanity can manipulate, dominate, even annihilate nature.[5]

In such a world, Vonnegut's consolations seem few. Love when you can. Laugh if you can. Believe fervently in what makes you happy while history goes about its wild dance toward catastrophe.[6] In keeping with the apparent pessimism of his novel's message, though, Vonnegut seems to qualify even these hopes. Love proves too momentary, too private, or too easily corrupted into lust or possessiveness. Laughter comes only at great expense. It always lingers too long until it becomes hollow and defensive—like whistling along a windswept country road. Vonnegut seems only slightly more tolerant of indulging illusions, the saving lie. With history condemned to rush off into a final catastrophic act of technological insanity on a scale that will dwarf similar acts at Auschwitz, Dresden, and Hiroshima, each person searches out the comforting lie of purpose, the pleasant (and painful) necessity of fashioning fictions of causality to sustain him or her as history self destructs: cold comfort, indeed.

Yet the willingness to accept the world's end according to John/Jonah leaves several questions unanswered. Why, for instance, is Vonnegut's apocalypse delivered in such fantastic terms? Why does a book that begins with such matter-of-fact realism evolve into something finally so unreal? This unreality is achieved not only by the creation of the *ice-nine* crystal (although the researcher Asa Breed does repeatedly dismiss it as a crackpot scheme), but by the whole collection of eccentrics assembled on San Lorenzo who bumble toward the apocalypse in such music-hall fashion. The opening is factual enough. John, a free-lance writer, begins research into what key figures involved with the Hiroshima bomb were doing on the day of the bombing and visits the research complex in Ilium, New York, where some of the theoretical work on the project was completed. Then the plot twists into a fantasy of improbable coincidences, unbelievable caricatures, and exaggerated events—all of which strain to thump home the simple point that science is pure evil and that scientists, even their offspring, are vaguely cannibalistic and lying "sons of bitches."

Yet, why does John himself seem so unpleasant, more so than any scientist encountered in the novel? Intensely self-centered, oddly paranoid, John is a man disconnected from the world—an abrasive loner who finds friendship difficult to cultivate, who takes instant dislikes to people, who is uneasy with even the idea of love and repulsed by the sexual act itself. He is preposterously vain and unbecomingly possessive. He is hardly a profound thinker; his speech is hollowed with cliches and lapses occasionally into baby talk. He fails to respond honestly to an abstract painting and reads album notes while a jazz album plays. Despite his profession, his credentials for factual reporting are dubious. Not only does he barely conceal his bias against Dr. Hoenikker as he begins his book on Hiroshima, but when he is sent on a magazine assignment to write about Julian Castle, the saintly jungle doctor on San Lorenzo, he freely admits, when he finds his subject quite hostile and caustic, that he will have to do some considerable doctoring of his own to make a palatable presentation of this latter-day Albert Schweitzer. And there is the matter of his unforgiving diatribes against scientists and, more generally, against people who think too much. But thinkers are far from alone; John makes hateful remarks against women, midgets, mongoloid idiots, and blacks.

And why, finally, does John the free-lance writer assume the name Jonah? If the name John is associated with the radiant optimism of the visionary Revelation apocalyptic, Jonah recalls a rather minor Old Testament figure. The biblical background, however, is crucial in understanding Vonnegut's messenger. Vonnegut has often reserved the right to refuse the message of his own characters.[7] In *Cat's Cradle*, this distancing strategy—keyed to the narrative device of the biblical antecedent—changes the apparent cataclysmic tenor of the novel. Indeed, *Cat's Cradle*, like the Old Testament Book of Jonah, delivers a most reassuring apocalyptic message. And Vonnegut turns to the very stuff of which his John/Jonah despairs—history—and fashions from it a way out of imminent cataclysm.

A brief review of the Old Testament Book of Jonah will help. God selects Jonah, a staunch Jewish nationalist, to deliver a message of warning to the Gentile people of Nineveh, who are traditional enemies of the Jewish people: reform or face the visitation of God's apocalyptic wrath. Jonah refuses the commission, not so much uneasy about venturing to Nineveh as he is simply unwilling to be instrumental in any attempt to redeem Israel's long-standing foe. He heads out to sea on a boat bound for Tarshish (a name that means literally "the ends of the earth"), as far west as he can sail from Israel, where, as Douglas Robinson points out in his critical survey of the biblical story, Jonah naturally assumes God dwells (143).

God, of course, intervenes, sending a fierce windstorm that moves the ship's crew to press Jonah for details about his flight from God and finally to throw Jonah into the sea at Jonah's own insistence, in order to quiet the winds. Certainly, death by drowning would thwart God's directive to reform Nineveh. But a great fish swallows the floundering Jonah, and, in its belly, he comes to acknowledge God's directive. When the fish spews him up, Jonah goes to Nineveh to deliver the ultimatum: reform in forty days or face the wrath of God. But Jonah, confident that such reformation is unlikely, withdraws to a position above the city to await the onslaught of God's justice. Much to his chagrin, however, the people of Nineveh, led by their king, embrace the message Jonah brings, and God spares the city. The apocalypse is averted. Jonah simmers, feeling foolish and deprived of a chance to watch Israel's hated enemies perish. He censures God, who seems to have changed His divine mind. He rails at God for sparing Nineveh, for being too tender, too easily moved by His own creations. The longer Jonah talks, the more spiteful his indignation sounds.

To teach the vindictive Jonah the difficult message of compassion, God sends him a leafy vine to provide his hut shade from the blasts of desert heat. But even as Jonah reclines gratefully in its shade, God sends a worm to destroy the plant. Jonah is mortified as his sheltering plant withers. God speaks to him and asks him if he can pity a mere plant, why then can he not have mercy on an entire city? And although critics of the Book of Jonah, among them Robinson, presume a closing moment of insight for Jonah—a certain reclamation of his narrowed soul—the book itself closes without Jonah's reply. And *Cat's Cradle* also moves to a moment when that book's Jonah leaves unanswered a critical question that could measure how expansive, how compassionate he could be toward those he reviles. The Old Testament book leaves open the question of whether Jonah learns the lesson of God's "immense capacity" (Lacocque and Lacocque, 78) for compassion toward even the most undeserving or the lesson of His faith in the impossible possibility that evil in humanity may turn toward the good.

Commentators on the Book of Jonah have argued that the book is a corrective to rabid Israeli nationalism that refused God's mercy to any but the chosen.[8] But, unlike other major prophets—Jeremiah, Ezekiel, or Isaiah, for example—a historical Jonah is doubtful. Rather, his little book is a deliberate narrative, one told (like *Cat's Cradle*) with comic touches and just enough verisimilitude to teach as well as to entertain. The book centers not so much on the reformation of Nineveh, which is accomplished in a spare five-verse passage, as on the question of Jonah's education: the dilemma of Jonah and his argument with God is the focus of the book. God does not "change His mind" about the fate of Nineveh, as Jonah angrily charges. The writer of the biblical book is only secondarily concerned with God's intentions to save the city. God commissions Jonah in an attempt to reform Jonah's narrowed soul. It is

a book that stands, Robinson asserts, as an "exceptional call for...
tolerance" (142). As a messenger of imminent cataclysm, Jonah is clearly
wrong: the message he delivers is twisted by his own prejudices and
hatreds. Jonah's name, Hebrew for "dove," certainly makes ironic commentary on his anticipation of Nineveh's destruction and on his petty
argument with the God who, as Robinson argues, seeks conversion rather
than destruction. The narrative works on the contrast between character
and creator—between what Jonah, a character driven by the eager
impulse of the cataclysmic imagination, wants to see happen and what
his God, the tolerant Creator, plans. Jonah, the character, listens only
to the soured voice within and resists the expansive voice without,
which is the sublime, compassionate message of the Creator (Lacocque
and Lacocque, 118–23).

Like the narrator of the Old Testament book, Vonnegut studies his
Jonah from afar. He manipulates a careful distance between his narrating
voice and the reader, who learns little about Jonah despite the first-
person narration in a book that is otherwise imbedded with other characters' biographies and often-lengthy reminiscences. Vonnegut clearly
discourages any close identification with his Jonah. Apart from references to his work as a free-lance writer, we learn in a quick paragraph
that he attended Cornell, married twice, smokes and drinks to excess—
tidbits that suggest Vonnegut himself. This is ironic, given the treatment
John receives once he metamorphoses into Jonah, but disturbing, given
the more recent movement in Vonnegut's fictions.

What we do learn, however, is that (much like his Old Testament
counterpart) Vonnegut's Jonah is obsessed with pattern. Both Jonahs
come to believe that the trials they endure and the distances they travel
(Jonah to Nineveh; John/Jonah to San Lorenzo) are part of a pattern
directed by God (in Jonah's case) or by a force simply beyond human
comprehension (in John/Jonah's case). Both Jonahs think that this pattern
ought to culminate in cataclysmic destruction visited upon the locus of
evil in the world (Nineveh, for Jonah; the entire technological-scientific
twentieth-century world, for John/Jonah). Certain of their knowledge,
both second-guess history by creating for it finales of destruction—Jonah
in his gleeful anticipation of imminent judgment, John/Jonah in the
cataclysmic tale he tells of *ice-nine*. Both finales, however, show only
a heartless willingness to lock history into endgames that promise simple
inevitability. With both characters, their creators intervene to thwart
the cataclysm and to teach the difficult lesson of hope in a dark and
threatening time.

The key difference in the tales of the two Jonahs is the narrative point
of view. The biblical narrative is written in the third person: a voice of

instruction, steady and restrained, that assures the writer (and the reader) a critical distance from a character who proves less likeable as the narrative develops. But in *Cat's Cradle*, such distancing is obscured as Vonnegut, in effect, hands the pen over to Jonah and allows him to complete the book in his own belligerent first-person. As the frame introduced by the opening sentence insists, *Cat's Cradle* is preeminently a told story. And this Jonah takes the opportunity to fulfill in fiction (unlike the biblical counterpart, this Jonah is a professional writer) the cataclysmic notions that he harbors, unmoved by hope and unimpressed by compassion.[9] As Robinson notes, one danger that threatens the biblical Jonah during his uncertain journey toward moral edification is the option of simply withdrawing inward into solipsistic fantasies of destruction (146). Such is finally the nature of the apocalypse called down by Vonnegut's John/Jonah. The apocalypse of *ice-nine* is Jonah's creation, his fantasy for the end of a world that he regards with wearied and jaundiced eyes. John the free-lance writer carefully weaves into the realistic story-line of his research the absurd fantasy of Jonah the apocalyptic. Using the device of *ice-nine* (the insistent italics suggesting its fictitiousness), John concocts a blackly humorous finale of history that reflects what he thinks twentieth-century humanity deserves. He freezes our history, impelled by a chance remark during a brief interview and then compelled by the energy of his own penchant for the cataclysmic imagination. It is as if the biblical Jonah, eagerly anticipating judgment on Nineveh, had completed his own book, bringing down (at least on paper) the judgment he felt, in his arrogance and vindictiveness, the people of Nineveh deserved—the traditional firestorm from heaven.

To clarify and perhaps to suggest Vonnegut's dissatisfaction with his messenger, it might prove helpful to borrow a model suggested by Robinson in his examination of *Moby-Dick*, another apocalyptic novel that plays on the Jonah theme. Robinson argues that Melville splits the Jonah role—the belligerent, angry Jonah who anticipates the destruction of Nineveh and the more tolerant Jonah who, Robinson argues, emerges at the close of the book. Robinson demonstrates this bifurcation using Father Mapple, who delivers an angry, uncompromising, decidedly apocalyptic misreading of the Old Testament story, and Ishmael, who emerges as a more tolerant, more loving sort of Jonah who has been tempered by experience to the difficult message of compassion and compromise. Robinson finds in *Moby-Dick* a fanatic prophet of disruption and discontinuity (Father Mapple) and a prophet who dwells not in the extremes but in the difficult middest (156-67). In Vonnegut's treatment, the narrative exposes its own narrator as another caricature Jonah—another misreader of the Old Testament story and belligerent fanatic who is too eager for extremes, too ready to usher in the apocalypse, and too ready to snuff out the feeble lights that illuminate a dark time. Vonnegut himself emerges as the steadying voice of continuity and tolerance who allows his character to dance off into the darkness that he himself creates.

As Jonah's fantasy unfolds, absurd step by absurd step, clearly what drives his cataclysmic imagination is his own distrust of progress and his base hatred of science. Because Jonah tells the story, every fantastic detail in his world readily validates his every apprehension over science. Felix Hoenikker and the offspring of his "magic meat" (61) all, in effect, are vested with the trappings of evil appropriate to Jonah's simplification of contemporary history. Franklin Hoenikker, who is not only the son of Felix but serves as the minister of science and progress on San Lorenzo (hence doubly worthy of being Jonah's Antichrist), is pictured in a *New York Sunday Times* supplement wearing a sunburst medal on his blouse, with his hair swept up into an outrageous "wiry pompadour, a sort of cube of hair, marcelled, that arose to an incredible height" (60)—the very embodiment of the atomic mushroom cloud. His other children are similarly slighted. Jonah patronizes Newt as a curmudgeon midget and winces at Angela, "a horse-faced platinum blonde" (79). Jonah tries very much to make them seem to be "babies full of rabies," to borrow the words of the elevator operator at the Ilium research complex (47). But each child in turn displays emotional depth that defies John/Jonah's natural bend toward the simplification of stereotyping. They are able to love, to feel compelled by compassion, to release complicated feelings through aesthetic expression, and to look at the world with relentless, open curiosity. They are, in different ways, antidotes to Jonah's rabid misanthropy. Like a chorus, they bear collectively Vonnegut's message of apocalyptic consolation in a dark time.

To accept the cataclysm of *ice-nine* as Jonah's private, and hence harmless, fantasy would explain the drastic departure from the realistic (John) to the fantastic and the cataclysmic (Jonah). John himself writes in the opening pages that the book he had started to write "was to be factual" (11), implying the book that he presents is not. To believe in Jonah's apocalyptic vision, to swallow (as Papa Monzano does) the *ice-nine* chip, this scheme of history frozen to a pattern, is to assume a degree of reliability through a self-appointed apocalyptic whom Vonnegut continually undercuts. Vonnegut, much like the Old Testament God who spares Nineveh, deliberately distances himself from this Jonah and from the cataclysmic patterning of history by offering instead a guarded optimism—faith in a fluid time, in spontaneity, in history itself. Like the Old Testament Book of Jonah, *Cat's Cradle* is a deliberate attempt to edify a pseudoapocalyptic messenger who willfully abandons history to inevitable cataclysm: this messenger glimpses the frightening evidence of his own time, simplistically creates good and bad guys, and then simplistically consigns the bad guys to a final act of species extermination. To accept Jonah's fantasy is to peer into a tangle of strings pulled between the hands and then insist on configurations. But as Vonnegut suggests, there is no damn cat. No damn cradle.[10]

John, convinced as he is that science and progress have condemned humanity to doom, finds justification for his fantasy and for its sense of predetermination in the eccentric, absurd religion of Bokononism practiced on the island. Indeed, *Cat's Cradle*, Jonah's novel about the end of the world, is counterpart to Lionel Boyd Johnson's *Books of Bokonon*, the religious tract of the Bokonon religion quoted so regularly in Jonah's book that it becomes a subtext. In the closing scene of the novel, the prophet himself appears, an eerie, ancient figure in a blue and ruined world, to write the closing lines of both books. The problem, of course, is that both books contrive an either/or dilemma for contemporary history: meaninglessness and the cataclysmic chaos of nihilism or meaningful pattern that masquerades cheaply as the truth and points defiantly toward death. Lionel Boyd Johnson (or John's son) corrupts and alters reality, or more particularly the contemporary history of his adopted island of San Lorenzo, by creating the tension between jungle and city, between his role as Bokonon the prophet-seer and that of Earl McCabe, a fellow adventurer, who remains in the city to play the role of malevolent dictator struggling to squash the holy man of the jungle. It is a game on an immense scale dreamed up by the two to divert the impoverished island population from dwelling on the grim reality of their miserable existence on the worthless little island and, more particularly, from realizing how far the inept government of McCabe has failed to provide the rejuvenation it had promised the people. One lie replaces or deflects another. Like the prophet Bokonon, John/Jonah creates a book that indirectly points up the dangerous difference between reality and fiction in which reality suggests the complicated, the agonizing, the messy, the unpredictable, the open; and fiction the neat, the bordered, the directed, the closed.

Like the two Jonahs, Lionel Boyd Johnson is sham prophet, a heartless charlatan whose message—or religion, as it were—barely conceals an immense skepticism and a fierce hatred. Like the biblical Jonah and all those swayed by the unforgiving fury of the cataclysmic imagination, Lionel Boyd Johnson can offer only illusions moving toward destruction. In the aftermath of *ice-nine*, the prophet counsels island survivors to commit suicide, telling them God himself has grown tired of humanity.

But in the growing menace of a world where truth and reality become the enemy, those most adept at evasions and illusions come to desperate ends: McCabe is driven to suicide; Johnson goes crazy like Kurtz, another death-dealing, self-appointed holy man of the jungle; and Jonah himself, unable to express love for Mona or to find compassion for a dying world, writes humanity and himself into a cold, blue corner and awaits the end of the world, smug only in the certainty that he sees the folly of it all.

John, driven by exaggerated fears and anxieties over life in the nuclear age, turns away from the absurdities and complexities inherent in a contingent, centrifugal, atomistic cosmos and instead asserts that it "all fits together / In the same machine" (12). He pursues pattern like the Episcopalian woman who, in one of the parables of the *Books of Bokonon*, "claimed to understand God and His Ways of Working perfectly." The woman, however, is confused by the simple blueprints for a doghouse. Vonnegut here and at other moments in *Cat's Cradle* stresses both the limits of human knowledge and the wonder of curiosity, which implies an exciting openendedness. The woman, as the parable points out, "is a fool," as is "anyone who thinks he sees what God is Doing" (13). And Jonah, who concocts a fantasy that warns only of the imminent, absurd end of things—who asserts with pride that he understands the direction of the unfolding processes of history—is finally, in the expressive terminology of H. Lowe Crosby, a businessman who comes with John to San Lorenzo, a "pissant," someone who "no matter what you say . . . knows better" (92).

John is confirmed in his expectations of cataclysm long before his fantasy of *ice-nine* commences. After all, he chooses a most curious title for his projected historical account of Hiroshima—*The Day the World Ended*. The exaggerated reaction to the bombing of Hiroshima, itself a sobering political and military expedient, indicates John's pat equation of technology with imminent catastrophe, his exaggerated distrust of science, and, most important, his tendency to indulge apocalyptic hyperbole. John's "factual" book promises to be wildly biased against science, as Dr. Breed quickly realizes during an interview for the book that devolves into an assault by John on science in general. Indeed, John, while assembling material about Felix Hoenikker, talks to one of Hoenikker's sons, Newt, who freely admits hating his father; to Hoenikker's secretary, who complains that he was a complete mystery; and to Marvin Breed, a man who once loved the beautiful woman Hoenikker married and who, even years after Hoenikker's death, still calls him a "son of a bitch" (52). This can hardly be the basis of the "objective" and "accurate" portrait that John professes to desire (35). In the course of

his interview with Dr. Breed, John admits that he could not resist implying that scientists were "accessories to murders most foul" (34). But
Dr. Breed counters by asking the question that Vonnegut encourages his
readers to ask, "Where did you ever get such ideas? From the funny
pages?" (35).

Deaf to Dr. Breed's genuinely modest defense of the potential of
science and research, Jonah does listen to his offhand remark about a
crackpot scheme suggested to Felix Hoenikker by a marine general: tired
of having his troops wade through the mud, the general wondered if
Hoenikker could fashion a compound able to raise the melting point of
water. Such a scheme strikes John immediately with all its sinister implications of science and the military in league trying to contravene natural
law by tinkering with a potentially cataclysmic concept (after all, such
a compound, as John hounds Dr. Breed to admit, could destroy the
water of the planet should an accident occur). He asks several times
whether something like *ice-nine* had ever been developed. Dr. Breed
points out no less than seven times that it does not exist. But the concept
of such a device to a person already predisposed to crying "The end
is near!" and to seeing futility too easily (later, for instance, in looking
at Newt Hoenikker's abstract painting of tangles of lines, Jonah sees
"the sticky nets of human futility [113]) veers John toward Jonah and
toward the fantasy of *ice-nine*. As Dr. Breed accurately foretells to John,
"I suppose you're going to rush to market with a sensational story about
ice-nine now" (41).[11]

Cat's Cradle is just that book. Like the Old Testament book, here is
a comic story nevertheless full of anger, resentment, and hate: a book
that anticipates apocalyptic thunder. Yet the biblical book undercuts its
own character's eagerness by highlighting the apocalypse averted—both
the fierce windstorm at sea and the firestorm promised for Nineveh. In
Vonnegut's novel the yearning for endings is similarly calmed. Sensational and absurd, *Cat's Cradle* freely blurs history into fantasy and
pushes the strict objectivity of reporting into the casual reality of science
fiction. Where to draw the line, what to accept as face or as John/Jonah's
fiction is impossible to know. Artfully, Vonnegut manages to create
credence for his apocalyptic messenger and in the same breath under-
mine his every pretense to reliability, his every gesture, his every
thought. Does the world end or is John/Jonah punching it out fiercely
on his typewriter? Are we, as Robinson argues, the Ninevites to whom
Vonnegut's Jonah delivers the message: reform from scientific worship
or face our own absurd ending? Vonnegut has a wider purpose in mind
than running from science. A master of the exacting, imaginative
demands of speculative fiction, he has glimpsed the promise as well as

the threat of science. The novel, however, aims at those, like John/Jonah, who are willing to cry down the heavens now and turn science into magic—those who turn away from history, turn away from the pain, and escape in simple scenarios of extermination.

Of course, Vonnegut does not announce the moment when John will metamorphose into Jonah and history will spin off into fantasy. Clearly, the idea fascinates John as he interviews Asa Breed. Perhaps the fantasy begins in earnest when John, drinking carelessly in the "small saloon in the rear of the plane" (65), plows through the fantastic history of San Lorenzo during the interminable flight to the island and admits that his book is changing purpose.[12] Perhaps the idea that *ice-nine* really exists occurs to him as he attends the dying Papa Monzano, who is "radiating pain so hot and bright that the walls seemed bathed in angry red" (146), and Papa whimpers hoarsely, "Ice." Whenever, the idea of *ice-nine* plants itself in John's mind like a chip of the compound itself, freezing it, as it were, into a vision of imminent cataclysm. After he leaves Ilium (which Dr. Breed tellingly points out was historically a "jumping off" place for restless pioneers headed west), John evolves into a Jonah who, in turn, plots the improbable progress of *ice-nine* from the laboratory of Felix Hoenikker to the shores of San Lorenzo and then to the bedchamber of Papa Monzano. Along the way, he often inserts bits of rather angry correctives to other (factual) histories. For instance, Jonah takes exception to the *Sunday Times* article on San Lorenzo by saying that Franklin Hoenikker "didn't say so, but the son of a bitch had a piece of *ice-nine* with him—in a thermos jug" (62). John/Jonah is, of course, curiously vague about just how Dr. Hoenikker managed to concoct *ice-nine*,[13] saying only that Hoenikker borrowed "this and that," leaving no records, "until so to speak, he had baked the last batch of brownies" (41–42). Not only is such a description decidedly vague for a historical record (suggestive of John's narrative swinging off its realistic moorings), but it smacks of simplistic thought.

Like the biblical Jonah whose narrative reveals how unchristian and unlikeable he is, the *ice-nine* fantasy that this Jonah concocts to present his vision of the world doomed by its own faith in science becomes a catalogue of his own failings. Even before the *ice-nine* fantasy commences in earnest, John, despite his professed desire "to see what he could see" (23), often fails to see what goes on around him. The reality of things does not greatly concern him. He misjudges. He assumes. For instance, when he decides to visit Felix Hoenikker's grave, he sees in the cemetery "an alabastar phallus twenty feet high" (48) looming ahead—a great stone mushroom cloud that, he assumes, has been erected over the grave of the Father of the Atomic Bomb. He smugly decides as he approaches it that the monument would be fitting as a picture for the dust jacket of his book on Hiroshima, a perfect commentary on the association in *his* mind between atomic science, death, and sterility (a stone phallus sheathed by icy sleet). He discovers, however, that the mushroom cloud rises over the grave of Emily, Felix's wife. Over Felix's grave is a simple stone cube. Rather than puzzle out its implications (which would, of course, be a measure of curiosity), John promptly forgets the whole matter. Other times he guesses; he glances rather than looks; he jumps to conclusions, often satisfied with what turns out to be only part of the story. Just as he stays in an air-conditioned room on the tropical island of San Lorenzo, a room that obscures one's view of the poverty on the island, John/Jonah lives cushioned from reality, happy with partial views.

Furthermore, both John the free-lance writer and Jonah the pseudoapocalyptic reveal an inability to love. John mentions two failed marriages and in the course of his stay in Ilium has a lackluster one-night stand with a personable prostitute named Sandra, an experience that leaves him feeling "bristly, diseased, and cynical," his soul "as foul as smoke from burning cat fur" (27). And Jonah, immured in the world of San Lorenzo, is smitten by Mona Aamons Monzano, the angelically beautiful adopted daughter of the island's dictator. In Jonah's emerging strained allegory, Mona embodies the essence of goodness and love; indeed, much about her suggests an uneven pastiche of images borrowed from the figures of the classical goddess and the Christian angel. Even without meeting her, he imagines that "she could make [him] far happier" than he had ever been (64). She quickly becomes for him another exercise in illusion. With her simple white dresses and her gold sandals, her pale gold hair, her full hips curved like "a lyre" (98), she seems to hover above his apocalypse like an angel in Revelation, playing "When Day Is Done" on her xylophone. To Jonah's narrowed soul, she seems to bring a message of intoxicating love. She first introduces him to the island ritual of *boko-maru,* the erotic experience of rubbing the soles of the feet together. Jonah, when he accepts Franklin Hoenikker's offer to become the figurehead president of San Lorenzo, accepts as well an arranged marriage with the divine Mona. But Mona spends her days innocently performing *boko-maru* with anyone in her naive attempt to spread love as best she can. In what seems to be a crucial scene, Jonah demands that she cease such indiscretions. She reprimands him in her simple way for trying to possess love and threatens to leave him. He quickly (and rather half-heartedly) adopts her generosity with love and allows her the freedom to continue bringing the world love. With her diaphanous gowns, Mona seems to bring to the cataclysm of San Lorenzo an ethereal figure of innocent love doomed in a world damned to hasty extinction. Indeed, the nadir of the postapocalyptic world would seem to be the moment Mona touches her lips while reaching toward the frozen corpses on the island and, consequently, freezes herself, a suicide that Jonah witnesses. Even her name suggests a certain oneness, a healthy wholeness that Jonah's cloistered soul, so soured by hate, welcomes. In the initial rush after first performing *boko-maru* with Mona, Jonah seems stunned beyond words, moved toward a spiritual and emotional rebirth.[14]

Vonnegut, however, suggests that Mona is no more capable of love, regenerative or otherwise, than is Jonah, and that like Jonah she participates only in the urgent movement toward death. Her rite of *boko-maru* is a childish gesture (as the name suggests), an empty, sterile ritual that mocks on the crudely literal level the exchange of souls implicit in the act of love. It is, however, appropriate to a woman who finds the sexual act itself repulsive and the notion of reproduction distasteful (178). When, in Jonah's fantasy, he finally succeeds in making love to Mona (a "sordid sex episode," as he calls it [177]) in the bomb shelter after the *ice-nine* cataclysm, the chapter is titled "The Iron Maiden and the Oubliette." Jonah afterwards describes the sexual consummation as a "bizarre, grunting, sweating, enterprise" (178). Curiously vapid, barely literate, uninterested in love (she is indifferently paired off to whomever succeeds to the presidency of San Lorenzo), she echoes Jonah (as their names suggest), rather than emerging as some courageous counterforce of love. Disconnected in her serenity (she does not react, for instance, when her adopted father, dying of cancer, collapses in great pain on the military review stand during the reception ceremony; she is quite enthralled performing *boko-maru* with a pilot), she is as "anesthetized" and "frigid" as Jonah at one point suspects but refuses to believe.

Mona's suicide gesture in Jonah's fantasy of a world frozen by *ice-nine* reveals that the acceptance of Jonah's radical simplification of history, his cataclysmic vision that death is everything in the modern world, offers only the acquiescence to death. By her suicide, Mona, who has resisted all along the implications of living, reproduction, and sexual connection, shows a resistance as well to the complexities of trying to survive. Her death is quick, easy. *Cat's Cradle* is, in effect, Jonah's suicide note for the human species. For him the only significant action left humanity is the final folly of species extermination. But, as Mona remarks, "Suicide is all so simple, that's all. It solves so much for so many, so simply" (182). John's inability to perceive clearly and to love completely are finally symptomatic of a more profound spiritual failure.

He simplifies; he reduces; he refuses to engage complexities. Like the biblical Jonah, he comes ready only to watch his Nineveh burn.

When Jonah first arrives on San Lorenzo, the island experiences one of its frequent power failures. During his first night, Jonah is awakened by the thundering bang of an oil generator in the presidential palace coming back to life and the subsequent flood of light and cacophony of noise as appliances all over the castle suddenly spark to life. Jonah rushes out of bed in "brainless ecstasy" convinced that the situation "seemed...mortal" (130), a situation that deliberately plays on the traditional "bang and flood of light" of the midnight surprise of the Christian apocalypse. His entire fantasy of *ice-nine* is a similar fit of brainless ecstasy, a fantasy fostered by the slimmest anchor in reality.

What begins the *ice-nine* fascination is John's conviction that humanity is doomed, pawns of some "who think too much." When he tours the General Forge and Foundry Company in Ilium, he notices

> A winded, defeated-looking fat woman in filthy coveralls trudg[ing] beside [him]....She turned to examine Dr. Breed, looking at him with helpless reproach. She hated people who thought too much....she struck [John] as an appropriate representative for almost all mankind. (31)

Winded, defeated-looking, helpless. These are the people, Vonnegut points out, who share Jonah's rabid distrust of science and who embrace the ending of history rather than the struggle to live within its complicated universe; they have forsaken the humility of curiosity to live in a murky world of ignorance. Later in the tour, John strongly identifies again, this time with Francine Pefko, a secretary at the research center who is as mystified as John by what she calls the "magic" of modern science. Pefko "gurgles emptily" and laughs "idiotically" when she talks. She is confused by words such as *antithesis* and *charlatan*. When she ransacks her mind for something to say to the august group of scientists whom she ushers through the research center, she finds "nothing but used Kleenex and costume jewelry" (31). More important, when her mother questions what actually goes on at the plant, she merely chants, "I dunno, I dunno, I dunno" (31).

Against John/Jonah's impressive ignorance stands the curious figure of Felix Hoenikker. Whereas John opts for surface inquiry, Felix questions and explores. Uninterested in people and untouched even by family ties, Felix wonders at the natural world as he tinkers restlessly, endlessly in a laboratory littered with cheap dime-store toys. He is described by Asa Breed as a "force of nature no mortal could possibly control" (23). Uninterested in the moral complications of atomic weapons, Felix, during the height of the Manhattan Project, was easily distracted into studying turtles: he wondered whether when they pull their heads into their shells their spines buckled or contracted. That sort of curiosity and radical disconnection from events does, of course, lead not only to Felix's neglect of his family but to the larger, more difficult question of responsibility for Hiroshima. But Felix, as his name implies and as his childlike simplicity suggests, is strangely fortunate: the pure product of twentieth-century scientific research that "plays" within the natural realm, investigating it with the simple open eye of an eccentric child, as the epigraph from Oppenheimer that opens this chapter suggests. When he accepts the Nobel Prize, Felix simply says, "I stand before you now because I never stopped dawdling like an eight-year-old on a spring morning on his way to school. Anything can make me stop and look and wonder, and sometimes learn. I am a very happy man" (17). Compared to the approach of John/Jonah, who molds from his profound ignorance a shoddy and fanatic certainty of knowledge, Felix's simple curiosity stands as bold corrective.

With Felix Hoenikker haunting the book like a shadow, Asa Breed emerges as the book's defender of science and the promise of research. Dr. Breed, "civilized, optimistic, capable, serene" (27), is one of those who "thinks too much." He explains patiently and quite sincerely the hope that scientific research holds out to the modern world, the importance of curiosity, and the dangers of reducing science to magic. Dr. Breed's commencement address to Sandra's high-school class, which still lingers in Sandra's mind as "some kind of talk" (25), argued that only superstitious people prevented science from realizing its potential. Unlike John/Jonah, Dr. Breed is quite capable of love. Years after Emily Hoenikker's death, Dr. Breed is still sensitive even to the mention of her name. *His* name implies a renewing fertility (rumors about Ilium name Dr. Breed as the father of all of Felix Hoenikker's children in an evidently prolonged love affair that would explain the phallus over Emily's grave; John dismisses the whole affair as "sordid"). Dr. Breed is genuinely disturbed by the story he relates of a mass murderer hanged in Ilium in 1782 for the deaths of twenty-seven people. He is stunned that such a man could have no remorse and could even go to his death singing. John, however, absently asks about the lyrics of the song and responds to the whole story with the rather callous cliche, "The mind reels" (28). Dr. Breed understands almost from the first word John speaks that he is closed even to the possibilities of science, that he is one of the superstitious. It is no surprise that Dr. Breed disappears from John's narrative once Jonah's fantasy commences in earnest. "Beautifully dressed" and a healthy "pink" (27), he would be sorely out of place in a fantasy where all the scientists must wear black hats.

Although Vonnegut has surely never proposed himself as arch-defender of science or technology, he senses the danger in the popular mystification of it. Given the grim evidence of this century's history, the promoting of science to religion—or, "magic that works" (147)—simplifies the nuclear age and reduces it to the possibility of a grim medieval showdown between good and evil. The elaborate drama created by Earl McCabe and Lionel Boyd Johnson was conceived with the idea that "good societies could be built only by pitting good against evil, and by keeping the tension between the two high at all times" (74). (It is, however, Vonnegut's jab at Lyndon Baines Johnson's simplifications of the renewed cold war, which pitched America into a hopeless morass in Indochina.) The insistence on good and evil as balancing forces able to shape contemporary events is inspired here by a Charles Atlas training manual. Rather than confront contemporary history honestly (as John's original book promises), Jonah, first and foremost a writer, recreates history and casts an absurd fantasy that denies ambiguity by insisting on a running struggle between a definable good and evil that points to inevitable finale.

Although McCabe and Johnson and John/Jonah practice these more public deceptions, the novel is replete with characters fleeing painful, if more private, realities: denied love, unhappy family life, ruinous marriages. The ugly Angela, trapped in a marriage with a scheming womanizer and heavy drinker, pretends to be happy yet blows soulful blues on her clarinet. Newt, a midget who has loved neither family nor friends and has been deceived in a love affair, paints haunted canvases. Franklin, unloved by his father and drifting in school, builds model countries in the basement of Jack's Hobby Shop. Emily, ignored by a husband too much lost in his own world, turns to Asa Breed for love. Like the marine sergeant who comes to Felix Hoenikker in the hopes of getting his troops out of the mud forever, these escapees try to deny reality. The problem of the book, of course, is that mud-turned-to-ice is a fantasy, and a dangerous one to boot. Vonnegut rejects his main character's immediate fascination with *ice-nine*. Vonnegut warns we must have mud—the messy, raw stuff of open history. Those characters willing to hole up in oubliettes of their own making, there safe from pain as well as life, merely accelerate the movement toward death. Vonnegut chafes against such pretense and against the idea of history itself, with its pretense of patterning (read, for instance, the delightful spoof of history books in the account of the history of San Lorenzo). In a novel so deliberately framed by a man such as John/Jonah, there are few moments when anyone speaks up for abandoning illusion. On the plane to San Lorenzo, Ambassador Minton, explaining his summary dismissal from the State Department for a letter his wife wrote that dared to suggest that Americans might not be universally loved, cautions that American foreign policy thrives on lies and that it should rather "recognize hate than imagine love" (72). And the dying Papa Monzano urges the others to discontinue the charade by killing Bokonon the Jungle Prophet so that the island can get on with looking at life straight on (147).

Like Minton and Monzano, Vonnegut senses the dangers of turning away from reality. Vonnegut freely makes light of his characters' tendency to simplification when Jonah finally sends the world into its apocalypse: as *ice-nine* hits the ocean, it does so in one "grand Ah-Whoom!" (174), much like the printed sound effects on a comic-book page. Jonah creates for himself a secret "cozy bomb shelter" that he happens to discover, which is absurdly stocked with Virgin Island rum, Campbell's chicken gumbo, and bound copies of twenty years of *National Geographic,* and there stays, dutifully like his adopted namesake, for three days. Vonnegut not only parodies the biblical story but spoofs the survival novels so much the fashion in the speculative fiction of the cold war 1950s. By casting a certain "Walt Disney charm" (184) about Jonah's fantasy of *ice-nine,* he cautions that such cataclysmic approaches to the twentieth century reduce history to cartoon, much like the bombing targets floating in the ocean off San Lorenzo on the day of the military air review: likenesses of the Kaiser, Hitler, Mussolini, and "old Joe Stalin"—contemporary history's bad guys pressed into easily destroyed cutouts. Cataclysmics in the nuclear age, Vonnegut cautions, are confused by their scientific world, terrorized by their own history, and threatened by the centrifugal universe that modern science seems more inclined to explore and define than to pull together into systems. They seek refuge in their conviction that rather than cope with history they need only to believe, as John/Jonah, in its approaching doom. Fatalists, they run scared from history into improbable, simplistic fantasies of cataclysms caused by "cutout" villains—evil scientists, fanatic military men, beetle-browed politicians. It is no coincidence that when the *ice-nine* hits the ocean, Jonah closes his eyes (174). So Vonnegut, more than aware of the necessity of facing history, invites the reader to enjoy this fantasy of a world ending, an apocalypse more vaudevillian than terrifying. Jonah's fantasy is like the "End of the World Delight," a drink served in the Ilium bar that he visits. On the day of Hiroshima, the bartender concocted a nauseatingly sweet drink—"a half-pint of creme de menthe in a hollowed-out pineapple, with whipped cream and a cherry on top" (27)—for a bum who came stumbling into the bar after hearing the news from Japan, convinced that Hiroshima would trigger the end of the world.

But Vonnegut is not concerned simply with undercutting Jonah's apocalypse as a harmless confection. Like the Old Testament Book of Jonah, *Cat's Cradle* works to correct a narrowing of the soul, a denial of compassion, an abandonment of hope, a loss of spontaneity and surprise. Jonah's apocalyptic rhetoric, after all, not only locks history into a simple choice between drift and doom, but sustains, in turn, a deep-seated hatred of humanity.[15] But, like the bird that flutters above the abyss (which is in this case opened up when the plane crashes into the Monzano castle), Vonnegut's message of hope—his "pootee-phweet" (174)—defies generic descriptions such as optimistic or pessimistic. It is instead the graceful, indecipherable gesture of the tiny bird resisting the cataclysm. Far from being a messenger of doom bent on excoriating the scientific community for destroying the dignity of humanity by creating the modern calculus of mass destruction and then entrusting such awesome power to politicians who are no better than sideshow performers, Vonnegut persists in maintaining a confidence in humanity. Nineveh, the most evil of God's kingdoms, will convert. The greatest lesson of Lionel Boyd Johnson's improbable religion is a message lost to John/Jonah, much as in the Old Testament Jonah resists the compassionate lesson of *his* book. The *Books of Bokonon* teach that man, dwarfed by the twentieth-century universe, is only "as big as what he hopes and thinks" (189). And John is shriveled indeed, a man unable to hope, who despairs of humanity's potential and is convinced that history teaches little but its folly.

At many levels, then, *Cat's Cradle* is a narrative in rebellion against its own narrator. Not only does Vonnegut undercut the dramatic showdown conceived in the fantasy of John/Jonah by pointing out again and again that such patterning is more a running away from history, but the characters assembled in John/Jonah's cataclysmic fantasy also work against his intended vituperation of the modern scientific world. Asa Breed, a scientist actually involved in the research on the atomic bomb, is balanced, reasonable, modest—hardly the Antichrist. Franklin Hoenikker, the minister of science and progress, tells Jonah that the greatest lesson of Bokononism is not the insistence on pattern, but the conviction that the only sacred thing in the universe is humanity. The Bokonon religion itself has as its cornerstone a parable of the Creation in which God leaves the invention of purpose to each person, thus explicitly refuting any one person's scheme as truth; Jonah calls this lesson in openendedness "trash" (177). Even Mona—the embodiment of love finally overwhelmed by the sadness of death—even Mona fails Jonah. She is as frigid and unloving as Jonah himself. The narrative of Jonah's fantasy, then, much like the narrative in the Old Testament, works to counter the actions, thoughts, and prejudices of its main character.

The hope of a world trusting itself to openended history is tempered by recalling that the reformation of Nineveh is rendered by *that* book's author as a rather comic and unlikely event. Indeed, the king orders even the animals to dress in ashes and sackcloth. But the faith in history is clearly preferable to the seething misogyny and willful embrace of cataclysm that characterizes John/Jonah. Vonnegut does not assume (as John/Jonah does) that the alternative to pattern is free-fall into contingency, the nihilistic energy of the "poor poet" Sherman Krebbs, who takes over John's apartment during his trip to Ilium and destroys it completely in a "nihilistic debauch" in which he sets the couch on fire and even kills the cat (58–59). Vonnegut wants only to free the complex, technological age from the ironbound logic of the cataclysmic imagination. But Jonah refuses the message. As he works out his fantasy, as his created world turns ice blue, Jonah positions his minister of science and progress (Franklin Hoenikker) still pursuing scientific data in stereotypically egghead fashion, seemingly indifferent to the cataclysm of *ice-nine*. Yet, as Vonnegut stresses earlier with Dr. Breed, Franklin's research investigates *survival* in the face of Jonah's narrative and its atmosphere soaked in death. Franklin, curious about how ants have managed to survive the *ice-nine*, constructs an ant farm. He tells Jonah, who is in no mood to listen, "You know why ants are so successful? . . . Because they co-op-er-ate" (187). Such deliberate syllabication is Franklin's (and Vonnegut's) closing effort to teach the willful Jonah that history in the technological age is as open to fables of survival and cooperation as it is malleable into cataclysmic fantasies. Jonah dismisses Franklin with a saying from Bokonon that, sadly, applies more to himself and the biblical Jonah: "Beware of the man who works hard to learn something, learns it, and finds himself no wiser than before. . . . He is full of murderous resentment of people" (187).

Billy Pilgrim, Vonnegut's other great pseudoapocalyptic messenger, learns a much harsher lesson from the pain of twentieth-century history. Against the advice of Malachi Constant, who pledges to keep looking back despite the pain, Billy is overcome by the suffering he witnesses in history and is driven to deny history altogether. If Jonah proclaims that death is everything in a technological universe, Billy Pilgrim is shattered to the point that he convinces himself that death is nothing. Jonah, terrified by the prospect of random events, constructs a pattern that is informed less by history itself and more by his own anxious distrust of science. He connects the dots, imposes configurations onto time. He pretends to understand. And the pattern he constructs, the cataclysmic fantasy detailed in *Cat's Cradle*, is finally one whose message is that humanity is helpless in time, able only to follow history as it moves toward swift conclusion. Vonnegut separates himself from such fatalism to offer at least the possibility that the "machinery of life" is open, fluid, "complicated," and "unpredictable" (51).

The tone considerably darkens in *Slaughterhouse-Five*. The apocalypse that will eventually consume the universe, which Billy Pilgrim "sees" in his Tralfamadorian fantasy, is an absurd accident. A Tralfamadorian test pilot accidentally blows up the universe while he is testing flying-saucer fuel (117). Unlike the fantasy of *ice-nine*, where humanity is at least the vehicle for its own extinction and where the apocalypse at least abides by cause and effect (albeit an eccentric pattern), history has taught Billy that such is not the case. Death for him is accidental, random, meaningless. There are no villains. No victims. No showdown. And no survivors.

If Jonah can be said to connect the dots into configurations, Billy Pilgrim wanders in the vast, empty spaces between them. Unable to master history by imposing patterns, Billy simply rejects linear time. Walking through the cratered world of Dresden-in-ashes, Billy sees only a world soaked in time and absurd death. The cruel lesson of Edgar Derby's swift execution destroys Billy. Its absurdity is magnified to include Billy's fantasy of his own death and the death of the universe at the hands of the Tralfamadorian test pilot as well. Like Lot, the biblical presence who dominates this Vonnegut book, Billy survives by refusing to look back. He withdraws into a universe that he creates as a defensive mechanism against a cosmos that defies explanation. His is a universe without history, time, or death; hence, it ends without fanfare, pain, or significance.

Like John/Jonah's fantasy, the story of Billy Pilgrim is another cautionary tale that warns against disconnecting from history. Both of Vonnegut's pseudoapocalyptics—the one of ice, the other of fire—offer only messages of surrender to helplessness before history. They evidence a profound inhumanity and a contempt for the species that dwarfs the historical atrocities that trigger both cataclysmic visions. Vonnegut cannot accept either strategy. Yet the consolation tendered in *Cat's Cradle* does not seem to work in *Slaughterhouse-Five*. History—so open and fluid, spontaneous and fascinating—is no longer on Vonnegut's side.

When he writes about Billy Pilgrim in the opening remarks, Vonnegut shows a sympathy with his character's dilemma. Billy and Vonnegut share the experience of Dresden; they both know its lesson. And Vonnegut demonstrates that he has known firsthand the sensation of being a "non-person," helpless in time and heading for meaningless extinction. When Vonnegut (like Lot's wife) turns to look back, history now threatens more than it did in *Cat's Cradle*. The historic event that centers *Slaughterhouse-Five* (the firebombing of Dresden) is more terrifying than the Hiroshima bombing that centers *Cat's Cradle*. Hiroshima, whatever its moral implications, was a political and military decision with a clear defense for its execution. The firebombing of Dresden on 13 February 1945 incinerated 70,000 *more* civilians than were killed by the Hiroshima blast. The official reasons for the attack have never seemed sufficient to account for the seemingly gratuitous destruction of an "open" (defenseless) city that was a center of art and culture. The promise of a fluid history that alone provided the corrective to Jonah's cataclysmic fantasy seems lost in *Slaughterhouse-Five*. History seems now more absurd, more dangerous, less dependable. To counter Billy's passivity to cataclysm, Vonnegut now can offer the thinnest hope left—a faith in today, the present that stands perilously near the grim evidence of the past, which, in turn, eclipses whatever promise tomorrows traditionally hold. Although Vonnegut once again rejects the message of his pseudoapocalyptic, it is a rejection delivered without the same jovial smirking that characterizes the undercutting of Jonah.

Slaughterhouse-Five is as much shaped by Vonnegut's look back at World War II as it is informed by the 1960s, a period of widespread and often violent expressions of doubt in the viability of long-standing institutions. Such periods are ripe for both the apocalyptic temper, with its reassurance of hope, and the cataclysmic imagination, with its warnings of destruction. Again in a Vonnegut novel, the two contend for control of the work's tone. Vonnegut anchors the novel firmly in the 1960s: he refers in his opening and closing chapters to the political assassinations of 1968 as well as to the ongoing involvement in Indochina—individually purposeless acts of aggression that seem to indicate, in aggregate, a pattern that points only to some greater absurd finality. Billy's message, however, is that when confronted by such chaos and uncertainty, such inhuman slaughter and purposeless suffering, humanity can disconnect from history by withdrawing completely into the sort of passivity that envelops Billy like an ether—like the bugs pressed in amber that the Tralfamadorians use to explain time. Like John/Jonah, Billy becomes a prophet of the cataclysmic imagination.

That solution seems to haunt Vonnegut as if it is only by the strongest act of will that he has managed to maintain his own ties with reality. In the opening autobiographical chapter, Vonnegut seems as unstuck in time as Billy. He wanders freely in his memory—to Dresden during the war, to his days in Chicago as a newspaper reporter, to his schooling, to his early years of marriage. Vonnegut, however, never loses himself in time. He operates, as it were, from the present. He looks back at the same events that have so casually destroyed Billy. He knows the sensation of becoming a Billy Pilgrim, driven to nerveless disengagement from history. When weather reroutes the flight Vonnegut plans to take on his return to Dresden (his own pilgrimage that repudiates Billy's fantastic time travel), he is left a "non-person" in a fogged-in Boston airport overnight. That night in the motel where he is herded with the other nonpersons who have lost their scheduled flights (much as Billy is cut loose from linear time), Vonnegut experiences that sense of disconnection from history that so alienates his character:

> The time would not pass. Somebody was playing with the clocks, and not only the electric clocks, but the wind-up kind, too. The second hand on my watch would twitch once, and a year would pass, and then it would twitch again.
>
> There was nothing I could do about it. As an Earthling I had to believe whatever clocks said—and calendars. (20)

So much in this stark confessional moment recalls Billy's own voyages in time: the harrowing feeling of helplessness that disconnection inevitably brings; the sense of confusion and the need to trust in some blind force controlling time, which seems only to pass rather than to progress; the suspicion that time and history are merely measuring games invented by the human mind; and the mood of alienation and critical disconnection from humanity suggested by the closing reference to "Earthlings." It is just this feeling that Vonnegut cannot accept. The solution of accepting what we cannot change—time itself—does not relieve Vonnegut of his anxieties about this century.[16] Billy, who streaks through the dark night of the twentieth century hoping to deliver (to any talk show in New York City) his news that time means nothing, cannot offer the apocalyptic message of consolation. His destruction at the hands of history merely drives him to the anesthetic inability to react to death of any sort—from the loss of a bottle of champagne to the cataclysmic destruction of the entire universe.

In Billy's fantastic universe of no-time, the present is lost to him. The imagined eternity that he offers quickly becomes as inane (and as infantile) as the child's endless singsong round "I Am Yon Yonson from Wisconsin," which Vonnegut talks about in the opening chapter. In opting to defy endings, to retreat from death, Billy immures himself in a world that can have no significance. The complexities of the present are simply divested of importance as Billy helplessly tumbles in time. The present, then, becomes much like the Tastee-Freeze concoction served at the three Ilium ice-cream stands of which Billy is part owner. A frozen delight that gives "all the pleasure that ice cream could give, without the stiffness and bitter coldness of ice cream" (61), this Tastee-Freeze is an artificial dessert, a processed confection. Against the barbarism and the technological cruelties of this century, Billy whips up a pleasant universe where "Everything Was Beautiful and Nothing Hurt" (122). But like *ice-nine*, it is a retreat from reality. It is a defensive strategy; like the domed cage on Tralfamadore, it both protects and traps. It is a simplification of history that signals a threat far greater than Jonah's rabid hatred of the scientific community. Billy refuses to engage life at any level. He numbs himself to the present. He must be told, as a POW in the barracks, that his coat sleeve has caught fire (97). In Vonnegut, the twentieth century can be conceived as a vast, uncertain ocean surging with evidences of humanity's cruelty and suffered indignities following one after the other like great, dark waves. In such a history Billy sinks from sight, much as he does in the YMCA swimming pool in which his father tosses him to teach him how to swim. At the bottom of the pool Billy finds only "beautiful music everywhere" (44), much like the reassuring timelessness of his fantasy, Tralfamadore. It is a withdrawal, however, that promises only to suffocate.

It is fitting that in the POW production of *Cinderella* Billy makes off with the airman's boots meant to serve in the play as Cinderella's glass slipper (145). Midnight will never interrupt his fantasy withdrawal from life. Indeed, his glass slippers are boots made of sterner stuff. But without that midnight stroke, Vonnegut suggests, Cinder-Ella is condemned forever to play at the fantasy of the ravishing, yet unreal, Cinderella (a child among the ashes, like Billy in Dresden)—swirling and dancing forever in a world of illusions, a world without clocks, a world without the stroke of midnight. Without that sudden, complete interruption of time—in short, without acknowledging at least the certainty of the apocalyptic moment—people in the twentieth century, jaded by the pattern of atrocities into ether worlds of their own construction, cannot live with any vigor in the present. Death reduced to fantasy robs life of its meaningful moments. To enjoy the ball, Cinder-Ella must anticipate the pain of the midnight hour. Without it, life is reduced to a game and death to diversion, much as when Billy, while on wargame maneuvers in the South Carolina hills, attends a Sunday morning prayer service during which his platoon, caught by surprise, is informed by a hovering helicopter that they are now all dead. "The theoretical corpses laughed and ate a hardy noontime meal" (41).

Robbed of the present by refusing to engage history, Billy, much like John/Jonah, cannot sustain love—his marriage is a loveless arrangement to a huge woman, "a girl nobody in his right mind would have married" (119). He drifts from his children. He indulges masturbatory fantasies in his Tralfamadorian universe. Like John/Jonah, a reporter guilty of distorting the facts, Billy is an optometrist who wears trifocals. Most of Billy's business comes not from prescribing lenses, but from selling frames and supplying safety glasses to Ilium factory workers. When Billy comes to look at history, rather than face the pain that Malachi Constant faces, he dons safety glasses of his own. Billy is an eyewitness to the twentieth century, the colossal tragedies of the technological age. But he attempts to take what he has seen and construct from it a mythology of timelessness, a fantasy of painless, deathless existence. Like the French photographer Andre LeFevre, who, in 1841, defended his pornographic postcards of a girl and a Shetland pony by insisting that his intention "was to make Greek mythology come alive" but was nevertheless sentenced to six months in a French prison (41), Billy simply cannot make a mythology from an obscenity. To live in an anxious age of technological obscenities demands seeing it as it is. Billy's myth, like the French postcards, is cheap. More to the point, his failure to confront history—to return to Dresden (as Vonnegut does in the opening chapter)—participates in a desecration of life far worse than the atrocities and private accidents and deaths that so distort his perceptions.

What is Vonnegut's prescription for the twentieth-century person haunted by a history that seems to eclipse the future? How is humanity to live in these latter days? Vonnegut resists the simpler lesson that Dresden teaches, the lesson of withdrawal, by fighting valiantly to connect. In the opening chapter, he speaks rather poignantly of troubled nights when history haunts him, when his breath stinks of mustard gas and roses (the smell of Dresden in the days following the firestorm), when he calls randomly on the telephone or has operators canvass the night world for his former girlfriends. He switches on the radio to connect with an all-night station in Boston or New York. He will even talk to his dog. Indeed, his opening chapter is one attempt after another to connect. He visits his war buddy. He travels to Dresden. He recalls his days working for the newspaper syndicate in Chicago, where every reporter working the city would be connected to the newspaper offices by "pneumatic tubes which ran under the streets of Chicago" (8).

With the determination to connect with history, Vonnegut, unlike Billy, does not surrender the present to forces he cannot control—past, present, and future. When he recalls taking his children to the 1964 New York World's Fair, Vonnegut writes of its display of the past and its exhibitions on the future, conceptions and inventions of Ford, General Motors, and Walt Disney—mechanistic and fantastic visions that did not allow for the present. It is there, on the the perilously thin ledge of the present, that Vonnegut takes his stand. "I asked myself about the present: how wide it was, how deep it was, how much was mine to keep" (18). This single sentence suggests Vonnegut's counterproposal to Billy's withdrawal from reality. As a confirmed apocalyptic, Vonnegut, nevertheless, does not reduce the lessons of history, as does his pseudoapocalyptic messenger Billy. The formula above is one shot through with anxieties and uncertainties. But the gritty resolution to accept the possibilities of living in the present is the best we can hope for in a technological world where yesterday seems fearsome, tomorrow dark. Far from denying the present, Vonnegut locates himself squarely in time and space (in defiance of his wandering character); he writes on 5 June 1968, eight miles from Hyannis Port, Massachusetts. And far from denying the implications of history (in walking through rebuilt Dresden, he senses the "tons of human bone meal in the ground [1]), Vonnegut proposes that our dignity, purpose, and ability to connect with each other rests in the honest resolution to accept this thin ledge of the present as all that we are given in an age of technological anxiety. Unlike Billy, whose acceptance of history forces him to be its passive observer, Vonnegut tries valiantly to understand history. He rummages through histories of World War I, histories of Dresden, chronicles of the Children's Crusade, even biblical accounts of Sodom and Gomorrah, in his attempt to find the key to understanding the twentieth-century pain. None, of course, can account for both the whirling firestorm of Dresden and the absurd execution of Edgar Derby, the events that destroy Billy. Vonnegut does not offer pat explanations. He stands mute before history, but he does not turn away.

In his two major apocalyptic tracts, then, Vonnegut rejects the strategies offered by his pseudoapocalyptics, who are enthralled by the cataclysmic imagination. Living in the latter days, Jonah, terrified by history, concocts a fantastic pattern that resolves history by directing it toward cataclysm: his is a simplification equivalent to a shrug of the shoulders; and he is like a cartoon character who watches a lighted fuse sputter and hiss toward a gigantic keg of powder. Billy, destroyed by history, lives indifferently in a world where, for him, death is finally as meaningless as twentieth-century history seems to imply it is. History leaves him stunned. It is Vonnegut, finally, who performs the traditional act of apocalyptic consolation in such dark times—separating himself from both strategies, which counsel only helplessness.

In the succession of novels since *Slaughterhouse-Five*, however, Vonnegut has moved by his own confession to "total pessimism" (Vonnegut,

"Address," 159). His long-standing dissatisfactions with technology, his disappointment with the abuse of such knowledge, and his anxieties before the implications of current events have directed Vonnegut to a harsh certainty that humanity is indeed headed toward a richly deserved catastrophe, whether nuclear, ecological, or technological. There are in his recent writings, both in the fiction and the plethora of nonfiction, echoes of his cartoon apocalyptic John/Jonah. In a commencement address delivered at Bennington College in 1970, Vonnegut rues the promise of scientific research by pointing out darkly that "what actually happened when [I] was twenty-one was that we dropped scientific truth on Hiroshima" (161). In the course of that address he warns: "I wish I could bring light to your tunnels today. My wife begged me to bring you light, but there is no light. Everything is going to become unimaginatively worse, and never get better" ("Address," 162). He tells of his belief in the promise of science, his naive faith as a boy that a scientist would someday take a "color photograph of God Almighty" (161). But he recounts that the promise was destroyed for him by the relentless revelations of history—by the fires of Dresden, the noiseless flash at Hiroshima, and the steady crematoria flames at Auschwitz. Although he advises the class to become less selfish, "to stop spending money on weapons . . . and spend money on each other" (168), such advice smacks of hollow cliche. His motto for the class is taken from *Henry VI, Part 3*: "To weep is to make less the depth of grief" (162). It is a measure of Vonnegut's emerging pessimism that he can no longer advise even the therapeutic balm of laughter.

Although it is pointless to draw judgmental conclusions about the quality of Vonnegut's recent novels, his fiction in the 1970s and 1980s evidences a certain lack of energy that reflects the apparent loss of his earlier determination that we will survive our own folly. Indeed, he now seems to simplify history.[17] He moves toward the perspective of John/Jonah in harsh excoriations against science:

> I say to you that the makers of such lies [nuclear scientists] are filthy little monkeys. I hate them. . . . They stink. If we let them they will kill everything on this lovely blue green planet. . . . They with their vicious stupid lies. (*Palm Sunday*, 71–72)

It is as if the jungles of the twentieth century have crept through the doors and pushed through the open windows of Vonnegut's House of Hope and Mercy in the Jungle. Indeed, in *Slapstick*, the setting is a deserted Manhattan Island; desolated by the Albanian flu, it is reduced to an eerie ailanthus jungle. In *Palm Sunday*, Vonnegut includes a letter (dated 1980) in which he writes that "the soul of twentieth century man is sick,'' sick finally beyond the cure of Vonnegut's enduring search for ways out of dead ends:

> What sort of soul would create a new physics based on nightmares, would place into the hands of mere politicians a planet so ''destabilized,'' to borrow a CIA term, that the briefest fit of stupidity could easily guarantee the end of the world? (70)

That is, of course, the very plot dreamed up twenty years earlier by John/Jonah, a defeated messenger of helplessness whom Vonnegut then could reject with a smirk.[18]

The apocalyptic message in Vonnegut now is a vision of history as fuse lit, a vision of time locked into pattern. He has become, as it were, a harbinger of catastrophe. Individual attempts to carve out meaningful existences are doomed by the mysterious, frightening web of Them, a force as powerful as it is stupid. The poignant paradise created by the love of the malformed twins in *Slapstick* is destroyed, after all, when the brother and sister merely reveal to their disbelieving parents that despite their overwhelming physical deformities they are quite intelligent and witty. That, Vonnegut seems to suggest quite darkly, is sufficient to justify the destruction of their private world of sympathetic communication and profound love. In this novel, the messenger bearing the traditional apocalyptic gesture of consolation, Wilbur Daffodil-11 Swain, is finally overwhelmed by time, history, and folly. Unlike John/Jonah and Billy, Wilbur dies, leaving his world cooling toward extinction.

In *Galápagos,* Vonnegut spins a most unremittingly bleak parable on the limitations and dangers of brains and hands—a throwback to John/ Jonah's petulant dissatisfaction with people who think too much. But *Galápagos,* a decidedly anti-evolutionary tale, offers the grim hope that in a million years humanity will be nothing more than seal-like creatures unable to do each other any harm or to conduct technologies that threaten the planet; they are unable to participate in any of the ''experiments with unlimited ambition performed by humankind'' (185). But these creatures are also unable to love, hope, create, cry, or suggest any personal identity. These are distractions that are not, however, sorely missed. The novel harshly satirizes the desirability of brains—characters suffer from brain tumors, Alzheimer's disease, rare hereditary brain disfunctions, assorted delusions, and clinical paranoias. The earth of one million years hence is a simple world of procreation and then death by sharks or whales—a fierce world of elemental survival where no one deals with complicated questions of how to make life meaningful. The tale is told by Leon Trout, son of Kilgore, who himself refuses to die after being decapitated in a shipyard accident. Like the very best of Vonnegut's heroes, Leon is curious, too curious to slip quietly away into the Blue Tunnel of the afterlife. He wants to find out what happens to his species and agrees to existence as a ghost for a million years to satisfy his curiosity. He watches as, absurd step by absurd step, humanity finally fulfills its evolutionary destiny by becoming brainless creatures. He is more than ready to enter the Blue Tunnel, abandoning humanity to its aspiritual survival among the rocks as creatures without dreams, laughing only at an occasional fart.

Despite the persistence of the comic style, Vonnegut's outlook has matured, much like Twain's before him, into a disconcerting contempt for humanity.[19] And although he still smirks, grins, and jokes, he now agrees with the cataclysmic imagination that so compelled John/Jonah— that history does indeed forecast its own approaching end. It is a most complete abandonment of the apocalyptic temper. To his readers, Vonnegut now is much like the oddly menacing figure of Dr. Felix Hoenikker, who, on the day of the Hiroshima bombing, fiddles with his cat's-cradle strings and coos to his frightened child, "Down will come cray-dull, catsy and all" (*Cat's Cradle,* 18).

Notes

1. It has become something of a formula in Vonnegut criticism to open with a defense of Vonnegut's immense popularity and the corollary idea that such accessibility inevitably implies shallow, sentimental thought (Wood, 24). See the introductory chapters to Stanley Schatt, James Lundquist, and Richard Giannone. And thumbing through Frederick R. Karl's exhaustive study of contemporary American fiction, one senses that Vonnegut is still treated with a certain disdain.

2. Although Tony Tanner (188–91) and Lundquist (69–85) discuss Vonnegut in terms of fiction making, Jerome Klinkowitz is Vonnegut's most consistent and persistent defender as an uncle to postmodern American novelists. He discusses *Cat's Cradle* as an "act of collaging," a "process" rather than a product (31); and he defends *Slaughterhouse-Five* largely as a novel about writing the novel. (64). He argues at length that Vonnegut felt impelled to experiment with form by a century in which traditional fiction was simply inadequate. For Vonnegut as fiction experimenter, see also William Thomas Hearron and James Mellard. Vonnegut, however, is less certain of his role as a master craftsman. Instead he defends the moral usefulness of the arts. Vonnegut speaks of writers as canaries in coal mines. They "keel over . . . in coal mines filled with poison gas, long before more robust types realize that any danger is there" (Lundquist, 15).

3. The image of apocalyptic ending figures in Vonnegut novels other than the two discussed here. *Player Piano* (1952) ends with a riot, as people rebel against the tyranny of their machine-dominated society; *The Sirens of Titan* centers on an invasion by a Martian force—hopelessly outnumbered and underarmed—which is devastated with nuclear efficiency by Earth's forces; Eliot Rosewater keeps a Doomsday Book and has a fierce vision of Indianapolis engulfed in flames; and *Slapstick* (1976) takes place in an America decimated by synthetic biological plagues that have reduced Manhattan Island to a jungle and the United States to a cluster of fiefdoms.

4. These two books received the only A+ grades that Vonnegut gave in the "report card" of his own novels, which appears on pages 311–12 of *Palm Sunday.*

5. A quick glance at criticism on *Cat's Cradle* confirms a rather widespread acceptance of John/Jonah's rabid dislike of science as the moral of the novel. Schatt decries scientists as "carefree, amoral children" (61); Lucien L. Agosta calls *Cat's Cradle* a "valediction" for humanity thrust into the apocalyptic moment by the "radical egotism" of scientists, the progenitors of the apocalypse; Lynn Buck cites Felix Hoenikker as the only villain in Vonnegut's entire canon; Charles B. Harris labels *Cat's Cradle* a "protest novel" specifically aimed at science; and Giannone, a most astute commentator on Vonnegut, asserts that *Cat's Cradle* targets science as the "intellectual abuse of our age" (60). Giannone himself mercilessly lampoons Hoenikker and his children as a "Charles Addams cartoon" (57). Apparently, Giannone never questions who is doing the cartooning—Vonnegut or his character John.

6. Although Buck actually lists these as such, they have become rather standard Vonnegut "hopes." For a particularly good treatment of love as Vonnegut's cure, see May's essay; for a thorough treatment of Vonnegut as defender of illusions, see both Tanner and Raymond M. Olderman, who treat the question of fact mingling with fiction.

7. Max F. Schulz argues for this particular feature of Vonnegut's fiction, although different critics have treated individual novels with more thoroughness. Schulz demonstrates that Vonnegut himself prefers to leave history indeterminate and, therefore, allows characters to assert bold moral stances while at the same time undercutting their credentials for delivering such statements. Schulz uses Eliot Rosewater as his example. Much has been done with Vonnegut's disagreement with Billy Pilgrim (see Donald J. Greiner and John W. Tilton).

8. See Andre and Pierre-Emmanuel Lacocque (19, 67–69), although this argument also defends Jonah as a character who is not only bigoted, but sincere in his amazement that God would treat the Ninevites with compassion; for other summaries of God's quarrel with Jonah, see William Scarlett's commentary on the Book of Jonah in The Interpreter's Bible series, Irene Nowell, and John C. Holbert.

9. Few critical responses have dealt with the Old Testament Jonah as the dominant figure of *Cat's Cradle*. The opening assertion ("Call me Jonah") has often sent critics to Melville and to *Moby-Dick* (see Olderman, for instance). Schatt mentions Jonah but asserts cryptically that Nineveh cannot hope to be spared in a Bokononist universe (66). Giannone, surprisingly, argues that the biblical Jonah suggests Vonnegut's character rising to moral responsiveness, trying to warn the world. Against considerable evidence, Giannone assumes that the Old Testament Jonah wants to reform Nineveh. Along similar lines, Robinson, who treats the Jonah figure in *Cat's Cradle* briefly on pages 152–54, asserts that even though John/Jonah's apocalyptic message is too late for his world (which is destroyed in purposeless absurdity), it is not too late for ours. John/Jonah becomes a sort of enlightened figure bringing an image of the end to act as warning to all of us. We become the Ninevites to be saved. Like Giannone, Robinson assumes redeemable qualities in both the biblical Jonah and Vonnegut's John/Jonah—qualities that are debatable, as this chapter argues.

    10. The Bokonon religion is often taken as Vonnegut's most complete statement of the usefulness of illusions and the reassurance of created patterns in the confusing tumble of the modern world. Yet such patterning is clearly more in line with the doomsaying, cataclysmic mentality of John/Jonah.

    11. It is crucial to establish how much Vonnegut emphasizes the extent to which Dr. Breed's casual mention of the outlandish *ice-nine* scheme possesses John. In the jargon of Bokononism, *ice-nine* becomes his *wampeter,* the center of his universe around which his very soul revolves. It is a measure of how death-oriented is this cataclysmic that he chooses to center his life around what he acknowledges to be a "seed of doom" (43).

    12. Such a framing device is used in a later Vonnegut novel, *Slapstick,* where the apocalyptic world of plague-devastated New York is part of what Vonnegut dreams while flying to his uncle's funeral in Indianapolis. John does visit the bar on the airplane and then relates, through a strange book one of the passengers gives him, the history of the island of San Lorenzo. The history is an odd mixture of *Robinson Crusoe, A Thousand and One Arabian Nights,* the Book of Jonah, bits of Lewis Carroll, and a strong suggestion of the wanderlust tone of romantic sea novels. It is perhaps the point of Vonnegut's rejection of John/Jonah that in his frame of mind, where one is bent on imposing pattern on history, the line between fact and fiction blurs too easily.

    13. Vonnegut has often referred to the historical origins of the concept of *ice-nine.* Irving Langmuir, a Nobel Prize winning scientist, approached H. G. Wells during the writer's visit to Cornell about the possibility of using the idea of raising the melting point of water. Wells paused for a bit and then rejected the idea outright. Even the most spectacular of science-fiction minds seems to have balked at such a preposterous scheme.

    14. The notion that love is *the* cure-all in Vonnegut's fiction is one repeated with much frequency. Leslie A. Fiedler, who treats much of *Cat's Cradle* with a patronizing sneer, does seem to think that the *boko-maru* ritual is an expression of emotion that could salvage the world lumbering off toward its apocalypse. One might do well, however, to examine the "poem" that Jonah is inspired to pen shortly after experiencing *boko-maru* with Mona for the first time (139–40). It is a fathomless mush of romantic cliches, ethereal adjectives (all capitalized), stilted lover's diction, and incomprehensible exaggeration—all elliptical to the point of nonsensical.

15. Jonah has a particularly strong aversion to midgets. Meeting Newt, who is barely four feet, inspires Jonah on numerous occasions to make rather insensitive remarks about midgets, who, he feels, are largely "diversions for silly or quiet times" (74). Significantly, the Bokonon religion asserts that the dignity of humanity as the "midget" in the absurd universe comes only from its recognition of that status and the determination then not to let the universe destroy it. Given Jonah's fantasy of world destruction and his proud charting of the way to the apocalypse, it is clear that he resists such an honest relationship with the twentieth-century universe.

16. Several critics, nevertheless, have written that *Slaughterhouse-Five* marks Vonnegut's acceptance of detachment and resignation. See Lundquist, Harris, Olderman, and David H. Goldsmith.

17. To get some perspective on this question of Vonnegut's simplification of history, see the opening chapter of *Breakfast of Champions* (7–16), which reviews the history of the United States in a particularly vicious manner, underscoring greed, ruthless competitiveness, and hypocrisy.

18. Here, for example, is a passage from *Cat's Cradle:* "What hope can there be for mankind . . . when there are such men as Felix Hoenikker to give such playthings as *ice-nine* to such short-sighted children as almost all men and women are?" (164).

19. In an interview centering on his plans to publish *Galápagos* (1985), Vonnegut asserted, in developing his own comparison between himself and Twain, that

He was angry at God for killing innocent people through illness. But we got those things under control now. . . . We don't get bushwhacked all the time, where you suddenly don't feel so good and then you die. The worst thing is, there's so much under man's control now, it gives me a different sort of bitterness. Twain was mad at the universe largely because of the germs, and I'm mad at it because humanity turns out to be such a failure. (Branculli, section F, 5)

Chapter 2
An Exemplary Settling Down in to the Self
Robert Coover's *The Origin of the Brunists*

[F]inally I get to where the boat is and I holler up and my brother he comes out and he looks down at where I am . . .and he don't say nothin that bastard he just looks at me and I shout up at him I says "hey is it all right for me and my wife to come over until this thing blows over?" and still he don't say a damn word . . .and I holler "hey you stupid sonuvabitch I'm soakin wet goddamn it and my house is fulla water and my wife she's about to have a kid and she's apt to get sick all wet and cold to the bone and all I'm askin you—" and right then right when I'm talkin he turns around and he goes back in the boat and I can't hardly believe it me his brother but he don't come back out . . .I beat on the boat with my fists and scream at him and call him ever name I can think up . . .and nobody comes out "Goddamn you" I cry out at the top of my lungs and . . .I turn around and head back for home but the rain is thunderin down like mad now and in places I gotta swim.

Coover, "The Brother"

The apocalyptic temper poses a most peculiar challenge to post-modern writers known collectively as the metafictionists: how to write about the end of the material world in a metafictional universe that works so arduously to discount that very materiality. Although apparently quite drawn by the metaphor of a world ending,[1] metafictionists, with their sly awareness of their works as harmless *ficciones,* displace the sobering

---

The title of this chapter comes from an article Coover published on the achievement of Samuel Beckett titled "The Last Quixote." Beckett's art, Coover argued, "is an exemplary settling down in to the self through all its pseudo-selves and posturing, disguises, imaginings with no illusions, doubting even the wherewithal" (143). Such a process of authentic self-exploration, it will be argued here, is accomplished only by the miner Vince Bonali.

metaphysics of Christian apocalyptics with their own playful fascination with the symmetry implied by the end. Compelled by an anarchic universe that mocks attempts at traditional mimesis and that threatens by its resistance to order, they invent reconciliation and create patterns with a self-conscious delight in the exhilarating exuberance of imagination. They pretend history without the investment of belief. They profoundly reject any insistent system such as Christian apocalypticism; indeed, they delight in upsetting and inverting just such patterns. The insistent linearity of Christian apocalypticism would seem merely refuge for those who fear sheer process, who retreat before the implications of an open universe of elaborate subjectivity.

Denied, then, the straight line, those in the metafictional universe navigate within the ceaselessly changing universe defined by quantum physics, where location is uncertain and time relative. In such an unreliable "multiverse," one must certainly relinquish objective patterns such as Christian apocalypticism, which has dogmatically decreed since the Dark Ages that the fragmented and freewheeling universe be scheduled and predictable. The investment to faith in such an outlandish scheme not only radically denies the evidence of four generations of quantum physics, but robs individuals of their greatest resource—the imagination to center subjectively a dynamic universe, to relish the intoxicating power of such creation, and to resist as unbearable tyranny any system handed down in place. The metafictional universe(s) would seem quite immune to any cataclysm, save the exhaustion of the imagination itself. Indeed, the ephemeral nature of any "given" universe constructed by a metafictionist would happily accommodate one apocalyptic reordering after another. The apocalypse would become, then, not so much the ultimate act of history as the required act of frequently reconstructing the subjective universes, which then explode harmlessly like a string of fiercely bright firecrackers. The metafictional universe could end with a bang today, with a whimper tomorrow, in fire the day after, in ice next week, etc. Forever, etc.

Given such a doctrinal predisposition against Christian apocalypticism, should a practicing metafictionist employ it, the intention would certainly be to mock its eager fanaticism and to dismiss as stifling its insistent linearity. Yet such a description affixed to *The Origin of the Brunists*, Robert Coover's 1966 novel, radically simplifies what is a most complicated work. Clearly, the novel is steeped in the religious frenzy of evangelical apocalypticism and in the rich language of Revelation; clearly, much about the Brunists does skewer Christian apocalypticism— a gaggle of widows, unemployed coal miners, religious fanatics, and assorted small-town mystics gather in white tunics one April night to await the end of the world, assured solely by the cryptic (often non-sensical) utterances of a brain-damaged coal miner who has miraculously survived a mining explosion. Like a Sinclair Lewis or a Theodore Dreiser alive in the latter days, Coover seems to indulge in a mocking, almost mean-spirited satire on the ennui in a small town sufficient to drive it "berserk with holiness" (Schott, 4).[2] Yet such an indictment of Christianity as an artificial (and comically absurd) construct accepted arbitrarily as gospel would hardly be news in the post-Christian age. Coover wants to ask a good deal more than what is wrong with the Christians.[3] Indeed, he ushers the reader toward an odd geography where the apocalyptic temper meets the metafictional impulse.

When it is treated at all, *The Origin of the Brunists* is dispatched quickly, a unicorn amid Coover's metafictions, one hung with that most damning of epithets (at least to metafictionists)—a "realistic" novel.[4] "Disappointingly" straightforward with a Dickensian cast of characters, the novel on the whole is radically unradical. A small midwestern mining town is stunned first by a fearsome mine explosion responsible for the deaths of ninety-seven men and then by the announcement that a survivor, Giovanni Bruno, claims, upon recovering consciousness in a local hospital, that during his time trapped in the mine he was visited by the Virgin Mary in the form of a white bird. In intermittent, lucid moments over the next several weeks, Bruno delivers from his bed bits of cryptic messages that seem to insist on the imminent end of the world. These messages inspire a cross section of the townspeople, who resist the implications of a universe where for no reason the mine could explode, so many men could be killed, the mine could be closed down, and a town could be allowed to die economically. They come to believe in the mine explosion as an omen of the apocalypse itself. After several tentative dates, they settle on 19 April as the date for world consummation. They move quickly from the (metafictional) joy of such a patterning to the joyless, dogmatic insistence on it as truth. As they begin to prepare for 19 April, the followers adopt the protective clique mentality of a cult. Other townspeople, not quite so ready to accept Johnny Bruno as a prophet but certain that a town full of religious loonies would do little to bolster West Condon, assemble into a so-called Common Sense Committee to restore West Condon to its sane, dull norm. These become, then, the armies of the light and of the darkness, a designation that shifts, depending on who is talking.

At the periphery of this apocalyptic showdown is Justin "Tiger" Miller, a more than slightly jaundiced editor of the local newspaper. Devoid of Christian beliefs and, by his own admission, of scruples generally, Miller drifts nevertheless into the intrigue of Giovanni Bruno, compelled by a fascination with Bruno's ethereal sister, Marcella. But he is even more lured by the game, and he sees in this gambit of the end of the world a game to end all games. He exploits it in his newspaper, running Brunist news that climaxes in a Good Friday special edition, which sends out the message of imminent consummation on the international newswires. Brunists gather on mountains and hillsides all over the world on the designated evening. In West Condon they cluster on the Mount of Redemption, a local make-out spot near the mine entrance rechristened from its more popular sobriquet—Cunt Hill.

Awash in the harsh kleig lights of television cameras, the robed Brunists wait and watch. An awesome thunderstorm, however, sends the mob scattering in a muddy, dangerous confusion that unleashes a frenzy of chanting, howling, stampeding, and gyrating in the tradition of West's grotesque street explosion outside Kahn's Persian Palace Theatre. During the confusion, Miller is attacked by an ax-wielding Eleanor Norton, one of the more fanatic members of the cult who is certain all along that the dark-eyed Miller is the incarnation of evil.

The closing chapter of the book follows Miller's gradual recovery from his wound, supervised by the plump, wholesomely sensual nurse whom he calls Happy Bottom. As the novel ends, Miller and Happy Bottom playfully enter into a covenant that promises sexual healing. In a mockery of the Christian resurrection story and of the Noah legend, Miller and Happy Bottom return metaphorically from the dead world of West Condon to establish, in their own language of joy and healing, a private passion in which they will resolve to delight in the immediate, the everyday, the common—the great realm unavailable to the apocalyptics. As survivors of the rainy apocalypse, they seal their covenant when Happy Bottom announces that she is pregnant, the "Sons of Noah" (532). They are healed, it would seem, and resolute in creating worlds every day like good metafictionists. In their passion they seem to find a healthy covenant that mocks the fanaticism and sterility of the Brunists, a particularly asexual clutch of boney women (mostly widows or virgins); sexually naive high-school kids; and frustrated, sexually indifferent men (such as Ralph Himebaugh, a fussy lawyer who lounges in women's silky undergarments and who listens with petulant disgust to a lengthy dirty story while keeping one boney elbow firmly pressed into his groin).

The "bad guys," then, are the assorted "religious monkeys over at the wop miner's house" (269), who fashion from private confusions and pain and from collective boredom an apocalypse that finally degenerates into a stampede and a public circus. (Indeed, the local businesses hurriedly assemble a small carnival and bingo tent to operate the same night as the expected consummation.) And the "good guy" is Coover's embryonic metafictionist, Justin Miller, who revels in life as a game and who stands apart, fascinated and bemused by the antics of the apocalyptics. Lured by their compelling sense of conviction, which his own life of studied skepticism lacks, he nevertheless skirts the Brunists' fanatic commitment to their conception of design and seems to leave himself at the close of the novel open to the wonderful immediate so crucial to metafictional games players.[5] But much in the novel undercuts, questions, and finally repudiates both Justin Miller as the novel's sane voice and the resolution offered by his sexual covenant with Happy Bottom.

In addition to his self-conscious use of Revelation, Coover clearly taps archetypal patterns borrowed from Genesis. A book primarily about origins, Genesis nevertheless moves within its opening six chapters to an account of God's methodical destruction of His creation—the fascinating myth of Noah and the ark. It is the cataclysmic spirit of Noah that hovers about the apocalypse of West Condon. Different characters at odd moments fancy themselves his reincarnation; Sunday school teachers and local preachers use the story as text in the intense weeks leading up to 19 April; rain falls steadily throughout much of the novel, which is taking place (as one character notes) during the months of February and March under the zodiacal signs of Aquarius the Water Bearer and Pisces the Fish; the very night of the apocalypse is rent asunder by a downpour of biblical proportions, one that quickly turns Cunt Hill into running mud.

Under the sway of Giovanni Bruno, West Condon becomes a community of Noahs who are intent, as he was, on the world's ending on schedule. The raging fire in the earth that explodes quite literally under their feet with an apocalyptic shuddering catches them all by surprise—Noahs unprepared, with arks only half-built. The inscrutability of the mine disaster seduces much of West Condon away from the incident itself and leads them to demand that it become a sign. They demand a second apocalypse—this one on schedule. The town determines that if history is going to end (for, in their case, they face not only the overwhelming waste of ninety-seven men, but the gradual economic extinction of the town when the mining company announces that the mine will stay closed), there will be a reason, a cause sufficient for such a cataclysmic effect. The alternative would be the unbearable absurdity that history merely surprised them. They would be reduced to Noahs caught in another dreary shower.

The apocalypse for which they plan is a refuge for the widows and the town—reeling from the surprise of history—much as the ark Noah constructed was a haven from the destruction of his world. Although much about the ark itself might mesmerize a metafictionist—an intricate construct with its nests of compartments and its complex of three tiers— Coover himself is no ark builder. He has little sympathy for Noahs who deny connection with the passionate spontaneity of history by withdrawing into patterns of cause and effect. Noah, inside the ark, patiently shuffling between animal stalls, hears nothing of the cataclysm just beyond the thick gopher-wood walls of his ark. The passages in Genesis that deal with the Flood rather quickly pass over the destruction of the earth; indeed, more space is devoted to God's instructions for building the ark. *The Origin of the Brunists* refutes this Noah complex, this disconnection with the brutal blood-and-bone unpleasantness of the physical world. Coover, as it were, invites the reader to forsake the insularity of the ark and plunge into the swirling waters outside: to reconnect, to open up to the uncertainty and surprise of history wrenched free of patterning and expectation. Only outside the ark can people be driven to engage the intensity and immediacy of living, facing there the grim uncertainty of mortality. As Noah's name literally means *rest*, that word implies not only a haven, but stasis as well—a mooring for those who tremble before the sheer process of open history.

No character so freely appropriates the Noah role as Justin Miller. Insulated by his own overly witty games playing and by his clever role playing, Miller (like Noah surrounded by the ark) never really confronts history without his defenses firmly entrenched. A consummate ark builder, Miller by the closing chapter has pulled into his own world as a mock Noah and is finally beyond the redeeming passions of life and love, which can only be earned outside the ark by engaging history directly. Coover understands that, after the Flood in the biblical tale, God Himself acquiesces to an openended history and refutes pattern. God acknowledges that His creation will not follow His great hopes for its destiny. He accepts the impossibility of the reformation of the wicked inclinations of His own creation. He does not purge evil by the Flood. When He makes His peace with Noah, God accepts human nature and humanity's failure to follow the pattern of holy living He first intended by His act of creation. God throws open the door to uncertainty, to the surprise of history.[6] He, rather than Noah, is the master metafictionist.

Coover himself exploits, upsets, and in general resists traditional apocalyptic patterning. He plants suggestions of it—typical antithetical images such as dark and light, good and evil, lamb and beast, and (more playfully) fat and thin—but he never lets such systems rest in place. He exploits to the point of absurdity characters who insist on engaging numerology with apocalyptic seriousness to concoct mathematical rhythms to history—how many miners went in that night, how many were rescued, what day they were rescued, how many letters in their names, etc.[7] But Coover's most intriguing undercutting of apocalyptic thinking is the narrative itself: he shelves the neat linear plotting suggested by the march to the apocalypse in favor of a far more complicated narrative patterning. Coover begins with an event nearing its end, then backtracks to bring the reader up to the moment that opens the section, and then slingshots ahead to the climax. This narrative patterning dominates the book itself (the novel opens on Saturday, 18 April—the night before the last day of the world—and then moves back in the second chapter to 8 January—the night of the mining disaster) and numerous instances throughout.[8] Coover upsets the linear narrative and suggests that one can't depend on history as a story neatly told or finished. To Coover, Noah's ark—unwieldy, insulating, intricate—is finally too passive (an ark, or course, is not outfitted with any steering or propelling devices).

If Justin Miller adopts the Noah role and thus loses credibility as the novel's sane voice, another character does forsake the ark to experience firsthand the actual apocalypse in the mine; to undergo a most fearsome series of surprises, disappointments, frustrations; and to move at the close of the novel hesitantly away from insistence on systems and roles. Vince Bonali, one of the miners whose narrative occupies a good deal of the novel, comes to a fearful understanding of the capricious, casual universe that is able to detonate at any moment and steps cautiously into such a metafictional universe of surprise. It is his epiphanic moment, while standing *outside* the deserted Bruno house long after the night of the apocalypse, that makes pale the games of Justin Miller and Happy Bottom and provides Coover not only his metafictional hero, but his novel's sane center. Vince moves hesitatingly toward the embrace of history that characterizes the apocalyptic temper. By his example, Vince undercuts the apocalyptics who whirl about the hills outside West Condon and reveals them to be caricatures appropriate to the cataclysmic imagination, their hearts filled only with expectation of the moment. These are characters who exploit the apocalyptic temper by appropriating its images, sense of time, and urgency but refuse its wider lesson of facing history, of resisting the game of guessing the hour and playing on people's hunger and hope. They are finally cartoon apocalyptics who recall Vonnegut's John/Jonah.

Like Vonnegut, who in *Cat's Cradle* offered the hope of the apocalyptic temper only indirectly against a dominating character lost to the easy fanaticism of the cataclysmic imagination, here Coover sets the steady, plodding Vince Bonali against the considerable charisma of the cynical, glib Justin Miller. Vince, like Vonnegut's Malachi Constant, decides finally to engage history, ready to learn, "gladder to stand the pain." History, for Vince, acknowledges the potential for devastation on public as well as private scales. Nevertheless, he stands firm. The meta-fictional multiverse of Coover is finally nothing less than the compassionate universe of the apocalyptic temper: a cosmos that surges steadily—at times mysteriously—certain only of surprise (the authentic apocalypse is nothing if not a surprise), and genuinely aware of the intricate implications of endings while vitally concerned with the affirmation of living.

The Origin of the Brunists, most fundamentally, is a novel about initiation: there are initiations into the Brunist circle; an initiation into the vigorously masculine brotherhood of the miners; various sweaty adolescent initiations into the mysteries of backseat sex; even initiations into a neighborhood kiddy terrorist organization of petty vandals who call themselves the Black Hand—the name inspired by a rather gruesome memento mori taken from the school gym while it served as a makeshift morgue the night of the mining disaster.

The reader is also initiated, but not into the cataclysmic world of West Condon. That world, with its eccentricities and hyped urgency, is deliberately left unavailable. Coover refuses to allow the reader to indulge seriously in the act of faith demanded by the Brunists. No Brunist attracts or engages the reader's sympathies. Not so much inhuman as unhuman, they are all pushed into preposterous poses of exaggerated performance: the too obviously comic (Eleanor Norton and her private, often frenzied communications with her spiritual mentor, Domiron); the too obviously tragic (the lawyer Himebaugh, who fasts himself to death); the too obviously pathetic (Marcella Bruno trapped by her devotion to her brother and by her powerful attraction to Miller); the too obviously cynical (Justin Miller himself); the too obviously fanatical (the red-haired, firesnorting preacher, Abner Baxter).[9] The list grows. It is not their hermetic world of approaching end that engages the reader. Rather, Coover initiates the reader into the world that Vince Bonali comes to see—one where history is freed from the necessity of describing an arc in the sky after every cataclysm, freed from the impossible burden of significance and order. History, Coover contends, must be engaged as a rapid-fire shifting of certainties, a world of surprise and suspense, a visceral world of blood, dirt, semen, and sweat. There is no more dubious an image to Coover than that of Noah as he feels, with a settled indifference, the first drops of the cataclysmic rainstorm. To Noah the cataclysmic, a pattern is merely being fulfilled. Coover's fascination rests more with the neighbors of Noah, those who must come to terms with the incredible fact of creation itself being destroyed. The huddles of those twisting in the angry waters *outside* the ark, hammering against its smooth, solid sides, failing to be heard, slipping back into the rising waters there to struggle with their very mortalities and to engage the apocalypse firsthand—these are Coover's initiates into the twentieth-century age of technological anxiety.[10]

To understand Coover's intention to connect with the grim, physical world, one need only examine the actual origin of the Brunist movement, a shocking moment that occurs during the mining accident. Ely Collins, a local preacher who works in the mine, faces the agony of an ad-lib amputation because his leg has been pinned beneath timber and "five hundred feet of mother earth" (41). One of the miners hefts an ax and begins the gruesome task of splintering the bone at the knee. With unnerving precision, Coover recounts the messy amputation: it takes two full swings and then several "short hacking strokes" to sever the leg. The initial stroke, however, spatters blood and tissue all about the cluster of trapped miners and baptizes one of them in particular— "Bruno, his face blood-sprayed, went dumb, mouth agape, and broke away in a silent fit" (42–43). Bruno never really recovers from this initial brush with visceral reality. It is a moment born of desperation and the complicated camaraderie of the miners (they do not want to leave Ely behind) who struggle to adjust to the apocalyptic surprise— to swim, as it were, outside the ark. The initiation destroys Giovanni. He retreats, cringing and pale, into meaningless babblings and eventual speechlessness. Even after his body has been dragged from the mine and scrubbed clean by the hospital staff, his sister Marcella notices that *"dried blood . . . seems to have sunk beneath the surface [of his skin], now mottle[d] with rose the flesh's pallor"* (108, Coover's italics). The Brunist movement commences, then, with a man overwhelmed. It begins as a movement in full retreat.

To point up the differences between the intensity of meeting history and the comic pathos of determining history as pattern, Coover begins his novel with two striking set pieces, both stories of initiation—one of Hiram and Emma Clegg into the world of the Brunists, the other of Tony Rosselli into the world of the miners. In the prologue, the reader follows the initiation of the Cleggs, who "were summoned by the Spirit" (3) to West Condon on the eve of the apocalyptic day itself. Coover begins the novel with the half-completed and meaningless utterances of Giovanni Bruno already translated into the message of imminent ending. Hiram and Emma are solemnly ushered through Bruno's house, which has been set up as a sort of cathedral to the Brunist movement and enshrines an improbable collection of relics, including a white chicken feather. The tunicked members of the Brunists speak with unabashed passion to the Cleggs (and to the reader) about the coming of the Kingdom of the Light in set speeches that are punctuated by applause with practiced regularity and end with a "chorus of 'amens'" (11). Like odd refugees from the Middle Ages, they speak straightfacedly about their persecutions at the hands of disbelievers and of their martyrs; they exchange ritual handshakes and speak in passwords. Once the Widow Collins and Eleanor Norton and even Ralph Himebaugh with his elaborate mathematical proofs explain to Hiram the world according to the Brunists, he is quite speechless at "how perfectly revolved this universe of ours" really is (11). The reader, glimpsing with amusement the Brunist world, is not tempted to make such a commitment of faith.

Once Hiram is properly robed in his white tunic, the Brunists decide to go out to the Mount of Redemption (with box suppers) to get acquainted with the spot and to rehearse the apocalypse expected the next night. The emphasis comes to be more and more on performance, for, as Hiram notes, of the hundreds of people "milling about" the Bruno house, half were "newspaper, radio, and television people: many cameras, much light, and unbelievable excitement" (4). Eleanor Norton, when she is not "discoursing to newsmen" (7), rallies the Brunists before they head for the Mount of Redemption with carefully polished rhetoric delivered in "a deeply moving performance" (11). In a ringing voice, the Widow Collins tells them that they go "to that Mount of Redemption, . . . not to die, *but to act . . .* " (12, Coover's italics). West Condon, caught by surprise by the mining accident, is now restaging history, ending it on schedule. The Mount will be their stage, flooded on Sunday night by the ever-present silvery wash of the television lights. And the cast, appropriately costumed, is ready now for its dress rehearsal. The air, as Hiram Clegg notes several times, is charged with excitement, like backstage on opening night.

Once the Brunists make it to the Mount, Coover quickly shatters this notion of history as theater by introducing an actual coming of the light—the headlights from the approaching cars of the town's vigilante Common Sense Committee. The coming of this light, however, brings only confusion, a free-for-all dispersal of the cultists, who fear possible violence. The worshipers cannot adjust to this surprise, and, despite their careful contingency plans should anyone disturb their meeting, they disperse in panicked anarchy. In the chaos, Marcella Bruno is killed by an automobile. *Accidentally.* That individual death disrupts the initiation of Hiram Clegg. The crumpled, bleeding body lying in the weeds in the ditch along the road leading from the Mount of Redemption defies the Brunists' careful chain of causality forged since the mining accident.

Hiram's mind undergoes a jolting initiation into open history. He cannot shake the emphatically real image of the bubble of blood coming from the mouth of the pale girl.[11] Marcella must be recast by the Brunists who, much like their founder at the moment of Ely Collins's amputation, cannot stomach such immediacy. Surprised once again by an accident, the Brunists recoil collectively into a reassuring, protective pattern—like Noahs retreating to the ark. Marcella's death becomes the sacrifice at the hands of the persecutors; she becomes the cult's Virgin martyr. Her limply raised hand becomes the subject of poems, songs, and paintings once the Brunists evolve into an institutional religion after the 19 April date. The bloodstain on her tunic, legend says, spread into the shape of a heart. Recoiling from the bubble of blood that so disturbs Hiram, the Brunists prefer the elaborate fiction of a heart-shaped stain.

Following this staged apocalypse, Coover thrusts the reader squarely into the most grimly realistic section of the novel—the fire in the mine and the desperate rescue efforts on the night of 8 January. The explosion in the mineshaft is a most effective rendering of the elements of the classic Christian apocalypse. When the mine is engulfed by a series of sudden gas explosions, each man trapped in the earth is confronted with his own mortality. And whether it involves the Herculean exertions of pushing earth, the amputation of pinned limbs, or the gambling that airshafts might prove passable, the miners (unlike the Brunists on the Mount) struggle to live. Here men face the very real. They must deal with the raw stuff of history freed from pattern, open to surprise and change—unexplained and unexplainable. There are no cameras, no television crews—only the dim shafts of the headlamps. The language is graphic, the reactions honest and confused, the only concern living, the suspense gripping. Unlike the prologue, where time is measured only as the passing of millennia, here time is unbearable, precisely measured—5:12, 5:28, 6:33, 7:32, the very moment of the ignition. Coover follows two sets of men, one under the direction of Vince Bonali that follows an airshaft to the surface; the other a cluster of seven men, among them Bruno, who must wait for help. Bruno will be the only one rescued.

Initiated into this world verging on its own consummation is a young man, Tony Rosselli, who comes to the mine for the first time on the night of 8 January. He is welcomed by a rather rough initiation ritual that would have climaxed with an air hose shoved up his ass had not one of the miners, Ox Clemens, halted it by brandishing a knife when Rosselli's pants were already down around his knees. To reassure Rosselli about the camaraderie of the miners, Clemens offers him a cigarette, despite the obvious hazard of smoking in a mine. The resulting detonation of gas long trapped in the mine not only initiates Rosselli (and Clemens) into Coover's very real surprise of history (both miners are immediately incinerated, standing at the very point of ignition), but brings its grim light rapidly to the entire mining crew. Indeed, Coover renders the apocalyptic moment itself in a section of clipped, urgent sentences (in contrast to the melodic sentences of the polished speeches performed by the Brunists in the prologue) that commences with the awesome simplicity of "There was light" (35). It is Coover's supreme apocalyptic moment, ushering men dramatically into the presence of their own mortalities.

To underscore further the difference between the apocalypse so carefully staged in the prologue and the apocalypse that ignites wildly in the mine, Coover moves from the men in the mine to the local high-school gym, where a basketball game is just getting under way when the mine erupts. Coover's deliberately artificial style, rendering the game as if it were a masque, translates the game into a series of carefully executed plays. No players are mentioned: merely the x's and o's of a coach's diagram board. No sweat, no emotion, it is a chessgame world of blacks and reds where struggle is artificially created and conflict only pretense, all subordinated to the diagram. There is no expectation, only execution. In its most rigorous form, it is a quasi-religious performance, one that anticipates the Brunists on the Mount of Redemption. The game itself is lost in the rhetoric of pattern making:

> He shams bounce to Red Four in the right corner, drawing Black Three out of the circle toward the foil, and then, alone and lit on his varnished disc, assumes his role: the Hook. A semicircling sweep, chasse, fade . . . stretch— but circle breaks as Black Two and Three puncture its rim in assault. Collision . . . . Whistle. Roar. Buzzer, unexpectedly prolonged. (46)

The mining accident has interrupted the masque. Indeed, the mob of spectators flows out of the gym to jam the road leading out to the mine leaving the scoreboard frozen at 14–11. The gym, the stage of the masque, will be converted quickly into a makeshift morgue. Coover's point is that when confronted with the surprise of history—their pleasant masque of diagrammed conflict halted by the grim, prolonged buzzer—West Condoners struggle fiercely to coerce *that* interruption into a new pattern. Struck by the sobering evidence of a universe that does not bow to humanity's determination of cause and effect, as one by one the miners straggle to the surface or are carried from the mines as blackened bodies with coroner's tags, the townspeople begin to assemble their own community masque—the riveting and artificial drama of the Brunists.

Two men, then, Hiram Clegg and Tony Rosselli, come to worlds on the verge of ending—one artificially, one authentically. To Hiram Clegg the apocalypse makes sense. He is struck speechless by its completeness until he must struggle with the image of Marcella Bruno. Rosselli, as well as the other miners, learns in the moment of the mine's ignition the lesson that Hiram resists as he grapples with Marcella's accidental death: history's stubborn resistance to making sense. Coover challenges the reader to face that universe; to engage its most difficult turns; to feel, as it were, the splattering of the blood from Ely Collins's leg without retreating. Tony Rosselli is initiated into a physical world of uncertainty and mortality, his face "smeared with blood and coal dust" (32). It is only in that world, far from the neat geometry of the Brunists' Magic Kingdom Come, that life can be engaged. To understand Coover's imperative, the reader must isolate the three characters most affected by the mining disaster—Giovanni Bruno, Justin Miller, and Vince Bonali—and see how each is tested by the surprise of history, and how two of the three fail.

At the close of the section of the novel dealing with the actual mining disaster, Justin Miller overhears a lengthy story at a local barroom that recounts the adventures of one of his pressmen at a whorehouse in a neighboring town. He selects one of his usual companions, but then is frustrated to discover, once they are alone in her room, that she is quite distracted, in mourning over the death of her brother in the mining accident: she is a "sorry-looking red-eyed droop" (122). Despite his best efforts at consoling her and trying, at the same time, to encourage her toward the bed, she remains quite unresponsive. Finally, he removes his pants and jumps her as she lies on her bed curled in a fetal position. Yelling a barrage of obscenities about her dead brother, he proceeds to have his way with bestial passion—"they punch and wrestle and peck and claw" (126)—all the while cursing her dead brother. Finally, they both "come in a tremendous simultaneous explosion"—"the greatest fuck they've ever had, if not indeed the greatest in world history" (127). He explains to her as they cuddle afterwards that he never really knew her brother but that he felt she needed something, even a lie, "to snap her out of her doldrums" (127). As the story finishes, Coover moves immediately to a phone call that Miller receives from Marcella, who tells him that Bruno, now conscious in the hospital, claims to have been visited by the Virgin Mary while trapped in the mine. The coincidence of the barroom story and the message from Bruno is deliberate. Giovanni Bruno's message is a lie told to revive a town that, like the whore, is stunned by a brush with history. His few, incoherent messages jolt a town to feverish activity, by reviving the fearful, the bored, the tearful, the lonely with the vision of a shattering universal orgasm—the apocalypse itself.

The problem—typical in metafictional work—is that Giovanni's "message" is accepted as the truth; it seriously admits faith. But it is accepted only by those who resist the implications of an open universe. It is embraced by those who resist simple mortality and the pain of its random surprise, like the Widow Collins, who admits that she clings to the Brunist movement to forestall accepting the loss of her husband; by those who resist chaos, like Ralph Himebaugh, who watches one icy night as a car spins out of control in wild, chaotic circles before hitting a telephone pole and who then kicks the machine, agitated that it should spin so wildly; by those who resist the routine of life in West Condon measured by the steady drone of "Tick talk tick talk" (22); by those who resist the saddening inevitability of loneliness—like the Widow Cravens, who sleeps around indiscriminately until she finds the Brunist cult. They mistake their resistance to the open universe for spiritual hunger, but they hunger only for the reassurance of the artificial construct. They most closely align themselves with the circle. They gather in circles (their emblem is a brown circle enclosing a miner's pickax); the movement even begins in the meetings of West Condon Evening Circle, a collection of churchwomen who meet every Sunday night.[12] The Brunists refuse to accept any universe not neatly run and well ordered. They are so desperate for accountability and hungry for pattern that they opt out of history. Yet the doctors who ponder Bruno's miraculous survival decide that Bruno, stunned by the amputation of Ely Collins's leg, must have wandered free of the tight circle that the others had made and lodged himself on a narrow shelf above them. He withdrew from the circle. Those in the circle did not move around much, did not stir up the air, and were asphyxiated—strangled, as it were, by their own circle.

Bruno, from the moment he is dragged from the mine, is essentially passive, a mere shell; Eleanor Norton even suggests that he died in the mine and that his body has been taken over by a spirit. He becomes to his followers another of their relics, one of their signs to be interpreted in a fascinating variety of ways. His followers range from intense and complicated mystics to curious high-school kids—from "lowgrade" Christians awaiting the traditional Second Coming to teenagers who use Bruno's message of imminent ending as a ploy for backseat sex. With his dead eyes and his passive mouth, Bruno manages to bring to the wasteland world of West Condon a convincing spiritual intensity, a mock Christ. Even before the mining disaster blasts away much of Bruno's awareness, he plays the part of a mock Christ. The reader first sees Bruno in the miners' locker room shortly before the descent passively accepting several painful flicks of a towel, which comically recalls the scourging of Christ. Indeed, the miners circle him, jeering and taunting. On a scrap of yellow paper that Vince Bonali wrestles from Bruno's hand is a poem called "My Mother," which begins with the line "From out of thy immortal womb" (25), suggestive of the Virgin Mary. In a brief tussle during which Bruno tries futilely to reclaim his poem, the miners pin his arms back, crucifixion style. The spectacle of the mining explosion, however, serves to invest this mock Christ with sufficient importance to be accepted as a neo-Christ, a classically nameless prophet (his name, after all, translates to John Brown) who has returned from death and whose message, like Christ's, is urgently apocalyptical and very cryptic. The mock becomes the real, but it is all still games playing.[13] The townspeople all too easily shuck off the hazards of life within the surprise of history[14]—the apocalyptic shock of the mining accident—and opt to live instead within the pleasant geometry of reassuring patterns typical of the cataclysmic imagination. By the close of the novel, the withdrawal is complete, and the cult has matured into the Reformed Nazarene Followers of Giovanni Bruno; the apocalypse put off to a more comfortable seven years; bishops appointed; creeds written (based on the words of Bruno, St. Paul, and Revelation); and hymns recorded (their ballad is number three of the Hillbilly Hit Parade).

As some have suggested, Coover may indeed have had a historical figure in mind when he created Giovanni Bruno: a Renaissance Italian poet and playwright, a dabbler in the new Copernican sciences, and, supremely, a philosopher named Giordano Bruno.[15] This Bruno, who was burned at the stake for heresy, is often hailed—because of his defense of the Copernican universe—as one of the fathers of modern science. It is more likely, however, that the Renaissance Bruno was executed for being a magician. Indeed, his disagreement with the Inquisition came less from his defense of Copernicus, which was not wholehearted, and more from his dissatisfactions with Copernican science because its constructed universe of orbiting worlds did not allow sufficiently for magic. To him the great Copernican sun suggested not mathematical centrality, but magical energy and great power. The mathematical universe robbed the cosmos of its very animation. To him this physical universe was one of innumerable, infinite universes. His was a heresy fostered not so much by Copernican science as by the Egyptian Hermes Trismegistus—the god-magician who posited the material universe as the eternal body whose soul was God. The Renaissance Bruno marveled at a rather unchristian universe, one forever in motion, forever expanding, radiant with life and charged with the energy of constant change (Yates, 408). It is a vision strikingly similar to the metafictional universe of sheer process. Coover contrasts such magic with the grim mathematicians of the apocalypse who come under the sway of Giovanni Bruno. Like Ralph Himebaugh, who plots on a graph the impending catastrophe, they deny life to the universe to the extent that their lives, in turn, are strangled (like the six men in the mine who die in their circle). They deny life: some of them abstain from sex, others fast (Himebaugh literally starves himself to death), others enjoy the raw sting of flagellation and corporal punishment. It is no accident that Coover names their town West Condon—the very name suggesting impotency—a town closed off, drained not only of its men by the mining accident, but of its youth who are steadily migrating north. In short, the Brunists share the restless hunger of the cataclysmic imagination; denied the exuberance of living, they twist into closed geometric figures themselves, withering away to bone like their prophet, a "tall boney miner" whose "thin ass" is blistered by Vince Bonali's towel (25). They are the mathematicians, so bottled up that when the thunderstorm scatters their apocalypse they erupt in a savage Walpurgis Night of dancing, sexual writhing, violence, and animal howling that recalls West's theater riot. And like West, Coover offers an apocalypse without illumination—the vicious thunderstorm is one oddly without lightning—offers, finally, a cataclysmic shadow show. Isolated from history in a flight that, as the novel progresses, becomes more and more eccentric and life threatening as it becomes more closed off from the animated universe of surprise, the Brunists wither in existences decidedly cut off from the very stuff of living.

If Bruno's followers reveal a disturbing inability to live fully, then Justin Miller, another cataclysmic, points up the devastating effects that the fascination with pattern can have on the human capacity to love. Unlike Rosselli and Bruno, Miller never faces firsthand the searing light of history. He refuses outright the dictum of Vonnegut's Malachi Constant to face history squarely. He records history secondhand, through the medium of his newspaper and through the lens of his ever-present Speedgraphic camera. In the first glimpse given of Miller, the reader finds him "shinnied halfway up" (53) the mine water tower, taking pictures high above the mine road jammed with the cars of anxious families of the trapped miners. Miller ranges high above the chaos, unaffected by it. Indeed, he will end up sleeping that night with one of the women who anxiously crowds the mine entrance waiting for news about her husband. He roams among the frantic townspeople, freezing into the neat images of his photographs their reactions to the surprise that history has so rudely dealt them.

This aesthetic exercise in fixing agony within a frame extends as well to his work as the tireless editor of the local newspaper. He accepts the newspaper's responsibility to lift the town out of its periodic doldrums, much like the man who assaults the whore with lies. Miller knows that the paper must be there to reassure the town whenever it is surprised by history. His newspaper—"a set of conventionally accepted signs" that fix life into "recorded and ordered history" (172)—shields the town from the very universe essential to the metafictional exuberance. He understands that the newspaper is a "benevolent hoax" (172); an "entertainment," he calls it, as he prepares to assemble the bits of history into neat geometric columns of news.[16] Yet, he professes, history is actually a "loose concatenation of separate and ultimately inconsequential instants . . . each possessed of a small wanton freedom of its own" (161). Long before Bruno experiences his visitation in the mine, Miller is keen to the hypocrisy of denying history by distortion. Even before Miller finds himself drawn to the Brunists, he runs a headline announcing the rescue of Giovanni Bruno that sets the stage for the emergence of Bruno the prophet—Miracle In West Condon (92).

Although he can recall with admiration the mystical moment during a state basketball championship game when Ox Clemens could shatter the tension by grabbing his crotch and gasping, "Oh Jesus! I jist wanna jack off" (527) and thus step completely free of expectations, free of the game, Miller cannot live with such surprise. At an odd moment of reflection, he guesses that to put out the newspaper every week he writes the equivalent of "a decent novel six days a week." He is the supreme fiction maker, the exaggerated caricature Coover uses to point up the deadening that such constant indulgence in clever fictions can produce.[17] Miller is lost to life. He is never an immediate character to the reader. He never invites the investment of sympathy. The "Brunist thing" catches Miller at a moment when he is momentarily tired of "the game he played, the masks he wore" (74), reduced to squashing roaches in his kitchen and declaiming melodramatically, "Do not despair . . . for our Lord Jesus has changed the shape of death" (75). The Brunists excite him in a way that the day-to-day routine fictions of the *Chronicle* cannot. The stakes are attractively high. And at the proper consummate moment as the Brunists cluster on the evening of 19 April, Miller, now *below* the water tower and gazing up at the heights from which he has been drawn down, acknowledges what the reader has felt all along— for all his pretense at cynical aloofness, Justin Miller is "one with the Brunists" (487), a pattern maker. He confesses at one point to reading Revelation at the age of thirteen, freely admitting that he never quite recovered from that exposure to the wonderful, pat world of exotic endings.

Marcella is Miller's most poignant failure. She represents his initiation into the surprise of history, his best chance to disengage himself from his games playing and to step into the *un*certain. She is attracted to him even before he comes to the hospital room to visit her brother, even before he finds out the name of that "radiant" woman wrapped in the Red Cross blanket, huddled outside the damaged mine. Her attraction to him is honest and immediate; her reaction reverently sexual. With his "*long legs and strong shoulders*," Miller strikes her as a wonderfully erotic/religious figure: a blend of "*forest greenness, and church masonry and northern stars a man to be loved...*" (120, Coover's italics). Little in this initial encounter, and little for that matter in all their subsequent meetings, suggests the doomed Virgin role that Miller insists she play from the moment he spies her at the mine entrance. Like the photograph that Miller sees as somehow "radiant," the doomed Virgin is an image of Marcella on which he insists. Marcella, he assumes, *needs* his saving love, his healing phallic touch. When they first kiss, he reverently kneels before her, gazes at "her young body," and rises "to enrich—he thought coolly—her experience" (238). White-skinned and hence ethereal and spiritual, Marcella is reduced to a precious figure to Miller, despite the completely natural and rather fecund touches that Coover gives her character as she tends her garden with a pagan lustiness.[18] Indeed, despite Coover's italicizing Marcella's thoughts, the first thing we see her do is blow her nose (82), hardly the stuff of doomed Virgins.

Miller generously casts himself as her rescuer from the insinuating web of the cult (although in her own thoughts she quite clearly rejects her brother's messages), from its unhealthy preoccupation with matters of the spirit and its morbid attention to the doomed and the damned. Before publishing the splashy, tabloid-style issue of the *Chronicle* devoted completely to the Brunists' anticipation of the end of the world, Miller decides to make his pitch to save Marcella from the cult and indirectly invite her to accept his role assignment, to become enclosed within *his* frame of the universe. His gift for her is appropriately a collar of "roughly hammered pieces of old brass" (316). It is a token of his game of possession. But even as he waits for Marcella to come to their rendezvous in the print shop, he panics, confronted by the potential of a surprise from history. In a ludicrous moment that nevertheless points up his radical dependence on scripted reality, he decides, "Better write it out. He realized he was back at his typewriter.... He rolled copypaper into his old Underwood, sat there for ten minutes, maybe longer, drumming his fingers on the keys. He wrote MARCELLA and added a comma. . . . Maybe it'd be easy'' (364).

Coover plays the scene in the print shop as it finally unfolds as an exchange of typefaces—Miller's characteristic roman face melds indiscriminately with Marcella's characteristic italic. Herein lies the distancing Coover insists on. Miller has never sought Marcella for sexual communion, in the way she has him. As he prepares his final scene with her (like the Brunists who rehearse their apocalypse), he relishes the idea of placing Marcella in the position of choosing the Lady (her brother's Virgin of the Mines) or the Tiger (as his cherished nickname from his basketball days recalls). He grins ''malevolently'' as he awaits her arrival (316). But the scene of long-anticipated passion mocks spontaneity. Miller, not the ''virginal'' Marcella, keeps hesitating. She must tell him, ''Do not be afraid''; and he asks *her* repeatedly to wait. He pulls back even as she pulls at his shirt and unresistingly unbuttons her blouse; she is *''momentarily chilled by the pace of distance between them,''* a distance she tries to diminish and that he pulls back to insure (368)— much like the ''immediate living space'' he later establishes between himself and Happy Bottom (526).

This miscasting of Marcella is Miller's greatest abuse. Whether she is dancing in the sun in her garden, devoutly attending her brain-damaged brother, slipping in and out of her erotically simple morning baths, Marcella belies the Virgin-in-waiting role that Miller (and later the Brunists) demands of her. Indeed, it is the realization that Miller's attentions have all been part of his private melodrama of rescuing the maiden and possessing her in marriage that destroys Marcella. It is a game that her frank, intense hunger for sexual consummation in the print shop cannot abide. When she flees the print shop, stunned by her surprise, *''something . . . revolved a final turn''* (370). Like her brother spattered with the blood of Ely Collins, Marcella retreats. She accepts the embrace of the Brunists, dons her white robe, and begins the killing fast that will disorient her sufficiently to drive her to the road the night of the rehearsal, there to be killed and translated finally into the bloodless symbol of the cult's Virgin. And it is this destruction of Marcella's vitality that earns Miller the sobriquet with which the overwrought Eleanor Norton curses him—the Antichrist. Indeed, he is the dominant focus of a book that Coover himself admits might have been better titled *Antichrist*.[19]

Happy Bottom's pseudonym suggests her own susceptibility to role playing. She plays at redeeming Miller from *his* preoccupation with the morbid Brunists much as he engages in the same game with Marcella. They are made for each other, pieces of the same game. Plump and decidedly frisky, she is, however, a reminder of just how unpleasantly primitive and disconnected from love are Miller's engagements of lust. Marcella's sincere offer of her "young body, all those subtle curves of thigh and belly" (238), is an attractive synthesis of the sacred and the profane. Happy Bottom, though, is animal relief. It is to her happy bottom that Miller turns when the goat in him kicks about on the first day of spring. He wrestles with her in the X-ray room even though he will profess his love to Marcella later that day. Happy Bottom even sends off to Miller's newspaper a series of terribly witty Last Judgments (fashioned in the same stylized language that Coover uses to set apart much of Miller's thinking). They are, in effect, co-authors long before the epilogue. Confronted with the staggering miscalculation of Marcella—*his* surprise of history—Miller turns to the easy profanity of Happy Bottom, and together they play out his game of mock Noah. Her sign of the covenant, her rainbow, is administered to Miller's ass with a sharp flick of her towel, a gesture that underscores the intentional parallels that Coover develops between Bruno the mock Christ and Miller the mock Noah. Miller even sees in her happy bottom the insignia of the Brunist movement—the pick surrounded by a circle. Indeed, as he recuperates in the hospital, he proposes that they create a cult just for two (forever witty and clever, Happy Bottom traces down to Miller's "peter" and puns, "And on this rock. . ." [524]).

The entire closing chapter is a lengthy—and at times, by necessity, tedious—exercise in religious parodying; the nearest antecedent to it is the (again lengthy) card-playing scene in which Lou Jones prepares to leave West Condon after he is fired for snapping pictures of Miller and Marcella that night in the print shop. It is a scene that plays off the decidedly profane slang of card playing and liquor with the sacred catchphrases appropriate to Passion Week. More than anything else, the closing chapter is a *recounting* of Miller's recovery, a self-conscious and self-indulging translation of it after the fact into the mock religious language of crucifixion, resurrection, and ascension. To understand just how this exercise distances Miller from history, one need only compare the moment of his wounding on Cunt Hill by the ax-wielding Eleanor Norton with the novel's other scene of ax-swinging, the grisly amputation of Ely Collins's leg. "It was done," Miller says, "dispatched by a priestess" (493). In a final moment of hyperbolic elegance, it is intoned that "Tiger Miller departed from this world, passing on to his reward" (493). It is all exaggerated in a manner that the recuperation itself parallels. Whatever despair wells up in Miller is one easily dispatched with an enema; whatever ills he has, quickly erased by coupling with Happy Bottom with the leverage provided by a telephone book. When the destruction of Marcella haunts him in his drugged and appropriately anesthetized state following his wounding, he casts himself as her Judas in the garden and, in his own way, finds solace in such role playing. Marcella herself means no more to him than she does as the Virgin to the Brunists.

The closing chapter affirms that Miller does not heal, but merely continues. He cannot love.[20] The title of the last chapter—"Return"—indicates Coover's acknowledgment that the book has indeed come full circle, returned to the same religious patternings that characterize Hiram Clegg's initiation into the Brunist cult in the very first section. Somewhere in the process, history—suggested most poignantly by Marcella—is decidedly lost, both to the Brunists and to Miller, their prodigal son. But the pagan coupling of Miller and Happy Bottom is hardly Coover's prescription for life in the anxiety of a contemporary quantum universe: he notes that their union created an "immediate living space" between the two. They are forever cushioned from each other, from the vital connectedness Coover suggests in Marcella's defiantly "unvirgin" hunger in the print shop.

It is no surprise that as he makes plans to live with Happy Bottom, Miller contemplates as well a career in television. Television implies itself into every significant moment in Miller's created reality, underscoring its scriptedness. He first kisses Marcella by the pale blue-white light of the Bonali television; his relentless coverage of the Brunists catapults them into international figures and brings the media to West Condon; he learns of Marcella's death during the commercials of a television program, even as he is explaining to Happy Bottom the Noah story. As he listens to Lou Jones's lengthy story about the whore, Miller watches a game show on the bar television. He is particularly attentive to the commercials, hawking deodorants and toothpaste (images of protection from the very natural world that Miller resists); and while watching the inane game show, Miller mutters to himself, "The Whole goddamn American populace [is] becoming a bunch of actors" (122). This is the America in which Miller most profoundly thrives. He is the poseur supreme. Not quite as fossilized as the master rhetorician Lou Jones and, hence, at odd moments able to be tempted by life outside the pattern (to weary of life within confining roles), he finally accepts his role of West Condon's most intricate, consummate ark builder. He is the inveterate games player (he has played basketball in high school and still plays semi-pro baseball) who recalls years afterward the "febrile moment" during a state basketball championship game when he felt the "bright flash of meaning" that came with the understanding that "patterns...worked" (155). As Miller toys with a career move into television, the reader recognizes its implications, given the penchant for patterning and artificiality evidenced by those fleeing from history—the television screen is a circle within a square, a double trap. The raw stuff of history—the stuff of the apocalyptic temper—eludes Miller's interest. Perched high above the scene of wrenching heartache at the mining accident, Miller enters the novel like a Noah glimpsing through the narrow windows of the ark the churning midnight waters below, which are alive with the thrashing of the desperate, those actually confronting their own history gone critical. The rainbow that Miller describes as mock Noah at the close of the novel represents a geometric pattern as closed as the circle and the square.

In the course of the novel, one character does open himself up to the heartbreaking surprise of history, the loneliness of authentic living, and the frightening reality of mortality. Unlike Bruno, who is destroyed by history, or Miller, who contentedly orbits it, Vince Bonali is initiated into it, into the harsh world that quite suddenly robs him of his pleasant illusions about living in an ordered universe commanded by a God who generously separates Vince Bonali from the rest of the "sonsabitches," a personal God to whom Bonali, when history seemed to turn against him, could always pray, "Come on, God! Get me outa this one" (250). His prayer to this God grows increasingly more desperate. Ambushed by a series of random and meaningless catastrophes (private apocalypses) that cause the steady dissolution of his town, his job, his family, and finally himself, he suspects that a protective God may be a useless fiction. Vince is the novel's only fully developed character who never comes under the sway of West Condon's urgent cataclysmic imagination. To him, the explosion in the mine symbolizes nothing more than the company's failure to ventilate the mine properly—a clear case of assigned responsibility. To a man so grimly engaged in the difficult grind of day-to-day living, the notion of an end to the world would actually be a relief, "to have done with this moronic business" in a "fucked-up world" (250). Unlike Miller, Vince is most painfully human. He struggles against the feeling that his future is just like a "big goddamn empty hole" (252); he struggles against an emptiness inside him, one he cannot explain or talk about with his family. Explanation eludes him, as does his Roman Catholicism, despite his efforts to return to it. At an epiphanic moment outside the Bruno house a few weeks after 19 April, he stands alone, facing the universe.

It is an authentic moment of honest confusion in a novel that works so deliberately with artifice and contrived understanding. One lush May night that is "laden with vegetable renascence" (504), Vince wanders to the Bruno house, now abandoned. He breaks in and sees the devastation wrought by the curious, by vandals, by the cult fanatics themselves. Troubled by such evidence of destruction caused by the pseudoapocalyptic fever, he picks up a fragment of a shattered chandelier as a souvenir of the hysteria. The moonlight that silvers the empty room creates a momentary, eerie rainbow in the house. Compared to the "rainbow" that Happy Bottom snaps onto Miller's ass, this rainbow glows with authenticity. Thrusting the glass shard into his pocket, he continues, exploring the upper reaches of the house. As he enters Bruno's bedroom, he hears police cars arrive outside. In his hurry to find a place to hide, he discovers the dead body of Ralph Himebaugh, the fanatic Brunist who apparently dragged himself in the closing hours of his fast to the very chamber of his prophet. It is a moment of shock for Vince Bonali. He bawls like a baby before the grim evidence of what loyalty to closed history demands—it is his initiation, his own birth. Finally, he walks resolutely—as few characters in the novel do—*out* of the Bruno house to make peace with his rapidly receding God. As he stands outside, the horror washes out of him (in sharp contrast to the mock release of Miller's enema), and he releases the glass shard that he has clutched in his pocket. He looks up into the "magnitude and care of the universe" (507), an awesome scope that dwarfs the doomed world of West Condon. He thanks God for his moment of redemption, all under that magnificent, open spring sky where the stars (despite the Brunist preoccupation with astrology) refuse configuration and deny messages.

It is just this open universe that Vince engages. He notes in one of his frequent moments of introspection: "History is like a big goddamn sea...and here we are, bobbing around on it, like a buncha poor bastards who can't swim, seasick, lost unable to see past the next goddamn wave, not knowing where the hell it's taking us if it takes us anywhere at all" (394). Vince, then, treads the waters that churn just outside Miller's smooth ark. Forever uncertain—as he remarks, "You think you know what the fuck is happening in the world...then suddenly you find out there's a lot more going on than you ever guessed" (366)—praying to a God he suspects to be a hoax, wracked by history and pained by its surprises, Vince resolves to carry on. He is the ideal metafictionist hero, resisting patterns and roles, engaging history without script or clever repartee, with only the will to keep going. He is also the ideal apocalyptic in a way that Bruno and Miller can never be; he is connected to history firsthand on the very real physical level—he sweats, he works, he cries, he fucks, he drinks, he eats, he is haunted in his dreams by the faces of the friends he lost in the mining explosion. And Vince releases the rainbow that Miller embraces.

This willingness to engage the everyday world is not palmed off as simple Pollyanna joy over being alive. It suggests engagement; it suggests the resistance to surrender, the acknowledgment of imminent discontinuity, and the fierce resolution to hope, to endure—all characteristic of the apocalyptic temper. Recall the parable, mentioned in the opening section, of the man hounded over a cliff by a hungry tiger and there, in the urgent confrontation with mortality, discovering the rich sweetness of the ordinary berry. Vince is aware of his mortality. He begins to feel his fifty years as he putters about the house while unemployed after the mining explosion shuts down the operation. His encounters with the apocalypse are immediate and nontheatrical. He is in the mine when it explodes. Although Bruno, stunned and dazed, is carried from the mine, his group slumps uselessly in a circle, waiting for help, singing "Amazing Grace" and drifting off to death; Bonali, however, leads his group to the surface via a tortuous and uncertain maze of airshafts. Later, when the Common Sense vigilantes set fire to the Widow Collins's house, Vince plunges into the sheets of flame to rescue the widow's daughter, admitting as he walks into the burning house that "he felt at home there" (322). Like the Christians under Domitian, like the first-generation Puritans, and like the world birthed fiercely by the thunderclap at Hiroshima, the apocalypse is no game to Vince; he lives in a world able to detonate at any moment. And it frightens him, haunts his dreams, alienates him from his family. When he talks about his uncertainties with Wanda Cravens during a brief affair with her, she counters by talking about the world of spirits where she finds comfort for her life of squalor and loneliness. Annoyed, he rejects such systems outright. It is no surprise that the boney Wanda Cravens will gravitate to the Brunist movement and will, by the close of the novel, refuse Vince when he comes to her house, determined to keep herself clean for the consummation. The affair, which erupts suddenly when Vince comes to her house on the night of St. Valentine's Day to bring her the relief check from the miners' association, is passionately (to the point of awkwardly) physical—her groping hands pulling mightily at his zipper, her boney knees opening hungrily, his big hand clutching the whole of her boney ass (210–12). It is much like the story of the whore told in the barroom. But Vince does not lie or calculate his moment. It is immediate, physical combustion, much like the mine explosion itself. Even the effects of his affair are immediate and physical—Vince is swept out of midlife doldrums by a surge of potency. He is revitalized in a way that Miller can never be in his campaign to win Marcella or in his pagan romps with Happy Bottom.

Vince, of course, does not move without deviation to his closing revelation. He is prone to the same destructive role playing that infects the entire West Condon community. He falls under the same idea that history is pattern when he accidentally retrieves the Black Hand from the fire at the Widow Collins's house. That hand is missing the same finger that Vince is missing. The coincidence unnerves him, and he sets off trying to find, or to fathom, a pattern to it, a message. It leads him not only to his momentary return to the church, but also to a certainty that he is marked for a prominent role in West Condon politics. He is caught up in the machinations of the Common Sense Committee and becomes one of its driving forces. He receives flowers from the mayor, who pulls up to Vince's run-down house in a Cadillac; he curries promises of political appointments once the "Brunist thing" is over; he begins to fancy himself the up-and-coming man in the community. On his front porch, as he rocks away the days of unemployment, he dreams of becoming mayor, of turning things around, of giving the little guy a fair shake. But the cost of this role playing is immediate. Vince allows himself to go along with the games of local politicking, with the committee's "social calls" to persuade Brunists by veiled threats to leave the cult. He even dresses up in a sheet as part of an elaborate drunken prank played on the hapless Ralph Himebaugh. He is, as he tells the mayor, "always game" (445).

But his willingness to play their game begins to rub his conscience. After the committee visits a confused high-school student under the sway of the Brunists and the boy then tries awkwardly to slit his wrists, Vince must go along with a newspaper release, prepared by the mayor, that Vince admits is "mainly the truth" (441). The release, however, claims that the boy came to them seeking refuge from the fanatic cult and then attempted suicide fearing reprisal. As the mayor callously tells Vince, "that's the game we play" (442). Later, as part of the "game," Vince, armed with a pickax, leads a vicious raid on the local church under whose protection the Brunists have flourished—an attack that culminates with the destruction of the church's Bible. As Vince begins to be troubled by what he must do to remain in their game, his delusions of leadership begin to fade. Even as he leads a group of drunken men out to disrupt the gathering on the Mount of Redemption the night of the apocalypse, he finds his followers slowly abandoning him in the bitter rain. During a final visit with Wanda, when he goes to break off their affair fearing it could jeopardize his political future, Vince continues his role playing, drunkenly begging Wanda for "one more for the old Mayor" (451). He drops his pants and begins to entice the resisting Wanda; but history has prepared one more surprise for Vince. The

Common Sense Committee, prowling about for Brunists, surprises him, pants around his knees. And although he manages to rescue Wanda from the drunken committeemen apparently intent on raping her, he does experience his own private, quite painful apocalypse:

> Four A.M. Staggered from the bed. Reached the bathroom door and up it came. Tracked through it in bare feet to the stool and got rid of the rest. Down to the bile. Sat on the side of the tub, head in hands. Sick. Not just in the gut. Sick in the heart, too. Fucked it up. End of the world. It was all over. (458)

It is a moment of honest recognition that his role playing, his pretend future, is lost. Divested of the neat pattern of future ascent that he had projected for himself, his world ends in an authentic (if private) apocalyptic shudder. It is not a showy apocalyptic pageant staged out on the Mount of Redemption, but a gripping moment of letting go, a moment of acknowledging his own foolishness. This private apocalyptic moment—vomiting down to the bile—is unplanned, spontaneous, and grimly physical. It serves to prepare Vince—once he is certain that political appointments are not coming his way, that his closest friends are leaving for employment up north, that Wanda's house is empty and for sale, and that his family is scattered and divided—for his final cautious step free of the fiction of a fixed universe.

Like *Cat's Cradle*, then, *The Origin of the Brunists* invites a contemporary world slouching toward its own extinction to reinvestigate the metaphor of the apocalypse: Vonnegut retells the Jonah story, and Coover replays the Noah story. Both suggest that the implication of the sudden and complete interruption of existence should rekindle dormant connections with the immediate—the world John abandons as he spins recklessly into Jonah; the umbrella of the universe that spreads over Vince Bonali's head one spring night. The idea of the apocalypse cannot lead humanity back to a medieval faith in patterns and symbols and numerology as the cataclysmic Brunists affirm. Nor can it lead to a complete understanding of the universe, which Justin Miller so yearns to possess. Nor can it afford the harsh, spitting anger of Vonnegut's John/Jonah. In the apocalyptic vision (and, in many critical ways, the metafictionist vision), the universe is governed by *un*certainty. It can draw people to the metafictional thrill of discovering a universe of change, expansion, animation by posing the notion of ultimate change, the final expansion, the culminating explosion of animation. It is a world of precarious uncertainty that Vince Bonali faces at the close of the novel and that the Brunists attempt to corral with their cataclysmic vision of neat, predictable endings. From the opening line of the novel

("Clouds have massed, doming the small world of West Condon"), West Condon is an enclosed little world, sapped of its life, scared to confront its death, and stilled, consequently, into a monotonous inertia where the promise of the New Year, the "vague hope its advent traditionally engenders," goes stale "only eight days" later (21). Under the intoxicating influence of the cataclysmic imagination, West Condon mutates into a world of closed history, locked into patterns that embrace endings like the fantasy of *ice-nine* that so fascinates John/Jonah as he stares blankly into photographs of neatly stacked cannonballs. The language of joy and healing able to counter such enervation belongs finally not to the arty irony of Miller or to the polished creed of the Brunist church, but to the bawling Vince Bonali at the moment he relinquishes the rainbow. His encounters with an awesome series of apocalyptic moments leave Vince with an authentic contact with his own self—he feels love, passion, loneliness, and the chilling onset of his own death; in short, he feels.[21] This has always been the value of the apocalyptic temper: not a cheap religious phrase, not a melodramatic despair over current history, not the hysterical sort of eyeless expectation of imminent consummation, but instead a way for people, eyes open and imaginations stirred (recall, for instance, John/Jonah's *closed* eyes and habitual cliches), to feel again what it means to live reconnected with a universe that promises only the slender miracle of the present moment.

Notes

1. Writers associated with the metafictional school who have experimented with the notion of the apocalypse would include Burroughs, Gaddis, Pynchon, Rudolph Wurlitzer, and, most prominently, Barth, although his fictional apocalypses are largely an exploration of literary constructs folding in on themselves rather than a concern for the larger question of social and historical constructs collapsing. Coover himself (who admits a literary debt to Revelation) has kept the apocalyptic temper in his fiction since the publication of *The Origin of the Brunists* in 1966, most carefully in two of his full-scale novel productions: *The Universal Baseball Association, Inc., J. Henry Waugh, Prop.* and *The Public Burning.* I have chosen to focus on the first novel because of the formidable work already done in analyzing the apocalyptic factor in these two later works. For such an analysis of *Baseball*, see particularly Jackson I. Cope, Arlen J. Hansen, and Schulz; for a thorough treatment of the apocalyptic attitude that shapes the perspective Coover brings to the Eisenhower 1950s, see Thomas LeClair's impressive effort.

2. The parallels between Coover and Lewis and Dreiser, at least in connection with his first novel, date back to initial reviews. Although not mentioning Lewis or Dreiser, Emile Capouya faulted Coover for a mean-spirited, bitter satire that was trying to revive the naturalistic novel by grafting onto it the surreal. Schott described the book as one plagued by "Hollywood giantism" and offered Coover the "reassuring" advice that, could he control that tendency, he could be heir to Lewis and Dreiser. Perhaps a panoramic look at a frustrated small town in mid-America will always suffer in the shadow of the turn-of-the-century realists, but even Karl, in his recent survey of contemporary American fiction, treats *Origin* as a failed political allegory burdened by a cast of flat, undistinguished characters more appropriate to *Main Street*.

3. It is safe to say that whatever critical work has been done on *Origin* has dealt largely with the book as a satire on religion, although the phrasing here is borrowed from the title of Leo J. Hertzel's article, the sole article in the body of substantial criticism on Coover's work that is dedicated to *Origin*. Hertzel claims that the book's "mass of detail" is held together solely by religion and that the origin of the Brunist religion is intended to resemble the roots of early Christianity. Larry McCaffery, one of Coover's most published critics, summarily treats *Origin* as a study of religion as one of the ways humanity tries to make sense of the world and of history through the marvelous invention of fictions. Kathryn Hume labels the citizens of West Condon examples of Coover's "naked" men, the vulnerable and the threatened who seek refuge from their universe in the comfort of signs provided by Christianity. Likewise, Lois Gordon lists religion as an expression of the human mind, a fiction vested with mythic authority.

4. Coover's description of his first novel as his "paying dues" originated in the interview with Frank Gado (148), but it has been repeated and expanded upon by Coover in subsequent published talks with McCaffery (67) and Thomas Alden Bass (294). This has led, at least in part, to the critical eclipse in which the novel has remained. Criticism has come a long way from an initial review that dismissed the novel as "an explosion in a cesspool" (Hertzel, "Christians," 19). The novel itself has had little close scrutiny; instead, it has been treated, trimmed, and simplified as a primer on metafictional impulses. Neil Schmitz is alone in praising the novel, citing it as Coover's unfulfilled promise before he lost himself in a series of fictions that are pure exercises in technique, without heart. The novel is long overdue for a thorough treatment on its own merits.

5. Justin Miller as the novel's "sane voice" (the term is from Karl [366]) is a critical commonplace. Margaret Heckard defends Justin as a lover of the "immediate, the everyday, the human things" (223); Richard Andersen admires the character and points out that Happy Bottom instructs Miller's cynical heart in the importance of things here and now; R.H.W. Dillard, Hume, and Gordon largely echo each other in accepting the sexual covenant struck by Miller in the closing chapter as Coover's way to salvage joy and passion in the contemporary universe.

6. The notion of the reaction of God to His destruction of His own creation is lyrically (and forcefully) presented in Walter Brueggemann's *Genesis*. Although it argues quite passionately that God was in grief over His realization that humanity would not follow His pattern for creation, Brueggemann's thesis is clearly that the Flood put humans in charge of creation.

7. The instances of numerology in Coover's book have been methodically elucidated in Lewicki's chapter on Coover. For a particularly effective example of the length to which Brunists try to read the universe in the code of apocalyptic numbers, see Ralph Himebaugh's chapter, particularly pages 219–20.

8. To list all these slingshot instances would become tedious; a few examples will suffice: the novel begins with Hiram's contemplating the dead body of Marcella on Saturday night, then moves back to Saturday afternoon, and then moves on to the rescue efforts over Marcella's body; in the Baxter family chapter (part 2, chapter 6), the section opens with the arrival of the Widow Collins at Sunday dinner time and then replays Sunday, moving on to the quick disruption of the meal that the widow's visit causes; Vince happens past the Collins's house as it burns, and then we move back to the group of neighborhood kids who decide to visit the Collins's house and there see the vigilantes setting fire to it; Eleanor Norton mentions that the messages from Giovanni now include references to the Mount of Redemption, and then we see the scene when Bruno mentions it; after the 19 April apocalypse, Elaine Collins mentions that her longtime boyfriend, Carl Dean Palmers, is now in jail, and only later do we learn the circumstances of his arrest and then move ahead to Elaine's new love for Abner Baxter, Jr. Throughout, Coover works to upset and startle traditional narrative time. As Gordon points out, Coover is fond of beginning in medias res (24).

9. For a fine interpretation of a later Coover work (*The Public Burning*) as a novel with a similar theme of performance and exaggeration of performance, see LeClair, who argues that Nixon is a man driven to risk excess on the public stage.

10. In one of Coover's later experimental short fictions called "The Brother" (*Pricksongs*), he recreates the Noah legend from the view of Noah's brother, a man with a pregnant wife, who watches his crazy brother build an ark in the middle of a field. Noah, not surprisingly, comes off in the worst light—he is "lost in a fog" and stares out into space, not saying a word even when his brother screams to him as the rain begins to swell. Like Vince Bonali, who also sees history as an open sea that must be engaged firsthand, Noah's brother, after futilely trying to catch up with the disappearing ark, vomits and retches, realizing—with the same sort of terror that stirs Vince at his epiphany— that his world is rapidly ending. Coover's sympathies rest with Noah's brother, who engages the apocalypse in a way that his serene brother will never achieve.

11. Like the other Brunist followers who have accepted the cult's creed in response to the immediate evidence of mortality, Hiram Clegg will not become an involved member of the Brunists until after his wife, Emma, dies of a heart attack the night of the apocalypse. Hiram then ascends rapidly to the position of bishop in the new Brunist religion. Like the Brunists, he prefers the easy dimensions of universal catastrophe to the terrifying mystery of individual death.

12. There are many suggestions of the circle about the Brunists: when Eleanor Norton first senses that Bruno the miner might indeed be the spiritual event she has been awaiting all her life, she feels her confused past become concentric circles. But the association that Coover develops is the destructive nature of the circle. To give two examples: when Hiram Clegg notices photographers taking pictures of him in his tunic, he feels foolish, and a "circle" of Brunists attacks the photographer and forces him to give up his camera; and Bruno, in the mine locker room before the 8 January descent, is encircled by the miners and pummeled when he tries to reclaim his poem. In addition, the Common Sense Committee, steered by the mayor, is associated with a square (yet another geometric figure); indeed, as the mayor doodles on his office pad while on the telephone enlisting help in his campaign to fight the Brunists, he creates squares that become diamonds that become squares until he has sketched a complete checkerboard. This circle and square imagery makes the television, which comes to dominate Miller's fortunes, a particularly ominous image.

13. The association of Bruno with Christ is one that Coover plays with long before the townspeople of West Condon take over the game much more seriously. For example, when the miners are preparing to descend into the mine, one of the miners addresses Bruno angrily, "Christ, go play with yourself somewheres else" (36), the "Christ" as much a noun in direct address as it is an expletive.

14. Coover makes it quite plain that it takes very little to convince the townspeople that Bruno is the neo-Christ rather than the mock Christ. In her initial visit to Bruno's bedside, Eleanor Norton grows excited as his impassive, semiconscious face nods absently to her leading questions, such as "Are you the One who is to come?" He nods and then drops back into unconsciousness. It is enough, however, to satisfy her hunger.

15. The connection between Giovanni Bruno and Giordano Bruno has been mentioned; see Karl (365–66) and Gordon (22).

16. The ambiguous nature of the truth as it relates to Miller's newspaper work is underscored when he whimsically feeds a UPI reporter a completely false report about the miners' recovery—a "lie" that nevertheless goes out on the national newswire as a quite acceptable "truth" (108).

17. The accusation that the metafictional fiction maker runs the risk of reducing his or her work to passionless finger exercises is a criticism that haunts Coover's own work (see Heckard, although she finally accepts Coover's humanism; and Schmitz, who most emphatically does not). To understand Coover's own fears (fears that go a long way in showing just how unacceptable Miller is as the novel's sane voice) one need only listen to Coover's words: "the first and primary and essential talent of the artist is to reach the emotions. . . . It may mean only a kind of sense of reaching people on a visceral level, that is to get them to think of the body. . . . Otherwise we look at it and say it's a cute act, you know, but it doesn't touch me at all. But sometimes it hits inside . . ." (Hertzel, "Interview," 26–27). Vince Bonali, rather than the ironic Justin Miller, engages the reader at this level.

18. Perhaps a brief look at the erotic suggestion of Marcella in her garden would help stress the point that Coover refuses Marcella the role Miller wants to give her. She emerges, fresh from a bath, singing, swinging, leaping in the sun. She revels in the spring and in being in love. A bird's "*liquid laughter* *sends wildflowers shivering up her spine, and out she dances to drench herself in the hot and holy sun"* (297). With pagan abandon, she goes on to plant her seeds in the rich earth, all the while the *"sun gloriously hot on her spring-frocked back"* (299). It is a scene—interrupted by the coarse description of how Cunt Hill got its name—that is vital to appreciating Marcella's connection with the fecund world so elaborately denied by the hill, which miners have plowed to resemble a woman's pudendum.

19. In Bass's chatty article on Coover, he mentions seeing on Coover's cluttered desk "yellow ruled pages on which are penciled the outline for *The Origin of the Brunists.* In a precise hand there is written on top of the outline: *"Antichrist* a better title?" (293).

20. Although Miller is the most developed example of the failure to love, he is far from alone in the Brunist cult. Eleanor Norton is swept up in a mystical ecstasy while walking along the sidewalk one day and in her excitement professes her love for the spirit Domiron; Ralph Himebaugh strokes his cats while he wears women's undergarments; Elaine Collins comes to her true love when he whips her with a tree branch during the frenzy of the rainstorm; Wanda Cravens samples any number of gentlemen before finally seeking the solace of reclaimed virginity in preparation for the world's end; Tommy Cavanaugh, high-school Lothario, loses his virginity by using the threat of imminent apocalypse on an impressionable high-school girl. The point is that the Brunists, by divorcing themselves from the open universe, close themselves off as well to the passions of being alive.

21. Perhaps a quote from a recent interview with Coover will make clear this idea that the Christian apocalypse is a phoney device used to divorce people from history, people who every day experience the hazards of private worlds detonating:

> Apocalypse is a magical idea borrowed from Christian mythology . . . . But short of apocalypse there's always disaster, which we have visited upon us day to day. We have had, in a sense, an unending sequence of apocalypses, long before Christianity began and up to the present . . . . And we can be pretty sure there's more to come. I mean, who can stop it. (McCaffery, 78)

Coover has frequently cited the apocalyptic temper as the dominant mode of contemporary fiction (see, for instance, the McCaffery interview and the Bass article). Clearly, however, he rejects the cheap phrasemaking of Christian apocalypticism and prefers people to turn away from grand-scale apocalypse to face, like Vince, private endings.

Chapter 3
With Sunlight in Their Eyes
Sinners and Saints, Apocalyptics and Prophets in *Love in the Ruins* and *The Thanatos Syndrome*

> *My heart is overwhelmed,*
> *My pity is stirred.*
> *I will not give vent to my blazing anger,*
> *I will not destroy Israel again;*
> *For I am God and not man,*
> *the Holy One present among you;*
> *I will not let the flames consume you.*
>
> **Hosea**

> *Q: How is such a belief possible in this day and age?*
> *A: What else is there?*
> **Percy, "Questions They Never Ask Me"**

In both Vonnegut and Coover, characters heroically resist this century's oppressive sense of exhausted hope—or fail to do so—solely on their own strength; our resiliency alone is tested. God, that most traditional consolation associated with the apocalyptic temper, diminishes (as it does for Vince) to a distant, obscure presence. But the nuclear age is far from a simple secular construct. What of the fate of orthodox Christian belief in a claustrophobic age charged more with the sense of closing possibility? If the awesome energy implied by a divinity sustained John's fledgling Christians and, centuries later, could make a paradise from the inhospitable wilderness of Massachusetts Bay, then what of saints in this age of sinners, in this age of disbelief? How do saints manage the trick of faith, as Graham Greene's Scobie despairs? After all, these latter days of the Christian age would seem a particularly inhospitable time for authoring Catholic Lives of the Saints. In the objective/empirical universe so relentlessly erected in the age of science,

Catholic hagiography reads now like heavy-handed (and rather bad) satire.[1] Writers still swayed by the credo of Catholicism must bring their message of its continuing vitality to a world convinced that the brave crusade, launched in the superstitious gloom of the Dark Ages and sustained too long in the harsh light of scientific evidence, has finally exhausted itself, that Christendom itself has somehow failed. For these writers, the communication of the traditional virtues of Catholic saint-hood—joyful dependency, resilient constancy, and the resolute accep-tance of alienation as humanity's natural condition on earth—can be accomplished now only by indirection. They offer two prototypes: the troubled (yet authentic) saint, wrestling with doubt, threatened by a world that stubbornly withholds belief in the transcendent, and denied the assurance that typifies the traditional beleaguered saint (atypical Greene); and the sinner who makes pretense to sainthood, a vile sham and strutting hypocrite whose incorrigible pride merely underscores how rare is true sainthood (vintage O'Connor). In either case, the dis-cerning reader must be responsible to canonize the legitimate saint or to damn the pretender.

Percy chronicles these latter days of Christendom ever sensitive to the dilemma posed when the "old words of grace are worn smooth as poker chips" (Percy, *Message*, 116). His characters search after, pretend to, dream of, and, in rare instances, ascend to authentic sainthood. And they must do so in a world trembling with apocalyptic shudderings. For if the Christian world is exhausted, the Secular City, which emerged during Christianity's decline, is in sorry shape as well. Percy uses nothing less than the apocalypse itself as the litmus test to separate his many sinners from his few saints. Percy's characters live under the constant threat of endings. But in a world robbed of its God and the omnipotence of the transcendent realm, such an apocalypse never comes off. Binx (*The Moviegoer*) wanders about New Orleans in his queer malaise, pon-dering the terrifying ennui of a world where the bomb does not go off. Will Barrett (*The Second Coming*), driven by his own determination to know God beyond the questions of other Christians, proposes to wait in a cave until either the Second Coming or his own death by starvation. It is a dramatic proposal, and, of course, absurdly vain. Lancelot recounts with the cold logic of a madman his own determination to prove God by documenting the existence of evil and sin—he videotapes his wife's sexual indiscretions with a Hollywood film crew staying at Lancelot's restored southern plantation. Convinced as he watches the films that he does indeed know sin, Lancelot proceeds to execute his own apoca-lypse: he levels the plantation in one shuddering fireball, a gas explosion that he feels punishes the wicked. Although his self-appointment as the descending judge is a delusion, he continues in his role as divinity by planning, after his impending release from the mental asylum, to commence the millennial new world in Virginia (appropriately enough) with a fellow inmate, a girl purified (he claims) by a vicious rape. These characters face with various degrees of distortion the grim evidence of the dissolution of Western civilization and search after nothing less than the traditional Christian finale itself. Imposing the apocalypse unsuccessfully on the slow collapse of the Secular City, the saint comes to recognize God's omnipotence and puts aside the hunger for the apocalyptic stroke; the sinners, however, pursue it without letup.

Love in the Ruins is Percy's most compelling examination of the apocalypse; with unrelenting urgency Percy here tests saints and sinners by having them confront both the enervated, spiritless state of Christendom and the rapid defaulting of the promise of the Secular City. Tom More, the troubled apocalyptic who narrates the novel, spends a harrowing weekend around the Fourth of July in an America of the not-too-distant future, watching as his Louisiana parish (and the world, he believes) pitches momentarily toward the consummation. But his brush with the apocalypse seems to move More from a spiritually disordered life, riven by rages and suicidal depressions, to a hesitant return to the Catholic church he abandoned some years earlier following the death of his young daughter Samantha and the subsequent departure of his wife, Doris. His is a spiritual rebirth that is achieved on Christmas Day, no less. Indeed, the novel seems a calculated (to the point of forced) tale of one man's reclamation in the ruins of the age of science. More seems to move erratically but unerringly from his self-destructive state at the beginning of the novel—a sinner, an alcoholic, a casual fornicator, an absurd Faust dabbling with a machine to heal original sin—to a condition in which, as Martin Luschei has offered, he is open to the possibility of grace. More is generally conceded to be by the close of the novel one of Percy's twentieth-century saints.[2] The incessant longings that trouble Tom More, his alternating depressions and elations, his recurring ennui, his radical disillusionment with Catholicism, even the grim specter of the dying Samantha that haunts him—all seem to resolve themselves in Percy's sentimental coda set five years after More's perilous weekend. The reader's final glimpse of More finds a humble prodigal happily married with two children, working the land and fishing the stream with Christian simplicity. The quintessential alienated man at the beginning of the novel—unexplained sniper attacks force him to wander about a most precarious landscape; his own cataclysmic certainties compel him to outfit three rooms in an abandoned Howard Johnson's as shelter for his three girlfriends—More would seem in the novel's coda to be most radiantly at home, invigorated spiritually by his return to the Catholic confessional. And as he carries off his chubby Presbyterian wife to their new double bed ("twined about each other as the ivy twineth" [379]), More seems to have achieved Percy's existential reversal—"the discovery of the pearl of great price at the very heart of the objective-empirical disaster" (*Message*, 99).[3] He seems to have found the harmony of a utopian state (only proper to a descendant of Thomas More) in a chaotic world moving toward its imminent disaster, a world sundered by political, religious, and racial factions. He is, by his own accounts, a survivor of that lost world. He fancies himself "God's spoiled child, a Robinson Crusoe set down on the best possible island" (361).

But the ivy imagery of the novel's closing sentence suggests regeneration only ironically. The coupling of Tom More and his nurse-wife, Ellen, is spiked by the Old Testament vines promised to entwine the ruins of civilizations damned by the angry judgment of Yahweh. They are the same vines that Tom More sees sprouting all over his decadent world—on the highways, in the golf pro shop, in a tavern, around a bottle of Southern Comfort—vines that no one else sees but that trouble the self-appointed apocalyptic because they foretell biblical-scale devastation and indicate moral deterioration and spiritual aridity.[4] Like the owl that screeches far off in the blackness of the swamps that border More's enchanted bower to shatter the careful harmony of his Christmas barbecue, Percy stands apart from his narrative and warns that all is not quite as harmonious as his narrator may suggest. Once again, a writer stands in radical, important revolt against his own character—much as Vonnegut works against his cataclysmic messengers and Coover moves against the narrowed vision of his cavorting cataclysmics and mutant metafictionist.

Here, Percy urges the damnation of his "converted" saint. This saint, who anguishes over the approaching apocalypse of the Secular City (even at one dramatic point rending his shirt), is a particularly vicious sort of pretender to sainthood, Percy's exemplum of the egocentric sinner who assumes self-election. More's "Home, Sweet Home" satisfaction is a stubbornly secular comfort, a resistance to the saint's traditional virtue of dependency on the Christian God. More is confronted by an apocalyptic world of division (suggested not only by a *United* States where a host of northern "black cities" are seceding from the Union and by a Catholic church spliced into three sects, but also by More's private life—his lapsed Catholicism and assorted domestic tragedies). But rather than accepting the overwhelming evidence of humanity's vulnerability and then choosing the complicated act of faith in a

God greater than such apparent disorder, More opts for arranging his own world and convincing himself of the authenticity of such a new life. But his new life after the apocalyptic weekend merely mocks the traditional Christian promise of paradise.

At an odd moment, More confesses that when he was thirteen, while on a walk through the woods, he happened upon a house under construction. Enthralled by the "triangles of new copper flashing, scraps of aluminum, freshly sawn blocks of two-by-fours," he was so taken by such intricate work that he "caressed the glossy copper, smelled the heart pine," and finally "defiled" himself (234). This curious recollection shows More's enduring fascination with "man's excellent geometries wrought from God's lumpish handiwork" (234). The idyll depicted in the coda is just such an excellent geometry. Alienation—not domesticity—is the earthly condition of the Catholic religion to which More makes his halfhearted return. Humanity, created to inhabit that queer state between the beasts and the angels, is a pilgrim or, in the words of Percy, a "castaway, a stranger. . . in the world but. . . not at home in the world" (*Message*, 142). This More resists. As the ominously maternal Ellen says to More after the danger of the weekend has passed without the apocalyptic conflagration, "Let's go home" (356).

Despite his family heritage ("Wanderers we became, like the Jews in the wilderness" [21]), More seeks earthly shelter. The cataclysmic weekend, however, begins with the Bantu guerrillas' campaign to get More to move *out* of his house. Three sniper shots shatter More's (appropriately) enclosed patio on 1 July. More convinces himself with characteristic vanity that the terrorists are trying to steal his invention—the lapsometer—when actually they only want his house because of its access to a television transmitter. Here and throughout, More resists the loss of his home, rejects the burdensome uncertainties and the necessary loneliness of the pilgrim-saint on earth. In the coda, his bower of bliss is, like the suites at the Howard Johnson's that he absurdly outfits against the apocalypse, a radical (and foolish) assertion of pride and autonomy. Taken by "the sense of his own sovereignty," More quotes Huey Long: "every man a king" (360). His utopia with Ellen, a hermetic world anchored to the immanent, is on a par with the insane audacity of his lapsometer (a device fittingly conceived during More's short stay in a government asylum). They are both exercises in human *in*dependence— indeed, the novel takes place around the Fourth of July, and the Christmas season during which More returns to the church is one celebrated by children setting off strings of firecrackers. Tom More, quasi scientist who drinks away his long afternoons in a tavern called (appropriately) the Little Napoleon, readily accepts himself as America's last chance by virtue of his lapsometer's ability to weld the flesh and the soul and thereby refute Adam's fall. He is that most dangerous phenomenon of the age of science that has placed before humanity the illusion of virtual omnipotence: the sinner who plays a most convincing saint.

Love in the Ruins is clearly a satire, a dystopian vision of a rapidly approaching dark time in an America dead from spiritual neglect. But the satire Percy pursues—directed at political fanaticism, religious hypocrisy, suburban ennui, academic hypocrisies, and scientific deper-sonalization—is heavy-handed and, on the whole, traditional stuff. The more complicated satire Percy sustains, however, is directed against his narrator even as More returns to the church in exemplary Percy fashion. That return is deliberately discontinuous with the novel that precedes it—Percy suddenly leaps ahead five years: the apocalyptic cataclysm so anticipated by More never came off; the Bantu guerrillas, their invasion of Paradise Estates a bust, have now bought their way into the suburbs with money from oil improbably discovered in their swamp homeland. More's return to the church is on a par with the Bantus' deliberately absurd move into the white suburbs. The Bantus pretend to be refined Englishmen—sporting knickers, playing golf (badly), and shouting to each other, "Good mashie, old man" (371). The Bantus play at being Englishmen with the same unconvincing foolishness with which More pretends sainthood. Like the English sparrows that have moved into the martin house More's father built, they are out of place.

The compelling satire in the novel emerges from this tension between More, a desperate cataclysmic without the stability of God, and Percy, the steadfast apocalyptic. Like the traditional cataclysmic, Tom More broods over an amoral world teetering toward destruction. Like both John/Jonah and the Brunists, he sees only an inevitable future. Indeed, he is always scanning the terrain for thunderheads rolling in, for vines poking through sidewalks, for curls of smoke rising in the distance. But, as with the cataclysmics, he is a mere watcher, impotent and helpless, driven to rampant paranoias. Denied the transcendent realm (his eyes are narrowed, swelled nearly shut from his allergy to the gin fizzes he drinks), More can only be certain, as he says again and again, that the worst will come to worst. His conviction of catastrophe then impels him only to despair and to the queer sense of pleasure that tingles his scalp as he anticipates a moment of cataclysmic change. Divorced from a God able to mitigate the apocalyptic message of an inevitable future with authentic hope, More can only indulge in fantasies of a new start once the cataclysm has passed, improbable fictions that parody the Christian new time promised once judgment has been rendered. As he sips his Early Times whiskey (itself a suggestion of the tawdriness of his fantasies of new starts), More toys at different times with visions of fresh starts: living happily with his three women in the survival shelter he has created at the Howard Johnson's, eating Campbell's chicken-and-rice soup, sipping toddies, and reading from the shelf of the world's great books, "beginning with Homer's first words...and ending with Freud's last" (8); marriage with Moira, happily raising chickens and children (243); marriage with Lola, "doing [his] researches" like an "agreeable H. G. Wells nineteenth-century scientist type" (322) and then watching "evening fall" from the gallery of her plantation, which is an exact re-creation of *Gone with the Wind*'s Tara (321); living with the "clear-eyed vacant simple Massachusetts girl" Hester in her swamp-commune chickee, eating catfish, maize, and wild grapes, and raising "good sweet innocent children" (347). He even mentions with a certain wistfulness Fletcher Christian's new life after abandoning the *Bounty* "with three wives on faraway Pitcairn, green as green and unhaunted by old Western ghosts" (44). But More himself is haunted. His visions of the new time are all refuges, deceits, imagined pastoral shelters, safe from corruption, crisis, and death; all varieties of fairy-tale happy endings; and all of them radically secular.

Such secularity undercuts the apocalypse for which More so carefully plans. Like a "new Copernicus" (7), More reorders the Christian cosmos into a private universe with More himself as its center. In the opening sequence, More is at the center: an elevated observation point on the cusp of the interstate cloverleaf from which he commands a central view of his southern community. Unlike the true apocalyptic, More the cataclysmic can not only pinpoint the time of the end (within two hours, he says checking his watch in the opening paragraph) but can be certain as well of its causes—the Bantu insurrection, whose elaborate (and farcical) schemes he has overheard, and the fallout of noxious particles from the ionizer attached to his lapsometer. But More is a center that cannot hold. Percy dismisses the feeble apocalypse threatened by scientific tinkering and by social revolutions. More's apocalypse fizzes, like the gin fizzes he drinks. He is not only a bad Catholic, but a bad apocalyptic as well: he is much like his crackpot mother, a shrewd real-estate broker and part-time seer and prophet who peers into her crystal ball to forecast "business and political" crises (169) but is nevertheless oblivious to the Bantu rebellion that breaks out in her very town—she is scrubbing her bathroom floor when a breathless More alerts her of the crisis in the streets. After his feared apocalypse dissipates much like the summer thunderstorms that constantly move across his Louisiana community, More (outside authentic salvation) endorses belief in a pri-

vate new world that is as hopeless as the Secular City whose ruins he
scans at the very beginning of the novel—one equally dead at the center
and devoid of spiritual love. Without God, who alone can guarantee
linear history by His promised interruption of time, More's new world
grinds away in a sad, heavy cycle, like the theory of recurring history
promoted by Arnold Toynbee, a favorite author of More's. On his forty-
fourth birthday (and, appropriately, again on his forty-fifth birthday),
More intones darkly, "Nothing changes but accidentals: your toes rotate,
showing more skin. Every molecule in your body has been replaced but
you are exactly the same" (148)—an odd confession for an authentic
Christian apocalyptic, but an accurate summation of More's false apocalypticism and a telling remark that sorely strains the credibility of
More's closing leap to the church. Despite More's pretense at reformation,
little about him has changed in the coda: More still leers at a neighbor
woman, still feels the burning thirst for alcohol (indeed, as he barbecues
his Christmas turkey, he thinks, "The Lord is here, a holy night and
surely that is all one needs" [378]—yet he decides in the very next
thought to take "six drinks in six minutes"), still promotes the promise
of the lapsometer, still ambushes his wife with base carnality, and still
sees the vines creeping, creeping.

Set against More, the failed apocalyptic, is Percy, who gazes with
unblinking eyes on the very same age of crisis that drives More to despair,
and yet endorses a vision, not of an inevitable future, but of an alternative
future—a possibility of reformation by humanity's electing to return to
the joyful dependency characteristic of traditional sainthood. Percy has
written eloquently on the parallels between the contemporary Catholic
writer and the traditional prophet who acts to avert catastrophe, like
the canary in the coal mine that senses danger long before anyone else.[5]
"When the canary gets unhappy, utters plaintive cries, and collapses,
it may be time for the miners to surface and think things over" (*Message*,
101).

A remark by More early in the novel illuminates the differences
between this character and his author. Quick to discount the effects of
his domestic unhappiness on his scientific discoveries, More promotes
himself (with characteristic vanity) into an impressive pantheon: "After
all, van Gogh was depressed and Beethoven had a poor time of it. The
prophet Hosea if you will recall had a bad home life" (11). The mention
of Hosea recalls a minor Old Testament prophet whose story of betrayal
and brokenness moves steadily toward a final joyous celebration of for-
giveness and reconciliation with God that mocks the pretenses of More's
Christmas rebirth. Much as Vonnegut found a model in the Book of
Jonah and Coover revitalized the story of Noah, Percy rejuvenates the

Book of Hosea; that book, like Percy's novel of the apocalypse, deals with a choice—independence and certain destruction, or dependence and unconditional salvation. Like More, Hosea is alarmed by his nation's moral and spiritual laxity; like More, Hosea knows firsthand the bitterness of marital betrayal; like More, he projects on his troubled nation the domestic tragedies of his own household. Spurred by a ruinous marriage to an unfaithful wife, the prophet nevertheless sees in her faithlessness and his abiding love for her a powerful allegory for Israel's moral dissolution and drift away from Yahweh and Yahweh's willingness to forgive despite grievous betrayal. Unlike More, Hosea undertakes the difficult role of warning his nation that it has fallen out of favor with the God who first established it in the wilderness (a joint effort that recalls More's review of "the poor USA" as God's once-favored nation [53–55]). Unlike More, Hosea only indicts; the time is still there to move toward a new direction, toward an authentic new time. He neither anticipates the coming judgment (as More does when nervously checking his watch) nor pretends to read signs. From the ruins of *his* marriage, Hosea brings a prophet's message that promises destruction only if Israel fails to return to Yahweh's authority. By the closing chapter, Hosea is moved to offer Israel's response, a reaffirmation of its traditional obedience to Yahweh, who in turn is moved to love His chosen nation once more.

As a prophet, Hosea (and, by his own definition, Percy himself) fulfills three roles: he discerns the critical nature of his nation's chaotic moment in history, reading the historical "now" aided by divine authority; he reasserts the viability of a traditional way to harmony, a way thought unavailable or abandoned as unworkable by his own people; and he calls upon his nation to return to that tradition. The prophet's role is then educative, not punitive. His is a gesture of love in a dangerous time—the hope in a God greater than the threat of chaos. Forever seeking, forever longing, forever hopeful, the prophet ministers to the people in an age trembling with imminent crisis.[6]

Percy undercuts More's attempts as physician ministering to his few patients. Like his father (a failed-physician-turned-coroner), More is hardly a successful doctor. He uses his nurse Ellen to shield him from his patients; indeed, he has largely forsaken his patients—revoked, in essence, the tie that binds a prophet to a nation—to work on his absurd lapsometer (and build his own scientific reputation). As a physician to the soul, he betrays the transcendent realm to the immanent world. His drive to "bridge the dread chasm that has rent the soul of Western man ever since Descartes" is nothing less than a campaign against the soul itself. In a world robbed of its transcendent dimension, one must face the reality that—given such a relentlessly physical universe—death will be everywhere victorious. More struggles fiercely with death. Whether in the hotel shelter or at home with Ellen, More plots to cling to life. His suicide attempt on a past Christmas Day inspires this love of the immediate—"Seeing the blood, I came to myself, saw myself as itself and the world for what it is, and began to love life. . . . After all, why not live?" (92). Clinging to mere life and unable to return wholeheartedly to his God, he remains at the close of the novel much like his father—numbed by alcohol and surrendering to death. Without God, the physician of the soul can only be its coroner. And Percy suggests in the coda that the apocalypse has not been averted after all. The love More has discovered in the ruins is the same ruinous self-love that has leveled the Secular City. More is still the doubting Thomas, and death is everywhere still winning—save that now the vines entwine More himself.

What ails the soul of such a man who, by his own testimony, has felt the exhilarating illumination of the true saint, who has touched the "thread in the labyrinth" (241)—that exquisite certainty reserved for those who believe that humanity is made only to love God and that life on earth is mere passage? After More voluntarily commits himself to the government hospital in the days following his Christmas suicide attempt, he realizes, "tears streaming down [his] face," that it is God he loves "in the beauty of the world and in all the lovely girls and dear good friends, and it is pilgrims we are, wayfarers on a journey and not pigs nor angels" (104). But he cannot sustain such assurance in the ruins of his life after Samantha's pathetic struggle with a relentless cancer and then Doris's flight to start her own new life at an island retreat off the coast of Mexico. It is betrayal on two fronts: Samantha's disfiguring cancer destroys his Christian faith in life and betrays him to his death obsession; his wife's resolution to end their stultifying marriage destroys his Christian faith in the miracle of love and betrays him to a series of "anonymous," "transient" relationships—"fornications," as More calls them (112).

More opts for regression from authenticity—the world where "things are too naked" (102). Like John/Jonah and Justin Miller, Tom More, who has agreed to an unconditional surrender of life, suffers a contraction of the heart—a deadening to the simplest physical level, where original sin can be treated, memories erased by liquor, and love transformed into an uncomplicated carnal exercise. Unlike Hosea, whose cruel domestic betrayals lead him *toward* a vision of reconciliation, More chooses an uncontested divorce from the spiritual plane that, to his troubled and narrowed eyes, has abandoned him. More becomes a scientist; he returns to his childhood predilection for humanity's "excellent geometries," a turn of heart that is, as suggested by the childhood masturbatory act in the woods, soullessly egocentric, crude, and, most importantly, unfulfilling, merely satisfying. If, as More challenges himself often, the question posed by the novel is, Can the physician heal himself? then the answer is a most resounding no. More is Percy's Everyman of the Secular City, sick unto death from the very satisfaction and omnipotence promised by the technological age.

More cannot accept the full Christian implications of his daughter's death. Samantha's neuroblastomic face represents what simply cannot make sense, and will never make sense, to the scientist. That memory haunts his most pleasant moments of anticipated satisfactions; for instance, he suddenly spurts tears as he beds down with Moira, when he recalls the night he and Samantha watched an interminable Miss America pageant waiting in vain for Samantha's blind date to appear. Samantha's tumorous face, distorted by the neuroblastoma to the point that it resembles "a two-eyed Picasso profile" (69), is Percy's harsh example of "God's lumpish handiwork," the inexplicable, indecipherable stroke of the Christian God. And the lesson of the saint's joyful dependency and constancy during such a moment of crisis comes from the distorted mouth of the child herself in More's final recollection of Samantha. Near death, she cautions More, who she has noticed has stopped going to mass, that the greatest sin of all is to refuse the grace God gives "to believe in him and love him" (332).[7] This is the very refusal More makes when, after his daughter's death, he denies all but the physical world and opts for the "low road" (69) where as a scientist he can see "into the hidden causes of things and erect simple hypotheses to account for the glut of everyday events" (11). He refuses to take his dying daughter to Lourdes, not because of any scientific bias, but precisely because he fears that a miracle might indeed take place, undeniable evidence that would complicate the simplified physical world in which he has already begun to exist. His is a world where the soul's longings are measurable; where fears, depressions, and regrets can be numbed by alcohol, lost momentarily in sexual assignations, or even massaged away with the help of the ionizer that Art Immelman designs to attach to More's lapsometer; where miracles are medical sideshows, like More's "cure" of the apparently hostile and senile Mr. Ives before a capacity crowd in the Pit of the government medical facility.[8]

Unavailable to Catholicism and its God, More falls under the sway of Art Immelman, a Mephistophelian tempter who first comes to More's office during a fierce thunderstorm as More is listening to the tumultuous finale of Mozart's *Don Giovanni*—the moment of Don Juan's descent into hell.[9] He comes in the guise of an unctuous liaison for the National Institute for Mental Health and offers More unlimited funding for both an ionizer that could be used with More's lapsometer and a "crash program that will put a MOQUOL in the hands of every physician and social scientist in the U.S. within one year's time" (160). The lapsometer, which Immelman deceives More into signing over to him, becomes in the hands of Immelman a device that merely massages the soul's perturbations into a pleasant nullity—like the alcohol that More consumes. Not coincidentally, Immelman carries "an outsized attache case like a drug salesman" (156). Without the Christian perspective that accepts longing, More becomes intoxicated with the idea of actually healing humanity's fallen nature, to win back paradise, to revoke the very lessons of Samantha's death. When Immelman makes his most direct appeal for More's soul, he tempts him with secular satisfaction:

> Believe me, it lies within your power to make all three [women] happy and yourself too. Didn't God put us here to be happy? Isn't happiness better than unhappiness? Love them! Work on your invention. . . . Develop your genius. Aren't we all obliged to develop our potential? Work! Love! Music! That's what makes a man happy. (344)

As More listens to Immelman's description of hedonistic happiness on earth, he is also drifting off to sleep ("with a smile on his face as he thinks of such a future") under the influence of a tranquilizer—Percy's suggestion of a parallel between Immelman's earthly satisfactions and narcotics. When More finally does reject Immelman by mumbling a prayer to St. Thomas More, he has not quite disavowed Immelman's philosophy, as the coda bears out.[10]

Anchored to the physical level, spiritual longing and Christian alienation are nothing more than treatable conditions. And More is their self-appointed physician, the soul's repairman. At one point More characteristically simplifies the collapse of Western civilization by suggesting, as he contemplates his own silent appliances and the rusted cars that litter Paradise Estates, that it fell apart because "nobody wanted to be a repairman" (60). It is the job he accepts. But original sin is *un*treatable and *un*repairable. It is as relentless, as inexplicable, and as incurable as the cancer that destroys Samantha. She nevertheless clings to her carefully learned catechistic bromides even in the face of such purposeless agony, and that dimension redeems her. But More is a Cancer himself, as his mother (a dabbler in astrology) points out (166–67). His insistence on autonomy is clearly not in remission, as the absurd pretense of his reformation indicates. As a cataclysmic, More can never make his peace with the end. He can struggle with it, run from it, anticipate it, even pretend to overcome it. But he cannot, as Percy has written elsewhere of St. Thomas More, be "most cheerful with Brother Death in the neighborhood" (*Message*, 109). Unable to dance with death, as More himself remarks about St. Thomas More, Percy's cataclysmic finds life a most obsessive, nightmarish "feasting on death" (354).[11]

Doris may seem an unlikely foil to More. Yet after her initial anger at God over Samantha's death, she commits herself to the Christian search (although one slightly mysticized by her British guru) for something greater than the death that so grimly disfigures and then destroys their daughter. That death turns Doris toward the "high road," toward the awareness that without such a dimension life and love devolve into mere dust and lust. Some months after Samantha's death, Doris confronts More with her resolve to "make a fresh start" (62), an authentic gesture toward revitalization in contrast to More's own drunken fantasies of new starts. She accurately diagnoses the dilemma of her marriage with More—it is dead inside, their love reduced to mere carnal habit.[12] Even as Doris tries to articulate her decision to recover herself, More clutches her about the hips and tries an impromptu seduction. Aided by Alistair Fuchs-Forbes, a British lecturer and healer whom More derides mercilessly as a fag reciting "*I Ching* in a BBC accent" (64), Doris begins to see that the world is too much with her, that the physical is the lowest denominator of human experience. She points out to More that his abandonment of the spiritual dimension has made their marriage a burned-out star, one collapsed into itself, unable to give light, just "heavy heavy heavy" (64). It is a measure of just how accurately Doris evaluates More that later—long after she goes to Mexico and there dies accidentally—More makes love to Lola, whom he has just met at a Christmas party, under the fiery red of Betelgeuse, a star that is indeed burned out and collapsing into itself.

More, of course, snickers at Doris's decision to undertake her pilgrimage to the Mexican retreat of Cozumel and there to follow what she comes to believe to be her greatest hope—making "simple, good earth-bound things" (64) with her hands and practicing intense meditation. He mocks her notion that "love is spiritual" (68) and then even tries to "convert" her to his philosophy—he literally drags her down to the patio bricks, and they awkwardly make love for the first time since Samantha's death. Such a passionate outburst (so similar to the pulsating fire of Betelgeuse) gauges More's refusal to take seriously Doris's quest and the implications of her spiritual anxiety. To him, Fuchs-Forbes is simply (and it is a simple analysis) after her considerable wealth. ("That's how you would *see* it" [68, italics mine], Doris chides him.) But Doris assesses quite accurately More's fatal dis-ease: "You're not a seeker after truth. You think you have the truth, and what good does it do you?'' (68).

Certainly much about Doris's swift awakening to the spiritual dimension is skewered by Percy. Her lecture to More in his enclosed patio is an improbable hash of half-digested Yeats, Hesse, Longfellow, Holmes, the *I Ching*, and Buddha (the very absence of Christian influence would indicate Percy's wariness). Hers is an appeal more animated by emotion than reasoned by thoughtful consideration. Yet, Doris does *leave* her home to become a pilgrim, her eyes ''full of sunlight'' (63). She abandons More to his vine-encrusted enclosed patio and his dark world of roiling thunderstorms. Her stand in the enclosed patio recalls Vince Bonali standing alone under the stars, releasing the rainbow, his eyes searching an expanse of night sky where God only whispers, faintly. Although Doris's death at the Cozumel retreat merely reenforces More's certainty that such pilgrimaging is pointless, Doris—like Samantha armed with her *Baltimore Catechism*—has met death unafraid. To her, that death reenforced a purpose for living—the very message of the traditional apocalyptic. Without such purpose, More is left with the ''riddle'' (180) he ponders as he reads Stedmann's account of the World War I battle of Verdun, which ''killed half a million men, lasted a year, and left the battle lines unchanged'' (44). The Frenchmen, More argues to himself, chose to die for something. Like Doris and Samantha, Coover's Vince Bonali, and the traditional apocalyptic (recall the man dangling over the cliff), they have found life in the very face of death. But what about those (like More) who opt not for life, but for mere survival; who cannot embrace death, but merely run from it; who find then only death in life; and who become nervelessly, terrifyingly alive and dead all at once? *Love in the Ruins* performs an unrelenting autopsy on just such a soul-dead man.

More is dying from a self-admitted failing: religion—things spiritual—merely makes him more mortal. During a vacation trip with Doris to the blasted wilderness of the American Southwest, More journeys (pilgrim style) to a ''forlorn little Catholic Church'' located at the crossroads of a ''moonscape countryside.'' There, More feels the exhilaration of the traditional saint, touches the ''thread in the labyrinth'' in an allegorical setting suggestive of the refuge Catholicism offers in the Western wasteland dessicated by unbelief. But when he returns to the motel, More translates such spiritual energy into an energetic coupling with Doris, one exuberant to the point that afterward she asks, bewildered, ''My God, what is it you do in church?'' (241–42). Lost to the transcendent, More refers to the Eucharist as ''eating Christ,'' a vaguely cannibalistic sobriquet that even he mocks with heretical vulgarity as he nibbles Moira's sensuous kneecaps. More, we are told, once wrote a "prize-winning essay for the Knights of Columbus" that derided transubstantiation as a "piece of magic to fool the ignorant" (341). Unavailable to this traditional Christ and His message of Communion, More appoints himself as nothing less than a new secular Christ. It is a message that comes to him as he stares at his own reflection in the dark mirror behind the bar of the Little Napoleon. Conjecturing that the "old Christ...didn't work," More offers himself to the Western world on the verge of the apocalyptic moment as the neo-Christ, the "maculate Christ, a sinful Christ" (145). The heretical audacity of such drunken claims would be simple comedy if such self-conscious self-promoting did not figure so prominently in More's movement toward spiritual rebirth.

That process commences in a deserted Catholic church during the Fourth of July weekend and culminates in the "sour darkness" (373) of the confessional five years later. Determined to confront the sniper who shot up his enclosed patio, More makes an ill-planned raid on the Bantu stronghold in the country club pro shop. Easily captured, he is taken to the Bantu headquarters—the long-abandoned Church of St. Michael's—and left in the oppressive heat of the monsignor's darkened office. The closed-up room immediately suggests a womb to the self-conscious More. He commences his rebirth, however, with movement *out* of the abandoned church to which the authentic saint would most certainly cling. The rebirth is further distorted by an artificiality, an unnaturalness that anticipates More's pretense to sainthood. He sweats and nearly swoons in the heat of a rectory office that is lined with "huge Kodacolor murals" of the great "snowy peaks of the Alps" (294). Cleverly, More makes his way to freedom via an air-conditioning duct to the rectory garage. He unscrews the grill of the duct with the bronze sword that he removes from the office statue of St. Michael, arming himself with the very sword that chased Adam and Eve *out* of paradise. Desperate for relief from the sweltering heat, before More reaches the garage he turns on the church air-conditioning system by simply throwing the master switch, which starts up not only the air conditioning, but the church carillon as well. It was stopped in midcarol five years earlier during the Christmas season in a previous Bantu uprising. When More kicks out the panel to the church garage, he does so with an exaggerated awareness of the symbolic import of his liberation, typical in a man so easily convinced of his own importance: "out I come feet-first, born again, ejected into the hot bright perilous world" (295). Percy demurs over such reclamation. Certain that the panel will fall with much noise, More waits to kick it out until the last "piercing obligato" chord of "White Christmas," a secular rather than sacred Christmas carol. Like the murals of the Alps and the carols lofting over the southern community sweltering in July heat, More's self-conscious process of rebirth is rife with the unnatural.

This indulgence of role playing, this secularity, this disconnection from the past mark not only More, but also the three women he chooses for his survival plan—with whom he will rekindle the human race after the apocalypse. There is Lola Rhoades, the striking, six-foot Texan horsewoman and cello player. She plays her cello with the same intensity as she swings her loaded automatics, rides her favorite sorrel, or digs in her garden. Her heart, according to More's lapsometer reading, is full of love, and More invests her with a mythic fecundity and passion. But her love is given uncomplicatedly only to her cello, which she clasps erotically between her sweating knees. She clasps More with the same fervor, running her calloused fingers along the small of his back and hissing her cello music to accompany their lovemaking. She is unavailable to natural potency, like her father (who boasts of organizing the world's only golf tournament run entirely at night, under the artificial illumination of arc lights), and like her plantation ("a preposterous fake house on a fake hill. . . dredged up from the swamp by the state of Louisiana" [172]). Sweaty, muscular Lola plays at the aggressive, thoroughly masculine role of protector to More, who is her ever pliant manchild, her "Tom-Tom." She is hungry to win and to dominate. During one interlude in the Howard Johnson's, Lola locks her legs around More's waist "in a non-erotic schoolboy's wrestling hold," and when More reacts in pain she claims that "Nobody ever beat Lola at anything" (323). Not surprisingly for one so self-assured, the apocalypse that More anticipates hardly bothers Lola—she stoutly urges More to come to Tara and there face the "twilight of the Gods" with Valkyrian daring. After the weekend, Lola abandons More to pursue fame as a cellist on the concert circuit in Texas.

Moira, the marvelously sensuous, simpleminded romantic (her favorite poet is Rod McKuen), has only a child's comprehension of time. As her name suggests, Moira trains her uncomplicated mind on idyllic tomorrows. She is lost to the past and indifferent to the present. Her initial reaction to More's plan to hold out against the apocalypse is abhorrence—she has nothing to wear. She spends the anxious moments in the Howard Johnson's oblivious to the danger More tries to explain to her, placidly pursuing her marriage plans with More until he drags her to the window and points out the distant smoke from the Bantu rebellion. More must concede that Moira is not terribly strong on history, either. An old container of Coppertone that she finds in the alligator weeds around the hotel pool compels her to compare the hotel in ruins to Pompeii. She thinks the "great motels of the Auto Age were the haunts of salesmen and flappers of the Roaring Twenties" (127). Undisturbed by ruins (unlike More), Moira takes More all the way to Silver City, Arizona, for a passionate weekend in a ghost town. If Lola delights in the erotic abandonment of her music and the competitive dominance of her partners, Moira provides More uncomplicated sensual satisfaction, her berry-brown, supple body quite unlike the sweating hardness of Lola. But as she settles down to wait out the apocalypse, reading her favorite author—Helen Gurley Brown—and listening to classical music— her Montavani tapes—Moira suggests simple physicality uncomplicated by intelligence.

The third woman, Ellen Oglethorpe, is a nurse. Ever in her starched uniform, she would seem ideal to minister to Percy's ailing physician. At once robust and ripe and a strict churchgoing Presbyterian, Ellen would seem to exemplify the balance of body and soul, flesh and spirit that More needs after the tragedy of Samantha. Indeed, Ellen crusades against More's relentless indulgence of self-destructive passions. At one point she invades More's office, where he has retreated once again to sit at his father's old coroner's desk, listen to Mozart, and sip toddies. She brings him a patient, stows his whiskey bottle, turns off his opera music, pops a chlorophyll tablet into his mouth to cover the lingering scent of alcohol, and then wets her thumb and smooths his eyebrow "like a mother" (147). She tends to him, frowns on his careless rendezvous with Lola and Moira, keeps him informed about the ongoing cataclysm, and works hard to insure his success as a physician. She seems, in short, More's best choice, a guardian angel for his final reclamation.

Percy, however, invests Ellen's character with dark implications. On More's forty-fifth birthday, she gives him after-shave lotion called "Hell-for-Leather," scented strongly like cloves (148). She is most taken by Immelman, Percy's Satanic tempter, and she is quite ready to accept his offer of a job as his traveling secretary. When Immelman disappears after More's ludicrous "prayer," Ellen watches him "turning slowly away" with trembling pity ("I think you hurt his feelings" [356]) and even makes a move to follow after him. She remains with More not to make complete his reclamation, but to oversee his damnation. She is a woman without faith, committed only to a creed of beliefs,[13] an institutional religion (Presbyterianism) with its conventional suspicions of other institutional churches. (She frowns particularly on More's ashes and sackcloth as unpleasantly Catholic rituals.) Unable to assert a transcendent faith, she cultivates only respectability, the good-folks image that More accepts in the closing line as he prepares to make love to her on the proper bedding from Sears. Ellen "does not believe in God" (145), "doesn't need God" (148), "doesn't have much use for God" (361); in fact, she is emphatically "embarrassed by the God business" (362).

She is indeed an apt nurse for More's closing affirmation of secularity. Unconcerned by spiritual longing or pilgrimaging, she ministers only to More's most basic hunger—she is in the kitchen for most of the coda, watching with matronly eyes as More settles down to a "plate of steaming grits and bacon" (361). A joyless neo-Puritan, she labors over the alcohol-dazed More (at one point reminding him of a Puritan woman leaning over her washtub), ever scolding, antiseptically passionate (they have slept for five years in separate, convent beds—quite narrow and made of white iron [368]), and the very embodiment of the soul-death reserved for More in the coda: moral rather than religious; efficiently procreative rather than loving; satisfied rather than fulfilled; content, as good Christian folks, rather than full of longing like authentic Christian pilgrims. When More embraces her at the close, intertwined like ivy, he embraces death itself.

The love he shares so generously with these three women leaves him only helpless and enervated—the mere sight of one of them leaves him aching, blows his speech center, reduces him to docility and passivity. More, who beds down with the three women in the Howard Johnson's suite under the leering smile of Hans's *The Laughing Cavalier*, knows that even the pitched ardor of such carnality can never quench the greater yearning that still haunts him long after he has resolutely divorced himself from the church. Under the narcotic influence of Immelman's ionizer,[14] More articulates the litany of such radical love:

Who am I?
I am he who loves. I am in love. I love.
Who do you love?
You.
Who is "you"?
A girl.
What girl?
Any girl you please. You.
How can that be?
Because all girls are lovable and I love them all. I love you. I can make you happy and you me. (202–3)

As More's lovemaking moves from the patio porch to the golf bunker to the humming bed and finally to the new Sears bedding—as he joylessly beds down with women who are as unconnected to a substantial past and as unconcerned with the vital transcendent realm as he—More underscores Percy's lesson about just how hungry the fed can be. Despite his best efforts to suffuse his couplings with spiritual import (at one point he whines, "Why did God make women so beautiful and man with such a loving heart?" [51]), he fails to see what a fellow inmate at the government asylum so correctly diagnoses: "You don't love God, you love pussy" (44). And clinging to the apparent satisfactions of such love, More finds only hunger, compared to the satisfaction he would feel after "eating Christ" at Communion with Samantha years before. He is the secular animal, the creation of the age of science, adamant in his belief in the "laws of materialism" and in the "cult of objectivity" (258–59). It is no coincidence that when More passes out on the golf course, he comes to on the shiny steel tables of the treatment room of the animal shelter—he reduces love to the bestial plane. He cannot love fully—his soul is soured by the sense of betrayal, his heart dead. At one point he mistakenly believes that he is having a heart attack; in fact, the bleeping on More's chest comes from the Anser-Phone clipped to his shirt pocket. Because More is so thoroughly dead inside, the physical love he pursues is diseased; this is suggested, for instance, by the burning wheals (from More's allergic reaction to the gin fizzes) that erupt on his skin wherever Lola touches him as they make love in the golf bunker on Christmas Eve.

Untouched by love, More pursues his resolute insistence on autonomy. He moves through an apocalyptic landscape determined to act alone: he searches out the sniper alone; he leaves the hotel alone to warn his mother; he leaves on trips to retrieve Lola's cello and then Moira's sachet. But each foray brings More only to a position of helplessness. He is captured, thwarted, spotted, surprised from behind. And other characters must come to his rescue: Victor Charles, a black deacon and longtime friend of More's, must intervene to protect him from the racist anger of the more militant Bantu guerrillas when More is caught in their country-club command post; when More is trying to escape from the rectory garage, Lola insures his freedom by breaking into the garage, her automatics at the ready. Percy emphasizes More's absurd determination to "go it alone" and then skewers that tale of self-sufficiency by exposing it as a masquerade, telling a comic tale of More's complete dependency, even as he celebrates his spiritual rebirth on *In*dependence Day.

A character so lost in self-deceptions and role playing (from Christ to Copernicus to Einstein to Hosea to Jonas Salk to Faust) has no stable identity; indeed, in the course of the weekend, More answers to a variety of names—Doc, Tom-Tom, Tommy, Tom, Chief, even Chico. All this prepares him for his greatest role, saint, which he executes in the coda with the guile of a consummate sinner. He models himself particularly after his namesake. He names his children Meg (like More's daughter) and Thomas More, Jr. He moves into the Old Slave Quarters, which resembles an English charterhouse. Indeed, his Louisiana parish turns radically British: English sparrows flit about, the local country club serves up roast beef and Yorkshire pudding as a Christmas feast, and even the Bantus appropriate British accents and dress. More plays his role with ease, even resolving that, should a good-looking woman flirt with him, he will guffaw heartily "like some ruddy English lord, haw haw, har har, harr harrr" (369). But this anglicized world is the world of Renaissance England that marked the nascence of the secular tradition that engendered the world in ruins at the novel's opening. The cycle, then, is complete. The reassuring linearity of the apocalyptic tradition is curved here into unbroken, unyielding cycles of emergence and ruin and reemergence. What is missing is the transcendent. The English, as More points out when he derides Doris's British companions, "are the most decent people on earth. . . . Because they got rid of God" (258).

The ashes and sackcloth, then, are merely the appropriate costuming for More's masquerade as saint. They underscore the superficiality of his conversion. Barbecuing his turkey on Christmas night, More still confuses the sacred and the secular, singing Sinatra tunes along with the *Salve Regina*. He celebrates his return to the confessional, dancing not only like David before the ark but also like Walter Huston (yet another actor) in *The Treasure of the Sierra Madre* (that jig a spontaneous reaction to the discovery of gold). Earthly wealth is exactly what comforts More. His search to reunite the flesh and spirit, to return humanity to paradise, has simplified considerably. He is less interested in unity and more distracted by union—he has organized the local chapter of SOUP: "Southerners and Others United to Preserve the Union in Repayment of an old Debt to the Yankees Who Saved It Once Before and Are Destroying It Now" (377). SOUP, however, is thin gruel indeed compared to the saint's communion, with its tantalizing promise of uniting the divine and the profane. But for More, the search is over. Tested by nothing less than the apocalypse, he has managed to find only himself, to find only love *in* the ruins. He settles for love of dust and lust. And as the haunting image of his daughter reminds the reader, mere survival is the stuff that can never render fulfillment.

Is there any character, then, who feels the exhilaration of the thread in the labyrinth and resists converting such wisdom into the base exchange of secular profanities? Percy has written elsewhere of his ideas concerning the modern saint. He has argued that the condition of the Christian is analogous to a castaway on an island. People divide into two categories: geniuses who bring news about the island itself and apostles who bear messages from across the sea. The geniuses (an appellation More appropriates for himself frequently) deal with the objective, the verifiable, the news relevant to the predicament of life on the island. A watcher of "The Today Show" who has been written up in *Time, Newsweek,* and even the *New York Daily News,* More deals with news. He explains to the three women about the approaching disaster ("the bad news" [301]) in sentences as "grave, articulate, apocalyptic, comforting as a CBS commentator" (302). Indeed, More's initial realization of the imminence of the apocalypse comes from watching the news on the motel television and seeing Art Immelman passing among a crowd, massaging them with the ionizer. But such news is, as events prove, invalid. The television in the motel has "bad color" ("green people in a green field under a green sky" [305]), is two-dimensional, and gets only the local channel. Happiness depends not on such news, but on authentic communications from a higher authority. And it is the apostle, the saint, who listens.

Father Renaldo Smith is clearly one such man of God. An obscure prelate, still faithful to Rome, he is the object of More's condescending description: "a good and faithful if undistinguished priest for twenty-five years, having baptized the newborn into a new life, married lovers, shriven sinners, comforted the sick, visited the poor and imprisoned, annointed the dying, buried the dead" (131). Compared to More's tingling anticipation of the apocalypse, Father Smith, unable to support himself by ministering to the scattered Roman Catholics who make up his congregation, spends his nights as a fire watcher, trying to avert, like Percy's prophet, the conflagration. Father Smith, who meets More during More's stay in the hospital, confesses to him that during a sermon he abruptly stopped. "Excuse me," he had said after a prolonged silence, "but the channels are jammed and the word is not getting through" (175). He refuses to improvise the message. It is this Father Smith who counsels More that death is everywhere winning in the world and that none are deader now than the living—it is the message More needs to hear, but refuses. It is no surprise, then, that Father Smith is distracted by More's charade of the Christmas confession—Father Smith's constant checking of his watch indicates time running out for More. He is certain, as spiritual advisor to the soul-dead More, even as More recites like learned lines the familiar confessional ritual (his eleven-year catalogue of sins is abbreviated to a simple sentence), that More cannot be led to responsibility for his sins, remorse, or any firm purpose of amendment—

all proper to traditional confession. More can only admit embarrassment
for his sins. Abandoning More to the secular realm, Father Smith advises
him to at least improve his relationships on earth—to become a better
father, a better husband, a better doctor.

Despite Father Smith's dire diagnosis that death is everywhere winning
and despite More's bedding down with Death, one character clearly
"wins" in Percy's sense, clearly clings to the traditional faith in a time
of upheaval and finds as reward for his resiliency a sense of place and
commitment to a clear future. Percy invigorates an apparently minor
character—Victor Charles (whose Christian name suggests Percy's
intent)—to counter his novel's overwhelming fascination with cataclysm, its shuddering surrender to this century's death wish. Like Vonnegut and Coover, Percy smuggles in the gesture of hope; he locates
the willingness to engage living in a dark time in a character who does
not hunger for center stage. Vonnegut, Coover, and Percy offer novels
dominated by the incendiary drama of the cataclysmic imagination. In
the exhausted fantasies of *ice-nine* and of the Brunists, characters find
riveting the simple arithmetic of the approaching zero—the clean, clear
lines suggested by the end—far more compelling, in fact, than the routine engagement of life in the middest. Just as the evening news concentrates on the mesmerizing images of catastrophe—houses being
swallowed by fierce fires; family automobiles pressed into odd configurations that suggest abstract sculpture—the literature of the nuclear
age concedes the powerful sway of glimpsing the unglimpsable, thinking
the unthinkable, as a civilization dares to peek at its own approaching
extinction. Much as Vonnegut can sound his tempered optimism only
against the caterwauling of his John/Jonah, and much as Coover plays
Vince Bonali's apocalyptic act of faith against the flashy sideshow of
the West Condon Theater of the Cataclysm, Victor Charles here is a
slender presence who moves nevertheless in steady, if eccentric, orbit
about the collapsing world of Tom More. Vonnegut, Coover, and Percy
warn (as Pynchon and DeLillo will later) that our century has become
absorbed in the drama of its own ending. Their novels here play out
the cataclysmic urgency in appropriately grandiose fashion, like emphatic signs that demand attention with the simple pronouncement of The
End Is Near. But that investment, these writers caution, is profitless. In
an age dominated by the uncomplicated image of the mushroom, hope
demands the complications of nuance. Vonnegut, Coover, and Percy
surrender center stage to their pseudoapocalyptics, each of them generic
showmen, pitchmen of cataclysmic inevitability. Like John/Jonah and
the Brunists, Tom More cavorts there in the pale of the stage light in a
grimly comic *danse macabre*. But the dance, each writer assures, must

finally exhaust itself. While the energy of each narrative may be compelled by the fierce internal combustion of the cataclysmic imagination, each novel turns toward the gentler energy of the apocalyptic temper for resolution. It is hope offered in spare strokes. They address a death-haunted community impelled by the intoxicating drama of its own civilization coming apart at every nail: in such an age, hope is a rare match flick that is illuminating because it is the sole spoke of light in such a darkening landscape—much as these minor voices emerge strongest in a wailing chorus of the exhausted, the defeated, and the lost.

Percy's apocalyptic, Victor Charles, works as an intern at an animal clinic and as a deacon at the Starlight Baptist Church. He heals, as it were, body and soul, nurtures the animal as well as the spirit—which More's absurd lapsometer can only attempt to do. Victor is a most reluctant Bantu guerrilla. He cannot hate whites simply for being white. He remains More's steadfast friend because More once stayed with Victor's dying aunt. And now Victor helps More, who in his insistent autonomy disdains such assistance. (Indeed, More barely conceals a virulent racism that recalls in its intensity the bigotry of Vonnegut's John/Jonah.) But Victor is there when More collapses on the golf course, and he carries him (Good Samaritan fashion) to the animal clinic. There, Victor not only treats More's physical needs (a communion of corn bread and buttermilk), but offers him the very advice that could redeem his soul. In effect, Victor delivers Percy's message to become as a pilgrim: he tells More to move *out* of his house. He goes on to deliver the soundest advice More receives: "You ought to trust people more. You ought to trust in the good Lord, pick yourself out a nice lady like Miss Doris, have chirren and a fireside bright and take up with your old friends and enjoy yourself in the summertime" (140). Unlike More, who tries to fashion a new Jesus, Victor proclaims with unshakeable faith, "Blessed be Jesus," even as Uru mocks his belief, claiming that such devotion to the white man's religion has made blacks subservient too long. He mocks Victor by ridiculing the white man who long ago abandoned belief in the Jesus that Victor still embraces: "You out-Jesused them, Victor, that's what's so funny" (288). Percy, of course, finds such resiliency commendable. Victor, in responding to Uru's remarks, accurately summarizes the condition of Tom More at the close of the novel: "Only a fool says in his heart that there is no God" (142).

Victor hovers about More's troubled wanderings like a guardian angel. He protects More from the wrath of Uru, smuggles More's carbine (confiscated by Uru when More is caught in the pro shop), returns it to him to protect More's mother, and helps More when he catches him emerging from the air-conditioning shaft in the church rectory. Steadfast in his faith, compassionate in his fellowship, Victor Charles tells More at the novel's close of his plans to run for Congress, to launch an authentic campaign of renewal through the sort of active efforts that More cannot accomplish, withdrawn as he is to his private world. Aided by his faith, Victor prepares to maneuver effectively in the world that so stuns, depresses, haunts, and finally destroys More.

It is only fitting to turn to Will Barrett, Percy's exemplary saint, for a summary diagnosis of Tom More, Percy's dis-eased sinner. Both live in worlds threatened by imminent cataclysm, both have religious temperaments tuned to registering every apocalyptic quiver. Yet, by the close of *The Second Coming,* Barrett has moved away from the simple, immediate realm and has begun his own pilgrimage toward the realization of a vision of cooperation between the spheres of the immanent and the transcendent. For him the apocalypse has passed now to God's hands. The ending of that novel is, appropriately, less a conclusion than a beginning, a hesitant gesture toward the difficult quest ahead. Earlier in the novel, however, Barrett writes in a letter about the dilemma of the modern unbeliever who, unlike the disbeliever, *chooses* not to believe. It is a scathing passage and one particularly appropriate to Tom More:

> The present day unbeliever is crazy as well as being an asshole... because he finds himself born into a world of endless wonders, having no notion of how he got here, a world in which he eats, sleeps, shits, fucks, works, grows old, gets sick, and dies and is quite content to have it so. Not once in his entire life does it cross his mind to say to himself that his situation is preposterous.... No, he takes his comfort and ease, plays along with the game, watches TV, laughs, curses politicians... and does not exercise his own freedom to inquire how in God's name he should find himself in such a ludicrous position. (118)

This is Tom More, mock-apocalyptic-turned-mock-saint. His quest for comfort and ease in a world splintering apart comes to be translated easily into the search for mere physical satisfaction, for spiritual rest rather than quest. But Percy's saints are determined travelers, aided in their trek across apocalyptic landscapes only by a map showing a destination beyond the end. They are pilgrims, like Doris, with sunlight in their eyes. In an apocalyptic novel ringing with Percy's snickers at the pretenses of scientists, psychologists, black terrorists, and white suburbia, Percy saves his loudest snicker—the last laugh, if you will—for his own narrating voice.

When Percy continues the chronicle of Tom More in *The Thanatos Syndrome* (1987), More himself admits the inauthenticity of his reformation and his reclamation by the church. On parole after serving two years in a minimum-security prison in Alabama for trafficking in narcotics (appropriate for one so lured by illusion), More concedes now he is only "a Catholic in the remotest sense of the word—I haven't given religion two thoughts or been to Mass for years" (45–46). And Ellen, still favoring iron convent beds, has completed the process of anglicization—as the novel opens, she moves to yank More's two children out of parochial school and enroll them in Belle Ame, a private school "on the English model, with tutors, proctors, forms, and suchlike" (45). She has converted, becoming "one of those Southern Anglicans who dislike Catholics. . . and love all things English" (46).

But prison life has altered more than More's shaky affirmation of Catholicism. Now at midlife, More rejects his concerns for the human condition. His scale, he confesses, is now "smaller":

> I don't have to plumb the depths of "modern man" as I used to think I had to. . . . At one time I thought the world was going mad and that it was up to me to diagnose the madness and treat it. I became grandiose, even Faustian. (67)

And if prison has moved More away from his faith, it has also worked to restore his humanity:

> I still don't know what to make of God, don't give Him, Her, It a second thought, but I make a good deal of people, give them considerable thought. Not because I am more virtuous, but because I'm more curious. I listen to them carefully, amazed at the trouble they get into and how few quit. People are braver than one might expect. (81)

As More begins to listen, begins to treat patients again, he finds that patients he counseled before his stint in Alabama have curiously lost their more disturbing fears, their more profound anxieties. Although they appear happier, More senses "they're somehow diminished" (85). They seem strangely disinterested, disconnected. More notes a critical lack of self-awareness, a loss of "the old ache of self" (85). Anxieties have been replaced by a disconcerting sort of vacancy, a "curious flatness of tone" (168); More, who as an "old-fashioned physician of the soul" (16) is uncertain about such remarkable recoveries, begins to investigate.

With the help of a local epidemologist and her roomful of computer terminals able to tap into a network of data, he uncovers an unauthorized project, Blue Boy, that attempts mass behavioral adjustments by contaminating the water system of Feliciana parish through the diversion of heavy sodium waste released from a nearby nuclear power plant.

The "truncated cone" (137) of the plant's cooling tower looms ominously in Percy's landscape. The chemical contamination suppresses certain cerebral activities and stimulates others. The project has uneven results. By strengthening the ego and "cooling the superego" (195), the treatment promises to reduce crime, suicide rates, teenage pregnancy, clinical depression, chemical dependence, anxieties, and even AIDS. The sodium treatment stimulates memory and concentration (Louisiana State University engineering students no longer use calculators, and Ellen masters bridge by being able to compute in her head the distribution of the cards). The treatment encourages less repressed sexual activity, a certain loss of inhibition and regresses communication skills (those treated "use two word sentences" [197]). The project, More discovers, is conducted without public consent or even the knowledge of the government. One of the project coordinators likens the sodium to fluoride, which was added to the public water supply in a similarly secretive fashion to treat dental enamel. One enthusiastic project supervisor promises:

> Instead of a thousand young punks hanging around the streets in northwest Baton Rouge, looking for trouble, stoned out, ready to mug you, break into your house, rape your daughter, packed off to [prison] where they cost you twenty-five thousand a year, do you want to know what they're doing? . . . Cottage industries, garden plots. . . . Plumber's helpers, mechanic's helpers, gardeners, cook's helpers, waiters, handymen, fishermen. (197–98)

Treated, they have become useful, industrious, and placid.

As More uncovers the project and threatens to make it public, he is offered a position within the network—his work on the lapsometer, after all, suggested treatment of complicated anxieties and neuroses by chemical means. But More, renewing his humanity, acknowledges there is more to the soul than "neurones" (88). He challenges the morality of altering human will and conditioning people to be good by making them docile. He divides humanity into categories—feisty jaybirds (the doers) and romantic bluebirds (the dreamers, the be-ers). The treated, he argues, are more like chickens. Like More's own lapsometer, the heavy sodium promises a "regression from a stressful human existence to a peaceable animal existence" (180). The backers of the plan, however, argue results. "Who's going to argue about knocking back crime, suicide, AIDS, and improving your sex life" (217). "It's war. In time of war and in time of plague you have to be Draconian" (218). But More discovers that the water treatment, besides gelding the self-consciousness of his patients, has led as well to a sordid ring of child molesters and child pornographers operating at Belle Ame, the children there mildly stimulated by steady intakes of treated water. More realizes as he gathers the offensive evidence—home movies, crude video cassettes, still photographs—what evil can be done in the name of what passes for the good. The treatments result in a loss of self, vulnerability to exploitation, and submission to indignity.

It is, as Father Smith's harrowing confession of his experience in 1930s Germany, the lesson of the Holocaust, of Verdun, of Hiroshima. It is the lesson of the twentieth century, the age of Thanatos. Rather than participate in its intrigue, More moves to stop the "aberrant local project." As the novel closes, More welcomes back a former patient, one who had been treated by heavy sodium. She "opens her mouth to speak" (372), to recommence the painful handling and the careful examination of her soul, the process so crucial to being alive. As a companion piece to *Love in the Ruins, The Thanatos Syndrome* eases More away from his self-delusions (he has neither had a drink nor taken a pill in two years), his embrace of the secular, his search for comfort, his acceptance of death, his life in the ruins. In the end, says Father Smith, who returns to act as More's spiritual mentor, "one must choose. . . life or death" (257). Although the machinations of the plot here are cumbersome as More skulks about the Louisiana bayou backwaters scaring up clues to the conspiracy, More's affirmation of his own humanity and of life itself is deliberate and emphatic. More still pages through Stedmann, still defines the century as the age of Thanatos, but by the close of the novel he no longer participates in the promotion of death. More challenges the notion of comfort on earth. He rejects Lucy, who steadily mutates into a latter-day Ellen, ominously maternal (at one point she even plasters his eyebrows with her wet thumb, a la Ellen) and protective. He rejects a future with her that is certain to be "sunk in English Tory melancholy" (348); rather, he assists Father Smith at a hospice filled with the haggard young victims of AIDS, ministering to the dying and finding there a strange celebration of being alive—the very message his daughter Samantha offered years before. They are the brave, the human, the alive.

More promising, however, although his religion and his God still elude him, he restrains himself from the pretense of shallow reformation that so distorts *Love in the Ruins*. Here, he refuses to assist Father Smith at the mass, fearing such participation would be "deceitful" (363). Don't worry, Father Smith counsels, "It is to be expected. It is only necessary to wait and to be of good heart. . . . You have been deprived of the faith, all of us have. It is part of the times" (364–65). Father Smith reassures More that in this century,

"God agreed to let the Great Prince Satan have his way with men....All he had to do was leave us alone. We did it. Reason warred with faith. Science triumphed. The upshot? One hundred million dead...one must not lose hope even though the final war seems inevitable as this terrible century draws to a close....Perhaps the world will end in fire and the Lord will come—it is not for us to say. But it is for us to say...whether hope and faith will come back." (365)

And Father Smith, more certain now of More's reclamation than when he listened wearily to More's rehearsed confession years before, warms to his disciple, "You are on the right track. I have watched you. Carry on. Keep a good heart" (366).

From mock saint and mock apocalyptic, More turns toward a gesture that promises reformation. Nursing the dying, ministering to the soul-sick, reclaiming his humanity, More has found his way to the genuine comfort afforded by the traditional apocalyptic temper. No longer reading cataclysmic omens like a weather chart, no longer anticipating doom, More delivers the compassionate message of Percy's saints: in a dark time, keep a good heart.

Notes

1. Although Protestant sects adapted (and altered with their suspicions of humanity's inherent unworthiness) the format of Catholic hagiography, the prototype of the genre is Catholic. This explains in part why Percy's major creations (with the exception of the wandering Binx) fall so strikingly into saint and sinner categories: Tom More, as I will argue, the sinner who pretends to sainthood by mistaking happiness on earth with sacred fulfillment; Lancelot, the thoroughgoing sinner who insists on questing after evil itself and then rendering his own apocalyptic judgment against the sinners; and Will Barrett, Percy's complicated saint who combines the trials of the other two sinners but emerges from his experiences healed in a way that the deluded More and the lunatic Lancelot are not.

2. Although some critics (LeClair and Thomas McGuane, for instance) do fault the novel for its sentimental closing, an impressive majority accept as authentic More's spiritual reclamation. See Eugene Chesnick, Robert Coles, William Dowie, Cecil L. Eubanks, John Edward Hardy, J. Gerald Kennedy, Luschei, and J. P. Telotte. William Leigh Godshalk argues at length the unreliability of Tom More as narrator, but concludes that by the end of the novel More has moved to a less distorted vision and a less apocalyptic outlook. More puzzling, Godshalk salvages More's character, suggesting that by the close of the novel More is less enamored of the material world.

3. Interestingly, this comes from a character analysis Percy performs on Tom Rath, the hero of Sloan Wilson's 1956 best-seller *The Man in the Gray*

Flannel Suit (Message, 99). Percy is stressing, however, how Rath merely mimics authentic reversal, plays at the role. This is quite important, given that More is similarly engaged in desperate role playing and fakery in his closing reversal of alienation. Both More and Tom Rath are death-haunted (Rath's father was a suicide, More's father the city coroner), and both are married to pushy women concerned about appearances. Like More, Rath dreams of a new life of material comfort rather than transcendent concerns. Rath, interestingly, lives in a run-down house with a ragged lawn and a weed-filled garden, perfect for More and his vines. In a questionable career move, Rath undertakes to promote the treatment of mental health like the treatments of polio and cancer—analogous to More's promotion of the lapsometer as treatment for original sin. Both novels end with unconvincing resolutions (Rath is moved at one point to assert that God's in His heaven and all's right with the world). The difference, of course, is that Wilson palms off such tripe as authentic; Percy undercuts More's resolution at every opportunity.

4. These vines underscore More's distorted vision. They are clearly manifestations of his unhinged mind. They are part of his overall determination as apocalyptic to convert the world to a Babylon ripe for judgment (at one point he compares his community to the hanging gardens of Babylon). But when he mentions the vines to other, more even-keeled characters—his mother, Max Gottlieb, and the bartender at the Paradise Country Club—they clearly have no idea what he is talking about.

5. Specifically, this idea appears in the opening passages of Percy's essay "Notes for a Novel about the End of the World."

6. For a more complete definition of the prophetic spirit in the time of crisis, see John Mauchline, Henry McKeating, and Brueggemann, who have written most compellingly of the prophetic imagination with particular reference to Hosea. Percy himself draws the specific parallel between the contemporary Catholic writer and the prophet Hosea in his lecture "The State of the Novel," reprinted in the *Michigan Quarterly Review*.

7. Percy, who has spoken of *Love in the Ruins* as a combination of the comic and the religious (Dewey, 287), plays a bit with More's abandonment of Grace. After Doris's departure and subsequent death in Mexico, Max Gottlieb (the name translates "God's love"), a doctor at the government clinic where More commits himself, arranges a blind date for More with an attractive and intelligent woman named Grace. Not surprisingly, the evening is a disaster (114–15).

8. The miracle—when More proves by his lapsometer that Ives's apparent senility is merely his refusal to respond to the overly solicitous care at the government retirement village—points out a larger issue than merely More's faith in such immediate, artificial miracles (as opposed to the miracles at Lourdes). Ives is an amateur archeologist and a career linguist, digging about for clues to decipher a hieroglyph. His quest leads him to a fountain on the grounds of the retirement village where he finally pieces together the message. That done, he tells the crowd at the Pit, he is ready now to return to his Tennessee hills, read a book or two, and die. Ives's secular quest is one easily

satisfied, and the solution achieved leaves him only death. Like the scientists from the clinic who search the swamps for the rare ivory-billed woodpecker, these scientists, More among them, search the immanent for the transcendent, confuse the realms, and mistake searching for authentic questing.

9. Given More's fondness for Mozart's dramatic tale of damnation, Percy seems to indicate again how much *his* tale veers away from salvation. The libidinous Don Giovanni resists countless attempts at reformation—as More does when he talks to Samantha, Father Smith, and Victor Charles—before finally being dragged down to hell—analogous, I would argue, with More's embrace of Ellen.

10. When More awakes dazed after his tranquilizer, he examines his pockets, trying to get his bearings. It is a most curious moment: he wants to "get a line of significance on my past and the hope of the future." What he finds is a collection of Phillips screws—clearly a reference to the air-conditioning grill he unscrewed at St. Michael's—and a "small dry turd" (344). That turd is unaccounted for in the narrative and must certainly be Percy's wry comment on More's future, the reformation detailed in the coda.

Much, however, has been made of More's "prayer" to his ancestor at this critical point in the narrative, a gesture that would seem to mark More's turn, or return, to traditional Catholicism and his rejection of the tempter Art Immelman, who swirls away after More utters the prayer. But More, in fact, composes other such hasty prayers during the novel—one during the hospital stay following his suicide attempt, another when he fears he is having a heart attack. Like the bower of bliss that he arranges in the coda, these prayers are not expressions or reaffirmations of faith, but immediate (knee-jerk) reactions to precarious positions: shelters, as it were, from the storm. More is moved to prayer only when Immelman appears likely to win over Ellen—an event that, given Ellen's own rather demonic temperament, is more a fait accompli. The prayer itself is a curious piece of devotional meditation, calling on St. Thomas More to help him beat this "son of a bitch." And Immelman, far from being cowed by More's expression of faith, simply leaves him in the capable hands of Ellen, who insures that the damnation of Tom More will be completed.

11. When More ponders the death of Samantha, he asks, "Is it possible to live without feasting on death?" (354). The answer, of course, is no, not without responding to faith. More, from his cataclysmic convictions, to his ghost-haunted past, to his closing embrace of Ellen, feasts on death.

12. At an odd moment during their encounter on the enclosed patio, More whispers to Doris, "I love you dead. At this moment" (65). Clearly, simple passion is dead at its heart, as Father Smith tells More at the hospital, "I am surrounded by the corpses of souls. We live in a city of the dead" (177).

13. This tension between mere belief and authentic faith dogs More, who cannot achieve either. His attempt to rattle off an edited version of the Apostles' Creed, the Catholic affirmation of belief, collapses into a heretical assertion: "I believe in God and the whole business but I love women best, music and science next, whiskey next, God fourth" (6). When he attends church with his mother on 2 July, he slips out right before the creed.

14. In its first use at the Pit on the day of More's cure of Mr. Ives, the ionizer reduces the Pit to a writhing mass of humanity. It merely serves to relax inhibitions and to bring to the surface a variety of perversions, prejudices, long-festering jealousies, and passions—both heterosexual and homosexual. Max Gottlieb is moved to compare the Pit to an infection of St. Vitus's Dance, a particularly debilitating disease that completely short-circuits control of the physical processes, a neuromuscular condition that suggests the physical out of control. It is what the lapsometer is all about and what More finally succumbs to by the end of the novel.

Chapter 4

Lessons in Love
and Silence

Gravity's Rainbow and the
Apocalypse in Gödel's Universe

*To those who have seen
The Child, however dimly, however incredulously,
The Time Being is, in a sense, the most trying time of all.*
W. H. Auden, *For the Time Being*

The image of the rainbow spans the Bible from Genesis and the Noah myth to Revelation and John's vision of God's judgment throne wreathed by a rainbow. In the Christian mythos, the elegant, simple arch signaled a sudden, hushed moment outside history. The luster of the mysterious, supernal rainbow promised continuation by reassuring the vulnerable underneath its arch of God's abiding covenant with His creation. Newtonian theories of optics and the property of light, however, divested the rainbow of such metaphoric sweep. The relentless scrutiny of the natural world betrayed the rainbow to the predictable, measured world of science. It became a manifestation of atmospheric data, of the complicated laws of the reflection and refraction of sunlight. The sweeping arch became merely a measurable parabola with a patterned spectrum of color.

It is a modern configuration—gravity's rainbow—that governs the apocalyptic world of Pynchon's 1973 novel: the relentless arc of the German rockets projected from continental launching sites and curving down into civilian London. This rainbow—bleached white and obedient to science and technology, politics and the military—far from fulfilling the biblical promise of hope to the vulnerable, insures instead the imminent decimation of those underneath its sweep. This rainbow does indeed belong to gravity, to the grim, predictable laws that lock even the planets into predetermined orbits, laws first described, appropriately, by Newton, whose simple laboratory prisms demonstrated the prosaic nature of heaven's spectacular rainbows.

Lodged beneath such a rainbow, Pynchon's is a world of nightmarish grotesques who cavort grimly under the white smudge of gravity's rainbow, compelled by anesthetic hallucinogens and profound passivity toward history until it either exhausts itself into entropic stasis or explodes in a final technological Götterdämmerung. In either case, history will prove faithful to the laws of scientific determinism. Powerless in this pre-apocalyptic landscape, Pynchon's characters indulge in mind-altering stimulants, creative paranoias, and sexual eccentricities as they wait for history to go "pure ballistic" (7) and succumb to the vicious curve of descent demanded by the unrepealable law of Newtonian gravity.[1] History has passed its own Brennschluss point, that awesome moment when the rocket hands itself over to gravity and the mathematics of calculable descent. Like the rocket, humanity itself faces inevitable, precise, and predictable fall in the aftermath of yet a second world war that gave the world the systematic efficiencies of the Nazi concentration-camp archipelago (Pynchon traces the fascination for the parabola that shaped the Wagnerian excesses of the Reich's master architect, Albert Speer) and the noiseless flash of atomic weaponry, both arch-metaphors for contemporary apocalypse and both central to Pynchon's novel.

Yet, curiously, a novel so centered on the devastating capacity of modern rocketry regularly highlights incidents of technological miscues, failed rockets, missed targets, premature detonations or descents and offers with straightforward thoroughness the eccentric and decidedly pointless investigations that cartoon science and its promise of calculation, its pretense to certainty, and its faith in cause and effect. Nevertheless, Pynchon warns, twentieth-century science has nurtured a way of thinking, a cataclysmic reading of history in which a grim past is anchored to an explosive tomorrow. Such certainty, however, denies this civilization its vibrant now—recall Vonnegut perched uneasily on the slender ledge of the present; recall Vince Bonali separating his now from the death-soaked fictions of the West Condon sideshow; recall Tom More, embalmed on Early Times, seeing about him a now crossed by the incessantly sprouting vines of imminent judgment. Pynchon moves to reclaim the moment, to celebrate its premise much as the biblical rainbow elevated its moment, making its now reassuring, triumphant, concelebrated by heaven and earth. In the now, Pynchon's characters thrive.[2] But to celebrate such release is to accept exposure, the vulnerability of standing clear of the protective shield of the parabola's shadow.

Pynchon plays out this choice between vulnerability and structure—between living and accepting death—in the very opening scene of the novel. In war-ravaged London, evacuees are herded "without resistance" like "sheep" through twisting, ever-narrowing streets cluttered with charred rubble until they are stopped under the "final arch" of a train station, under a nightmarish sky strung by the sweeping white trace of a German rocket. There, under this *double* parabola, the herded understand that "there is no way out," that they are to lie still and "be quiet," to wait the "final falling," the "absolute Zero." They are Pynchon's cataclysmics, awaiting judgment as if the rockets carried the authority of God. Huddled and defeated, they wait only the stroke of random death.

Countering such acquiescence is the example in the opening pages of Pirate Prentice, the apocalyptic. Hungover, noting the vapor trail of the same approaching German rocket (and calmly judging it smudged and "slightly torn") and recognizing that he has "less than five minutes," he resolutely *ascends* to his rooftop hothouse to pluck bananas for breakfast. As the rocket is "beginning its fall," he yanks at the giant clusters, "radiant yellow and humid green" (12), that thrive in the chill of Pynchon's death-haunted north. There, beneath the parabola of the German rocket, Pirate begins to concoct his breakfast of sweet banana confections, much like the man in the parable who, while dangling from the cliff, sucks the heady sweetness of the berries growing in the crags of the hillside. As Pirate prepares the breakfast, he notes casually that the rocket has proven "queer," a premature misfire that has exploded harmlessly, he surmises, out over the North Sea. His sumptuous breakfast of banana frappes comes off—"it is not often Death is told so clearly to fuck off" (11). Ever vulnerable, ever aware (much like the man dangling over the cliff), Pirate Prentice asserts, nevertheless, a vibrant now: in the spare five minutes left him by the arc of gravity's rainbow, he asserts his privilege to live.

Pynchon keys such moments of stepping free of the arc of history to the promise and magic of Christmas, which celebrates Western history's single genuine, unpatterned moment: a pure event, as it were, without cause. The novel opens in the hush of the Advent season, with history ready for just such a moment able to refute the ominous indications of its imminent dissolution. The Nativity serves Pynchon as a celebration of vulnerability—a baby crying in an open stable, his parents/guardians much like the Zone's Displaced Persons, who live under a government of oppressive evil. In such dark times, the Nativity illuminates. It is a moment of surprise, a gesture of overwhelming love. Such a moment is marked by nothing less than a star. Yet, the star that rested above the infant Jesus and signaled the commencement of His resistance to history from a position of apparent vulnerability has been supplanted by the bright spark of the rocket.³ Indeed, the glow of the descending rocket is often mistaken for a star. Yet, real stars do glint above the ruins of London and over the wasteland of the Zone, illuminating the slender interface between the descent of day and the ominous slouch of approaching night. The star appears in that moment between, and those who respond find their way to Pynchon's vibrant now, the moment poised between past and future.

In a trembling pre-apocalyptic world poised beneath the approaching rocket, Pynchon invites contemporary humanity to be reborn away from history in exhilarating private nativities that forsake the self-destruction of history when promise collapses into grim certainty, magic into mathematics, vulnerability into dumb paralysis, and assertion into unprotesting acceptance. This is the Christian promise of Christmas—"a season of birth, of fresh beginnings" (152). Indeed, *Gravity's Rainbow* opens amid an "orgy of Christmas greetings" (154), a crippled city resolutely displaying Nativity scenes, purchasing gifts, even sending sacksful of greeting cards.⁴ Roger and Jessica share a hauntingly beautiful Advent service in a chapel in the desolate countryside of Kent. Here, under the steady orange glow of descending German rockets that are still sixty miles up and will hang, starlike, over the service, and under the steady drone of the bombers that sing like mock angels, the war weary gather to savor the sense of magic, of defiance, of love suggested by the original Nativity:

> The plaster baby, the oxen frosted with gold leaf and the human-eyed sheep are turning real again, paint quickens to flesh. To believe is not a price they pay—it happens all by itself. He is the New Baby. On the magic night before, the animals will talk, and the sky will be milk. (155)

The chapel's "scratch choir" is dominated by a soulful countertenor (a musical range that suggests wonderful ascent) sung by a corporal from Jamaica (like Pirate's bananas, another tropical presence defying the north). The Advent service is a marked moment of hope, a communal celebration of a baby who, "tippin' those Toledos at 7 pounds 8 ounces" (158), nevertheless triumphed in a world of Caesars and Herods. It is, however, an Advent service, not a Christmas celebration—a waiting, not a fulfillment.⁵ The service is surrounded by reminders of the ongoing rush of the war—of shipyards in full swing, organ banks awaiting the wounded, dead soldiers in snowbanks whose ice-blue hands still cling to good-luck pieces. The communicants, however, return to the night world outside the chapel doors cherishing the image of Western civilization's most defiant, most vulnerable archetype—the infant Jesus:

> no counterfeit baby, no announcement of the Kingdom, not even a try at warming or lighting this terrible night, only, damn us, our scruffy obligatory

little cry, our maximum reach outward—*praise be to God!*—for you to take back to your war-address, your war-identity, across the snow's footprints and tire tracks finally to the path you must create by yourself, alone in the dark. (159)

Characters then appear vital in their willingness to move into the open, to dispense with the illusion of control. It is an exacting rebirth. Other characters, eunuchs who "capitalize the T in technology" (607), grow, perversely, to enjoy the frustration of their own powerlessness, like the disturbing number of characters whose erotic stimulation depends on the stinging lash of the whip. In one grim scene, Pynchon remarks on the desperate situation of a colony of homosexuals in the Zone who, freed from the Dora concentration camp, puzzled and finally terrified by the unconditional freedom thrust upon them by the Allied liberation, set up a sort of ghost camp with their own members acting the part of Nazi tormentors (775). Pynchon's invitation is to step into the Zone and to thrive, like a newborn child, in its anarchic openness. When Slothrop meets Argentinian exiles in the Zone, they describe passionately the history of their country and the emerging centralization of the Buenos Aires government as a tragic movement away from the pampas and the freedom of the ranging gaucho:

"All the neuroses about property gathered strength, and began to infect the countryside. Fences went up, and the gaucho became less free. It is our national tragedy. We are obsessed with building labyrinths, where before there was open plain and sky. To draw ever more complex patterns on the blank sheet. We cannot abide that *openness*." (307)

These are the alternatives in Pynchon's apocalyptic world: the pampas or the labyrinth. The most labyrinthine edifices in the novel are certainly the "White Visitation," the experimental laboratory that also serves as headquarters for the shadowy operation of the British surveillance, and the Mittelwerke rocket-assembly plant, a vast, sinister network of tunnels imbedded into a mountain in northern Germany. They contrast with the refugees of the war, who huddle together in open countryside in roofless houses that tilt wearily in the bombed countryside of the Zone, clinging only to each other, subject to the random exercise of the laws of ballistics.

Pynchon offers a novel that struggles to stay open, that is itself a kind of pampa. The novel is packed with marvelously labyrinthine sentences, freighted with digressive histories, threaded with assorted trivia and asides. Key scenes wind up in paragraphs that trail off with the reassuring open-endedness of ellipses.[6] The novel bravely resists conclusions.

But Pynchon is no Borgesian Dedalus, a self-indulgent maker of elaborate but ultimately closed mazes. The novel is more than a metafictional approximation of the cataclysmic moment that ushers its readers toward the terrifying claustrophobia of the closing scene beneath the descending rockets; it is more than merely an exercise in style that shelters readers from their own grim history by amusing with its aesthetic verve and daring.[7] Rather, there operates in *Gravity's Rainbow* an earnest survival mechanism. Indeed, in its very baroque construction, the novel approximates the apocalyptic temper itself—call it meta-apocalypticism—its very form resisting the end and concentrating its enormous energies on the unfolding now. *Gravity's Rainbow* is an extended strategy to stall conclusions, to thwart the ominous linearity of plot, to bend cause and effect absurdly, to resist periods in sentences that live wildly for line after line. In short, it stays open.

The question posed by the novel, then, is disturbing: In a ruined world-Eden where technology has provided so convincing and devastating an illusion of control (or plot), are there no surprises (such as love) left? Or is humanity merely to wait for the final, grim flash of the cataclysm? Technology has rendered history cinematic, imbued it with a sense of the mechanical, the unreal, and (what is far worse) pointed it toward an inevitable final reel[8]—it is the summary nightmare of the cataclysmic imagination. Pynchon sends characters out into the violence and confusion of the Zone (a fitting metaphor for the post–World War II age of casual atrocities and uncertain moral direction) and demands that they preserve their vulnerability, their willingness to grapple for purpose in the rooflessness. Not, in short, to build labyrinths, edifices that will prove ineffectual shelters should history lumber toward its finale. Much like Coover, who tests his characters against their willingness to engage an open universe of sudden change and stunning surprise, Pynchon challenges his characters to move to positions above the cataclysmic rush, beyond the slavery to gravity, to follow the example of Lyle Bland, Slothrop's uncle in Massachusetts. Bland is initiated into the shadowy brotherhood of the Masons, an organization Pynchon plays for all its "They"ness. Not only is the United States itself an extended Masonic plot, but Truman, who rubbed "the atomic clit of Miss Enola Gay" (685), was himself a Mason from Missouri. But Bland finds in the Masons only a tired ritual that has lost its "zip" (687), a failed system where passwords and secret gestures alone move the machinery of the organization. Bland responds by beginning to conduct journeys "somewhere out of his body" (686), spiritual excursions while his body, "the inert white container" (686), stays anchored to the davenport. He makes startling discoveries about the possibilities of living rather than obeying history. He finds:

> the wonder of . . . earth [as] a living critter, after all these years of thinking about a big dumb rock to find a body and psyche, he feels like a child again . . . still he is in love with his sense of wonder, with having found it again, even this late. . . . To find that Gravity is really something eerie, Messianic, extrasensory to Earth's body. (687)

This is Lyle's nativity and Pynchon's prototype of the exuberant nova of the heart. Restless within the failed system of the Masons, its webbings looking shoddy, Lyle (no longer bland) heroically taps the energy of Pynchon's resistance fighters. He responds to the pulse available when people step free of the technoscientific frame (in this case, the earth as a big, dumb rock) and find that gravity, far from being an integrative force, merely pulls down—curtails, as it were—the rocket's flight. As Lyle gathers his family about the davenport to bid them farewell and then prepares for a journey from which he will never return, he leaves behind the hapless slaves of gravity—that sluggish pull that holds down the mud, waste, and decay of Pynchon's Western industrial world. Gravity is the energy of the hammerfall.

Like traditional historical epics, *Gravity's Rainbow* assembles a cast of characters who must come to terms with their history. Each of the novel's four sections is dominated by characters who must choose between love and silence. Roger and Jessica in the opening Advent section; Katje in the first Zone section; then, in turn, Slothrop and Oberst Enzian must each seek the world that thrives *between* the grim necessities of the zero and the one: on the one hand, mere annihilation and, on the other, the nightmarish *Raketen Stadt,* the dystopia of conformity, control and operating paranoia. These characters are given opportunities to respond to love. Love, not gravity, is the energy that flows between the zero and the one, and what Pynchon explores in his search for an alternative to annihilation is whether love or silence will be the way of the contemporary universe: whether the nuclear age will be dominated by the covalent bond—the mutual sharing of electrons—or by the ionic bond—an invasion, a seizure of electrons (672). Each character, in turn, fails to sustain a moment's rush of freedom from under the arch of history; each character hisses away into silence, inching the world toward cataclysm. Only Enzian—yet again a minor character—edges toward the hope proffered by the passion of love. That alone invigorates the now with the energy of possibility. Pynchon's pseudoapocalyptics and rabid cataclysmics are each starved for love, much as in the other works studied here: consider John/Jonah's unfathomable misanthropy, the decided asexuality of the Brunists, the scripted romance of Justin Miller, the casual fornications of Tom More under the grinning leer of the laughing cavalier. Here, amid the swirl and confusion of Pynchon's cataclysmic world, Enzian bobs up (Ishmael-like) to teach the difficult lesson that love is the sole energy that resists scientific measure, that can defy both the nightmare of the zero and the enervating passivity of the one. It is, Pynchon argues, the Christmas passion.[9]

> Most people's lives have ups and downs that are relatively gradual.... They're the ones who never get struck by lightning. No real idea of cataclysm at all. But the ones who do get hit experience a singular point, a discontinuity in the curve of life—do you know what the time rate of change *is* at a cusp? *Infinity*, that's what! A-and right across the point, it's *minus* infinity. How's *that* for sudden change, eh?... That's getting hit by lightning, folks. (773)

Roger Mexico would seem to be one of the lightning struck, one of Pynchon's heroic resisters.[10] As a statistician, Roger accepts life as random. He renounces Pointsman's doctrinaire Pavlovian faith in cause and effect and challenges his unimaginative doctrine of absolutes, the one and the zero. Fascinated by the random scheme of his statistics, Roger can "survive anyplace in between" (63), that immense and open geography Pynchon offers to those who wrench free of the arc of gravity's rainbow. But, more important, Roger, in the opening Advent section, actually experiences the lightning bolt of love. Before his exposure to Jessica Swanlake, Roger was the "Dour, Young Man of 'The White Visitation'" (45), a statistician who carefully plotted the sites of German bombings with objective curiosity like a "spider hitching together his web of numbers" (45). By Roger's own admission, his life before Jessica was "a point on a moving wavefront, propagating through sterile history—a known past, a projectable future. But Jessica was breaking the wave. Suddenly there was beach, the unpredictable...new life...he might, with her, find his way to life and to joy" (147). This passion for Jessica moves Roger beyond the mathematical and the measurable—toward his "very first real magic"(44).

Roger and Jessica secede from the war. Their emerging passion dominates the Advent section, endowing their love with the Christmas promise: new beginnings that shatter rather than fulfill history. In their brief affair in bombed London—"Death's antechamber" (45)—they discover in the hushed evenings of their passion the magic of merging "into a joint creature" (44), "close as muscles and bones can press, hardly a word beyond her name, or his" (141). They withdraw to a "house in the stay-away zone" (47), which they occupy illegally. As they furiously make love, the night is punctuated by German rockets. Here are all the earmarks of Pynchon's resistance movement: an all-consuming, incandescent passion; the determined withdrawal from the curve of history; the vulnerability of passion behind heavy blackout curtains and of postcoital moments rocked by the sudden explosion of nearby rockets; and the renewal, the rebirth of the childlike. Under Jessica's influence, Roger turns a healthy "child-pink" (151), and Jessica "looks only nine or ten" (142). They play tickling games in bed until the shudder of a German rocket stops them cold. They become, it would seem, Pynchon's first refugees from history who, with the strength of their wartime passion, find the resiliency to assert, "[we] are in love. Fuck the war" (47).

And when the passion proves less incandescent and more incendiary, less sustaining and more destructive, Roger seems to continue his resistance even when Jessica decides to settle down with her other lover, the stodgy, pipe-puffing Lieutenant Jeremy Beaver, and chooses a career within the shadowy bureaucracy emerging in postwar Britain. When Roger begins to intuit how Pointsman has manipulated his affair with Jessica, sending her off to the Zone because he fears that she would distract Roger from his work as Pointsman's assistant, he launches an outrageous assault against Them. He punches his way through the labyrinthine headquarters of British surveillance, bellowing for Pointsman. With wild irreverence, he urinates over a polished, twenty-foot-long conference table while a meeting is in session. Later he tries to ruin an intimate dinner party to which Jeremy and Jessica invite him out of a sense of noblesse oblige. It would seem to be the complete liberation of the once dour, young statistician. Roger departs the novel after his performance at the party, singing the "Counterforce's Traveling Song":

> "But we're bringing down Their system
> And it isn't a resistance, it's a war. . . . " (746)

Yet Roger's love, his saving passion, is deliberately undercut by Pynchon. The lovers are inauthentic, theatrical, untouched by the very love that compels them to secede from the war. Jessica's love drives Roger not to the renewal of the childlike, but toward the petulantly childish. Pynchon carefully removes an ennobling dignity from Roger's rejection by Jessica. He grovels, he begs, he sobs "snot by the cubic yard" (133). In Pynchon's ongoing war of the counterforce, Roger Mexico is clearly a misfire, a dud. His childish rebellion against the higher-ups leads him not to the profound nativity of the heart demanded by the experience of love, but only to empty gestures that render him comic relief in Pynchon's vastly more complicated drive toward a sustaining counterforce.

Perhaps the difficulty begins with Roger himself. Despite the occupational necessity of combing through the "dumb inertia of cobbles and beams" (47), Roger remains largely untouched by the war, by its waste and its horrors. He measures and graphs it, asserting by his efforts that the war is amenable to mathematical scrutiny.[11] Like a baby playing with alphabet blocks unaware of the power of language, Roger plays at these symbols of randomness, unaware of its rich potential. This ignorance undercuts his assertion of passion because of his obsessive attempts to control the direction of that passion, much as his graphs seem to contain the war. In short, he seeks not to love, but to possess and dominate Jessica, who all the while is coolly weighing both her lovers.

Such a game of domination is underscored by a disconcerting element of role playing that comes to characterize the affair. Pynchon snickers that Roger and Jessica first meet in the tradition of the "Hollywood cute-meet" (44). Jessica wrestles with her broken bike by the side of the road. Driving past, Roger stops, distracted by a glimpse of Jessica's "most nonregulation black slip and clear pearl thighs above the khaki stocking" (44). He offers her a ride in his Jaguar. Jessica hesitates, unimpressed with him (she calls him even at this point "a little boy" [44]). Suddenly, a rocket explodes nearby. Pynchon notes the rocket is far enough toward the city to be safe, but close enough to send Jessica "across the hundred miles between herself and the stranger." Returning to the road with Jessica now by his side, Roger accidentally runs over her bike, and Jessica tells him, "I'm totally in your power." Here is a passion ignited by the lowest physical attraction, by a game of mock helplessness played against a Hollywood backdrop of rockets exploding harmlessly.

Much about their passion suggests Hollywood artifice. They play at vulnerability, as when Jessica childishly pulls off her blouse, "her small breasts bouncing free," while Roger drives down a crowded highway (143). They *elect* to move into a stay-away zone—they could have been all the while in some "snug hotel" (61). Indeed, Jessica admits privately that their rooms "do not even feel like danger" (62). But she enjoys the inauthentic experience; it is for her the scripted Hollywood wartime romance, a calculated attempt at spontaneity. Her passion will not survive the war—much as the war (or at least an exploding rocket) drove them together, the end of the war moves Jessica to the safer, more correct merger with Jeremy, the Eager Beaver. It is a disturbing measure of her giddy reaction to what Roger represents (rather than to Roger himself) that in their initial sexual coupling, she climaxes twice even before Roger enters her (140). With Roger she plays a most willing Fay Wray (65), one who knows the man-in-the-monkey-suit trickery of Hollywood, who knows that the passion is played before rolling cameras, that her beastly lover is a pair of mechanized paws driven by a hydraulic lift. Importantly, Pynchon's failed characters—Jessica, Katje, Slothrop himself—each play the Fay Wray role. In connection with Jessica, Pynchon offers an analysis of the "Fay Wray complex": "This is a kind of protective paralysis, akin to your own response when the moray eel jumps at you from the ceiling" (319). It is withdrawal from passion, represented by King Kong with his "coarse black hair, the tendons of need, of tragic love" (320). It is the consummate role of those who reject the life of vulnerability demanded by Pynchon.

Given her predisposition to insulate herself from raw passion, Jessica taints Roger's passion a most sinister red. She wears the color, she sports red lipstick, she knits Roger a red scarf (suggestive of the hangman's noose), and, when they make their most frantic love, "the light always gets very red for them" (140). This is not, however, the color of fiercesome passion. Given Pynchon's familiarity with twentieth-century physics, this is the hue of the red-shifting universe,[12] the spectrum color of light whose wavelength is becoming progressively longer—the color, in short, of a universe moving apart. Jessica plays roles—the passionate, reckless wartime lover of Roger; the correct partner and procreative mate of Jeremy. She lives a twinned life, never giving herself to the passion that Roger demands. Pynchon underscores such duplicity by Jessica's unusual last name—Swanlake. Tchaikovsky's ballet centers on the twinned figure of Odette/Odile, traditionally danced by the same ballerina. Although Pynchon wildly parodies the romantic tragedy (much as Tyrone Slothrop parodies Wagner's Tannhauser), the gloss to *Swan Lake* points toward Jessica's penchant for performance, her inauthenticity as lover, and her manipulative nature that makes her finally one of the herded. Attractive yet aloof, Janus-like, Jessica merges Odette/Odile: the Swan Queen, doomed, pathetic, hopelessly in love with the handsome prince; and Odile, the treacherous, cold, deceptive look-alike who tricks the prince into foreswearing his love for the Swan Queen. The faces of the Swan Queen and of Odile are both mirages, deceptions created by an evil court magician who has enslaved the Swan Queen. What creates Jessica's twinned nature is the war itself. It has, as she admits to Roger when he asks about her childhood, destroyed whatever identity she once had. She merges finally with Jeremy, even crops her hair to move toward the unisexual look appropriate for their future within the labyrinth. As his wife, she assists him in his first postwar assignment, reassembling captured parts of German rockets and then firing them off into the sea. In effect, she continues the arc of gravity's rainbow after the war has stopped.

To Jessica's parody of Odette/Odile, however, Roger plays an earnestly tragic prince. His has been from the first glance at Jessica's pearly thigh a wildly exaggerated passion. When Roger, fretting over losing Jessica, decides that Jessica is all that makes the world tolerable, he asserts with a tragic sweep (so sweeping that it becomes ludicrous) that Jessica is "the British warm that protects his stooping shoulders" and "the wintering sparrow that he holds inside his hands" (206), yet another image of his presumed power over Jessica. Roger goes on to less and less coherent attempts to express his hyperbolic passion; indeed, he frets (as he spills his confession out in some of Pynchon's purplest prose) that "he feels a raving fit coming on" (206). The loss of Jessica to Jeremy leaves nothing between Roger and gravity (826). His play at passion, at vulnerability, at openness, at magic has merely driven him under its menacing pull. In his gushing anguish after Jessica coolly rejects his desperate offer that she marry Jeremy but bear his baby, he accepts a decidedly cataclysmic world view, a shrinking of options to an either-or dualism (either death or life as Their slave). He joins, in short, those herded under the parabola, under the rainbow.

It is all, however, amusing. As a statistician, he plays at randomness. He never engages the war directly. As Pig Bodine reminds him, "You're still so fuckin' naive, Rog, wait'll you see your first European-gangster hit, they like to use 3 rounds: head, stomach, and heart. . . . that's a good autumn kind of thought to keep in mind" (828–29). As a lover, he plays at passion, preferring the salty explosions of simple lovemaking and mistaking possession and obsessive jealousy for love (he is haunted by the thoughts of Jessica and Jeremy in a variety of coital positions— "Does she do that for him too?" [41]). And as a jilted lover, he plays at revenge. His gestures against Them are futile, and in their futility merely assert a stronger sense of Them. His is merely a noisy surrender. When he urinates on the conference table, the astounded conferees actually enjoy the "warm piss" (741), and Mexico runs out of ammunition just as he swings towards Pointsman, his original target. The litany of vulgarities that he and Pig Bodine concoct to ruin the posh dinner party (carbuncle stew, hemorrhoid hash, clot casserole, etc.) becomes something of a surreal parlor game among the stronger-stomached guests, who chirp out their own bizarre concoctions. Pig and Roger exit not so much as destroyers of the party, but as its cheap entertainment.

Although Roger moves, he does not resist. His resistance, like the love he foists on the indifferent Jessica, is a waste of energy, a particularly dangerous notion in a universe that slouches so steadily toward entropic exhaustion. If Roger and Jessica are privileged to share the novel's most poignant moment—the Advent service in Kent—they clearly do not learn its lesson. And Roger departs the novel, quaking at Jessica's feet, crying snot by the cubic yard, running out of piss, and playing the fool.

If souls most touched by love are propelled to the vulnerability and wonder of a child, those most touched by history are shriveled to ashes. Much as Roger's botched passion play controls the opening Advent section, Katje Borgesius and her affair with Tyrone Slothrop dominates the second section of the novel—the bone-chilling, post-Christmas, midwinter months of Slothrop's first weeks in the Zone. Katje, touched by history, is one of Pynchon's "children who has learned how to die."[13] Although her face still retains "traces of baby fat" (107), inside Katje is "corruption and ashes" (109). As a Dutch girl at the time of the Nazi occupation, Katje suffered as a victim of the Nazi Captain Blicero and his pathological sex games—imprisoned, along with Blicero's other toy-child, Gottfried, in Blicero's house, hidden in the woods near the rocket-firing sites. In counterpoint to Roger and Jessica, who attend a Boxing Day stage production of *Hansel and Gretel* (where yet another rocket explodes harmlessly nearby), Katje has played a harshly authentic Gretel, facing a most ominous open oven door—as Blicero's slave, she has lived under the threat of the concentration camp.

Yet Pynchon makes clear that the "game" adopted by this trio in their "charmed house" (120) in the woods—the "strayed children . . . the edible house, the captivity, the fattening, the Oven" (111)—preserved a routine, a sense of form. It is a "shelter," against the war, the "absolute rule of chance" (111). Caged, degraded, terrorized, Katje follows Blicero's commands and nightly wears a variety of costumes and sexual paraphernalia—dodging, as it were, the greater threat of openness represented by the war beyond the walls of the charmed house. Accommodating rather than resisting, Katje learns to adjust to history by voiding her identity and playing at selves convenient to the moment. Ophelia-like, her spirit broken, her heart scraped of tissue, she becomes Their pawn—Blicero's, Pirate Prentice's, the British surveillance network's, and finally, the Firm's. In Katje, the Janus face of Jessica is splintered into a plethora of roles. Katje is virtually a one-woman repertory company. She forever primps, applying rouge, powder, and mascara. Indeed, she is introduced into the novel being carefully followed by a hidden movie camera.

Detached and passive, her own identity vacated, Katje moves easily from role to role. After slipping away from Blicero's cage and crossing military lines disguised in an old black dress and boots, she volunteers her services to Pirate Prentice's espionage organization and accepts roles that extend her range to the infinitely more intricate deceits demanded as she becomes pawn to the master games players. She will play, for instance, a Blicero-like role, Domina Nocturna, the surreal sexual Amazon who punishes and disciplines the aging Brigadier General Pudding in a ritual, played out deep within the labyrinthine rooms of the White Visitation, that includes humiliation, whippings, forced masturbation, and the ingestion of her urine and feces—all to help him atone for atrocities he committed during World War I. Katje conspires behind the elaborate artifice of such assigned roles. Her name indicates her nature— "Katje," the Dutch meaning "kitten," suggesting playfulness, helplessness, irresistibility, vulnerability; and Borgesius, a most uncommon Dutch name, but a most common Pynchonesque play on the name "Borges," the master labyrinth builder. Her roles are the substance of her surrender, her acquiescence. She moves freely only within the labyrinth, only from role to role, aping the Pynchon virtues of vulnerability and passion.

In their initial encounter, Slothrop "rescues" Katje from the giant octopus that grabs her—King Kong style—on a secluded beach cove in the Zone. Appropriately, here Katje plays the Fay Wray role. Much like Roger and Jessica's Hollywood "cute meet," however, the entire scene is rife with bogus vulnerability. Katje is never really at risk. The octopus, Gregori, has been trained to menace her by viewing films of Katje at the White Visitation; backup operatives from the White Visitation stand by to distract the octopus when Slothrop badly mismanages a rescue. Only Slothrop is deceived, and even he suspects that the encounter may have been arranged. Although the randy Slothrop falls immediately for Katje's smoldering, consummate sexual lure, the arranged nature of their "chance" encounter (indeed, they will make love that evening under constant surveillance) diminishes the passion. In a book that despairs of lives that wither under the parabola, it is indeed a dark sign when Katje remarks that their love has been determined under the parabola— she had lived near the rocket-launching sites, he near the points of impact (224).

Because Katje has surrendered to Them, she becomes the handmaiden of the cataclysm. She joins the herded under the rainbow. Indeed, when she meets Slothrop, she works at the roulette wheel at the Casino Hermann Goering, operating a *fixed* game. As an employee of the house, she wears its uniform, "a rainbow-striped dirndl skirt . . . which shimmers underneath the skylight" (242). She displays, as it were, Their colors. She nurses the certainty of an imminent apocalypse, sure that she is privy to the "secret lusts" that drive not only men, but the planets as well. Not surprisingly, she imagines the apocalypse as a plunging burning toward a terminal orgasm (260), continuing the mingling of death and sex suggested by her role as Domina Nocturna.

Hardly a celebration of sexuality, Katje and Slothrop's first coupling in Katje's suite combines images of mechanized, competitive sexual athletics with quirky Hollywood slapstick (a spraying seltzer bottle, a feather-pillow fight) and the thick ambience of a dream set "in slow motion" (228) that suggests vast distance between the two lovers. Katje, buoyed in her bed as if at sea, plays a convincing seductress. Indeed, when a suspicious Slothrop checks the closet in her suite, he finds a "crowded maze" (again the kitten in the labyrinth) of fancy evening clothes, never worn, that smell of "carbon tet"—the props of a Hollywood wardrobe room (227). Katje herself, however, is a disturbing figure in black and white. As Domina Nocturna she wears silver sable fur and black boots and dyes her pubic hair ebony; at the cove she is a "dim figure in a black bombazine frock" (216); in her suite she greets Slothrop in a "white pelisse" (226) that wraps skin that is the very whitest Slothrop has ever seen. But in the uneven wash of moonlight in the suite, the naked body of Katje takes on a dark, "ventral side" (228), the eerie silver light pocking her eye sockets and tipping her breasts black. Katje's passion thrives not under Pynchon's illuminating star, but in the shifting moonlight, reflected in Katje's walls of mirrors. She cannot give herself comfortably to passion; Slothrop moves her finally to the sheer physical relief of an orgasm.

Here again, passion is colored a most disturbing red: when she makes love, Katje's eyes glint momentarily red, like an animal's (225); they make impromptu love wrapped in a red damask tablecloth; and the evening before she walks away from Slothrop, departs yet another game, she wears a striking red gown of heavy silk just for him (263). Like a distant planet, cooled and inhospitable to life, Katje has moved finally too far away, beyond the touch of magic. She accepts the whiteness of her soul because on it any color can be painted, washed away, redone. In their last coupling, Katje is angry over Slothrop's deliberate interference with one of the surveillance team's operatives, and Slothrop is driven to attack her with karate chops, kicks, and bites, nearly raping her anally before they consummate their passion with bestial violence. The screaming struggle and its teeth-bared climax suggests the heresy of their love—how far they move from the earnest engagement of the healing magic. Much as she slipped the bonds of Blicero's "love-cage," Katje simply walks away from a sleeping Slothrop.

Katje later returns to the narrative in a poignant moment with Pirate Prentice. She meets him deep within the labyrinthine interior of the Firm's government offices, the kitten now safe within her labyrinth. There Pirate, who earlier had made the banana frappes under the menacing parabola of the German rockets, opens up to Katje in an extraordinary moment, despairs over their fate as intelligence agents "working under a shadow": "It will be possible, after all, to die in obscurity, without having helped a soul: without love, despised, never trusted, never vindicated—to stay down among the Preterite, his poor honor lost, impossible to locate or to redeem" (633). As he recalls with keen regret friends he betrayed, lovers he lost, family members who drifted from him as he moved within the organization, he confronts the direst notion: his approaching death, inexplicable and sudden as his name slowly comes to the top of some shadowy list. Trapped within the labyrinth, having bartered passion for security and the predictable curve, Pirate is waiting to die.

As they "trade some pain and a few truths" (634), Pirate, in a gesture of his own failing resistance, swears an ineffectual allegiance to Katje, who has always attracted him, and they embrace. In the labyrinth's dying light of dusk, the two affect a grim embrace—one beginning to fail, the other terminal (Katje's affliction is a "leukemia of the soul" [167]). Like Roger near Jessica, Pirate feels himself "caught in [Katje's] gravitation" (635), that eerie force of her attraction associated with Pynchon's controlling metaphor for the descent to death and decay. Katje is gravity itself.[14] Not surprisingly, she counts among her ancestors Dutch explorers responsible for the senseless slaughter-to-extinction of the dodo birds on Mauritius. Awkwardly, now, the two move to a balcony where they share, Pisgah-like, a surreal vision of a world-chain of copulating men and women—a dazzling, erotic connection of sexuality from which they are forever excluded. As the scene darkens (or, to borrow from Pynchon's insistence on the cinematic, as "they dissolve" [639]), they swirl in a dance, a faint shadow of the connections being made in the vision.

Like Gottfried, who perishes in Blicero's 00000 rocket wrapped in a shroud of protective white plastic, Katje, in her final appearance in the novel, wears white (starkly contrasting with the Zone's emerging spring landscape), pulls her hair back into a tight knot, and renounces in her thoughts Pan as a "lousy lover" (765). Unlike Lyle Bland, who moves beyond slavery to gravity, Katje is spiraling on her own trajectory, far past her own Brennschluss point, hurtling now like Gottfried in his rocket toward death. Katje can no longer feel any essential humanness, can no longer respond to pain, to passion, to vulnerability. Out of place in a green world, she is played out, bicycling about the Zone, tired of the actress's life of "easy work and cheap exits" (771). Wrapped in a shroud, she ebbs out of the novel in silence like Tyrone Slothrop, terminal and surrendered. It is her life sentence, as Enzian points out to her, to survive, "merely survive" (772).

When the Argentinian anarchists-in-exile discuss with the German film director von Göll the possibility of his providing inspiration for their anarchist cause by making a movie, von Göll suggests filming *Martín Fierro*, an Argentinian epic romance about a nineteenth-century gaucho-hero who resists the centralization of the Buenos Aires government, a brutal campaign of systematic exterminations and harsh labor camps. Fierro, a conscripted soldier in the government army, sickens of such tactics and finally deserts to live forever in the wilds a step ahead of government posses. Matched to this tale of resistance, however, is the second part of the epic, *The Return of Martín Fierro*, in which the gaucho-hero "sells out: assimilates back into Christian society, gives up his freedom. . . . a very moral ending, but completely opposite to the first" (450). Von Göll, suspecting that the first part might appear too antisocial as well as too unbelievable, advises the Argentinians to film both parts: "even the freest Gauchos end up selling out, you know. That's how things are" (451).

This curious exchange indicates the resolution strategy to Pynchon's own novel. In the closing two sections of *Gravity's Rainbow*, Pynchon, in essence, films two alternative endings: one, the heroic emergence of Oberst Enzian as leader of the Hereros in the Zone; the other, the gradual dispersal, the splintering of Tyrone Slothrop. They are contrasting tales, one of resistance and struggle, the other of assimilation and accommodation—in short, lessons in love and in silence. Under the ever-widening arc of the apocalypse (not only the launch of Blicero's rocket, but also the ominous suggestion in the closing sections that a still greater rocket is coming down), Slothrop opts to hiss away, Enzian to cling to what there is to cling to. What Slothrop finds is what he himself has lost but cherishes nonetheless—the spontaneous, urgent, creative passion of love.

In the opening chapters of the novel, the promise of Tyrone Slothrop is difficult to understate. He seems to embody the playful fecundity, the bravura of openness, the urgent sense of vitality that would mark a resistance to the cataclysmic dive into silence, fearful paranoia, and sterility. There is, for instance, his job: a bomb-site inspector who searches the rubble for signs of any life amid the destruction. There is his desk with its anarchic mess layered like an archeological dig, and his wall map with its colorful pins to mark successful sexual encounters, a track record that merely foreshadows his randy trot across the Zone. Slothrop would seem the modern picaro whose final defiance is his gradual dispersal, his refusal to die—in a way, his immortality.[15] Shifting identities with casual abandon, loving lustily even as Their cameras click, and Their eyes follow, Slothrop seems to cheat Them, frustrate Them, confuse Them, elude Them. He particularly thwarts Pointsman, the resolute Pavlovian who desperately dogs Slothrop to explain his ability to react to the rockets before they explode—in apparent defiance of Pointsman's faith in cause and effect. Pursued, threatened, nearly castrated, Slothrop nevertheless spreads his seed over the Zone in a life of openness, exuberant vulnerability, and love in the vacuum.

Yet, like Roger Mexico, Slothrop falls far short of his potential. Since he cannot be deterred from his single-minded and absurd quest for the answer to his erection problems, he never responds to the magic and openness that the anarchy of the Zone offers. He cannot be brought to his own nativity. Although the opportunities are frequent and he does allow himself hesitating moments of vulnerability and love with sincere and compelling women, Slothrop is finally death haunted, an obsession suggested by his physical arousal at the approach of the German rockets. He is chained, bound to his past—not only to his infancy as an experimental subject of Doctor Jamf, but more to the inherited Puritan legacy that compels him to question the visible, to be dissatisfied with mere appearances.[16] A temperament unable to trust translates easily into a fierce paranoia that allows Slothrop, shortly before he disappears from the narrative into slivers of personality, to read the world as signs—an ominous capitulation to Pynchon's cataclysmics. Bustling about the Zone, Slothrop is less a character free than a character pursued, a chesspiece with the illusion that his movements are his own. He is Their pawn, a figure in Their hands because he elects at key moments to invest Them with his faith. He is more comfortable with the image of the enclosing hand (late in the narrative, with Slothrop's dissolution well under way, he will appear in a vignette as Fay Wray, complete with bleached wig and "sequined number" [803]) and the pointing finger (the finger of God poking through a cloud is chiseled on the gravestone of a Puritan Slothrop).

This Puritan gloom counters the vibrancy of the opening Advent section. Slothrop is strangely out of place—a Puritan at Christmastime. If Slothrop is waiting, it is not for the Christmas moment, but (as he tells friends in the Operation) for the rocket he is sure has his name on it. As bomb-site inspector, touched so by death, so routinely examining its sudden obliterating power, Slothrop does not resist. Rather, he is scared by the rocket. Indeed, if once he prayed for life to survive the war, now, an alumni of the Battle of Britain, he sees little point in the prayer. Overwhelmed, fatigued, he grows convinced that death approaches. He talks the language of the exhausted, the cataclysmics crowded under the parabola who live by the terrifying necessity of either/or, the one or the zero. Slothrop, whose family history given in the opening section indicates a legacy of early death, dissipated business energy, and gripping inertia (the "pioneering" Slothrops never moved farther west than the Berkshire Mountains), feels not only the certainty of his own approaching, random death, but the certainty of a universal "hammerfall."

And the rendezvous that he keeps with the assortment of women in ruined London do little to relieve his haunted death obsession. The women (first names only) are random encounters, impersonal and unemotional, as suggested by the markers on his wall map. They are moments in days that are themselves growing colder, darker. There is, for instance, Darlene, "the adorable tomato in a nurse's uniform" (133). At her place, he is momentarily overwhelmed by an assortment of sweet wine jellies and gooey prewar candies. Their assault on the sugared confections recalls Pirate Prentice's heroic banana breakfast except that it is merely prelude to a voracious lovemaking session. Yet when a rocket goes off nearby as Slothrop and Darlene drift into sleep, the romance darkens. Roused from the stupor of his postcoital sleep and suddenly finding himself blood-engorged, Slothrop (as he has been conditioned) ravishes the confused Darlene. The response to their vulnerability here is not love, but a lust ignited by the ominous approach of the rocket and manipulated by Slothrop's own conditioning.

Once Slothrop moves into the Zone (or, more correctly, is released into the Zone like an experimental rat into a crazy maze), he moves with absurd dedication through a series of byzantine chases, reckless rescues, muddled missions and pursuits—many associated with his accidental connections to drug running in the Zone's emerging black market. All these adventures—whether he is delivering drugs or searching for clues to his connection with the rocket—merely suggest purpose; they are themselves played out in a most purposeless manner, all executed under the Firm's careful surveillance. They are his own labyrinths against the Zone's disconcerting freedom. His moments of vulnerability in the Zone are few. His most authentic connection is (appropriately) with a witch, Geli Tripping, who briefly puts Slothrop in touch with the magic of vulnerability, of stepping free of his mazes. Slothrop first approaches

Geli in the early spring ("Everything is fresh, washed" [338]). She is singing a bittersweet love ballad in the roofless section of Nordhausen. The lyrics reflect her own intense commitment to a Soviet intelligence officer named Tchitcherine, who is somewhat less than reciprocal in his feelings toward her; indeed, she knows how many women he has all over the Zone. Yet she can sing of a love that "never goes completely away / Never completely dies" (337).

The lyrics entrance Slothrop. They share a bottle of wine in a roofless room and become for a moment another of Pynchon's refugee-lovers from the war. Slothrop is fascinated by her apparent resistance to the war: "She might have spent all her war roofless and secure, tranquil, playing with small forest animals in a rear area someplace" (338). Her love, her magic, has sustained and renewed her, and will by the close of the novel draw her to a haunting reunion with the faithless Tchitcherine. In the momentary arrangement that Geli finds with Slothrop, she intends no infidelity to Tchitcherine. She tells Slothrop that he is at best his surrogate. Yet when they make love, the act places Slothrop in true vulnerability: in a roofless bedroom, in the rain, with two distinct threats hanging over him, one immediate, the other omnipresent and infinitely more threatening. Geli keeps an owl, Wernher, who has a peculiar habit of swooping down on Geli's unsuspecting lovers; in Slothrop's case, it buries its talons deep in the small of his back. And, as Geli hints, there is always the possibility that the wandering Tchitcherine could return at any moment and surprise them in their refuge.

Yet Slothrop stays, puts aside his inherited paranoia, and lives for one tenuous night on the threshold of vulnerability. He resists, in effect, the apocalyptic tremors suggested by the midnight flapping of Wernher's wings and by the terminal surprise of Tchitcherine. "Paranoid that he is, he snuggles down under the counterpane with the long-legged sorceress, lights a cigarette, and despite endless Tchitcherines vaulting in over roofless walls . . . even falls asleep, presently, in her bare and open arms" (343).

Geli attempts to move Slothrop into Pynchon's landscape between, but the tutelage of the witch is not sufficient. She takes him to the top of the Brocken on the border *between* the Soviet and American zones to watch the sun rise (the border time *between* night and day) and to watch as they cast gigantic, three-dimensional shadows across the valley, hints of the power of Geli's love. Geli dances in the dawn, and together they make love, "dancing on the floor of the whole visible sky" (384). In dawn's slender interface, they revel like giants. And yet Slothrop moves on, sensing the approach of the hapless Major Marvy. He leaves Geli behind as he ascends into the skies, heading toward Berlin in an absurdly bright yellow and scarlet balloon. As the gondola begins its ascent surrounded by curious children, the last to release her hold on the rising balloon is Geli, who, like Katje, is dressed now in bone white with her hair tightly locked into pigtails. Her "big serious eyes" follow Slothrop for as long as they can, then "she kneels in the grass, blows a kiss" (387). It is Slothrop's final moment of love before he succumbs to the awful silence of his eventual capitulation to history, suggested here by the sweeping silences of the sky into which he drifts before finally disappearing.

Once beyond Geli, Slothrop sheds identities with awkward, theatrical insistence; raises a moustache; negotiates for identity papers; sports outrageous stolen clothes and costumes. Pynchon follows Slothrop like a rapidly diminishing point on the sweep of a radar screen. Slothrop falls under the menacing spell of narcotic hallucination. He is inadvertently enmeshed in a sophisticated drug network and attends an odd assortment of decadent cocaine sorties. Drugged, coaxed into the world of shadows, Slothrop becomes an inveterate sign reader, able to translate events into plot using his Puritan acumen, the ultimately comforting illusion of deducing a They from the evidence of Their control. In short, he makes connections. Unable to feel the "wine rush" of defying gravity, he comes to believe that "random" is just "another fairy word" (460). In his final appearance in the novel before his dispersal begins, Slothrop is told the story of John Dillinger, who in *his* life moved free of the system, was hunted by Them, but lived (much like the heroic Martín Fierro) one step ahead of the posse—until an unimaginative agent, Floyd Purvis, surprised him outside the Biograph Theatre. Yet Dillinger is a model of the resistance phalanx, a hero of the anarchists (indeed, strips of Dillinger's bloodied shirt are treated like relics in the Zone) rewarded with a swift and certain death, in striking contrast to Slothrop's enigmatic and disturbing erasure. For, despite his inherited infection of death, Slothrop does not die—he hisses away. Responding as programmed, indulging hallucinations rather than reality, opting for sexual interludes rather than passion and exploits rather than living, Slothrop comes to make his final commitment to Them in a decisive moment shortly before Pynchon reports that Slothrop's dispersal has commenced.

Slothrop, we are told, during his time with Saure the drug kingpin has begun to roam about the mountains, tuning himself, it would seem, to the natural flow—suggested by the harmonica he finds and keeps in a stream so that the water itself bends the reeds of the instrument. He wanders about the mountains alone, naked, letting beard and hair grow, reestablishing ties with the insect and animal life. He rejects the absurdity of his quest, his search for discharge papers. He seems primed for the nativity of the soul, a nova of the heart. His soul, that "awkward albatross," seems set to stir. But he cannot let go of America, his tie too strong to the civilization that in the context of his Puritan ancestry suggests only shit, waste, and death. Indeed, the image of the United States comes to Slothrop like an aging vamp, as alluring and fatally decadent as the figure of Katje in her role of Zone seductress. "Poor asshole, he can't let her go. She's whispered *love me* too often to him . . . vamped insatiably . . . with come-hitherings, incredible promises. One day—he can see a day—he might be able finally to say *sorry*, sure and leave her . . . but not just yet" (726). This tie delivers Slothrop finally to the rainbow, to certainty, to death. The natural world is now a shape to be read. The flights of birds, the ashes from his fires, the guts of the fish that he catches and cleans, even the graffiti on shithouse walls— all speak to Slothrop. In a final stroke, Slothrop poises himself naked in the road under the sun and becomes a living intersection, a living cross, a living sign. As Slothrop exits the novel, he recalls a highway job he once held in the snowy Berkshires where one April he cleaned the refuse of the winter from the roads:

> picking up rusted beer cans, rubbers yellow with preterite seed, Kleenex wadded to brain shapes hiding preterite snot, preterite tears, newspapers, broken glass, pieces of automobile, days when in superstition and fright he could *make it all fit*, seeing clearly in each an entry in a record, a history: his own, his winter's, his country's , , , instructing him, dunce and drifter, in ways deeper than he can explain. (729)

Like Katje scorning Pan in the springtime, Slothrop moves through April making sense of winter, making things fit, forcing refuse to pattern. As the section ends, Slothrop stands literally under a rainbow; he ends where metaphorically he has been all along—locked under the parabola. And he cries. The rainbow is no reassuring sign to him; rather, it is like an "enormous stout cock" driven down into the "green wet valleyed earth" (729), suggesting the ravishment of the world-Eden that figures so prominently in Pynchon's discourses on Westerners' destruction of the earth.

Conditioned since birth—and, hence, a fulfillment of cause and effect, not its aberration—Slothrop, a pawn whose inbred paranoias effectively insure Their dominance over him, succumbs finally to the parabola. Trapped beneath the rainbow, he cannot make his way to the star, the interface between night and day. Rather, he hisses away into silence. When Reg le Froid, a mental patient in the White Visitation, escapes the hospital, he runs furiously to a point overlooking the ocean, a metaphor for vast anarchy much like the Zone itself. Reg resists the overwhelming urge to leap until a constable, trying to coax him back, suggests that the sea has a name ("Bert"), at which point Reg tosses himself into the ocean. Like Reg, Slothrop succumbs to the Zone as its vastness grows familiar. He begins to twist events into plot and coincidences into patterns; thus, he joins Pynchon's cataclysmics wailing under the rainbow.

It is finally Enzian who plays out the affirmation in Pynchon's apocalyptic world, who resists the notion of the system running down, the drift into calculation, the handing over of the earth to the erotic completeness of the terminal orgasm.[17] As leader of the Hereros' rocket project in the Zone, Enzian moves toward assembly and restoration, countering the sweet frustration of the powerless who have by their passivity made cataclysm inevitable. Contrasted to those led under the arc, or to those who opt for narcotic hallucination rather than confront their own history, Enzian is perhaps the character most thoroughly touched by the twentieth century. A bastard born of a Russian AWOL sailor and an African woman, Enzian is a Displaced Person from birth. A survivor of von Trotha's campaign of extermination against the natives of the African Südwest, Enzian was, as an adolescent, a lover of the Nazi Captain Blicero and finally brought to Germany to live as an exile in the Zone. With von Trotha and Blicero, Enzian experienced the very embodiments of twentieth-century horrors, merciless cultural extermination and the megalomaniacal faith in ballistics. It is a measure of Enzian's resistance that even after such exposure, such infection, he opts for the magic and mystery of standing apart from the arc. He finds, in short, what there is yet to hold on to.

As the emerging leader of the Hereros, Enzian combines the long-suffering resilience of Moses, the battered agape of the Christ, and the expansive humanitarian vision of John the Divine. The novel traces in the closing sections the threat to Enzian's command represented by the Empty Ones, the Hereros who, weakened by the extermination campaigns, terrified by the implications of history, and confused by the sense of homelessness in the dark Christian north, opt for tribal death, a passive acquiescence to inevitability through voluntary abstinence from procreative sex, indulgence in a variety of nonprocreative activities (masturbation, bestiality, homosexuality, among others), and a program of abortion and sterilization. It is this movement toward silence that Enzian counters with a message that he receives—magi-like—in a moment's illumination that gives him the key to living in the Zone. He intuits the urgent need to read not the rocket, but the ruins, to see the possibility of reconnection in the rubble, of power waiting to be restored.[18] As his followers laboriously assemble their own rocket from parts left scattered and abandoned all over the Zone, he knows their 00001 rocket will never be fired, a counterpart to Blicero's 00000 death rocket that will be fired with the doomed Gottfried inside. This rocket is assembled to draw the exiles together and unseat the Empty Ones from positions of authority.

The circumstances of Enzian's birth indicate his potential to resist the accumulative effect of history. In December 1904, his Russian father, a gunner in an armada headed for certain death at the hands of the Japanese navy, abandoned ship in a Südwest African port because everywhere on the ship he "could smell death" (408). Enzian's father met a Herero woman who seemed "a breath of fresh life" (409), suggesting again the life-affirming tropics against the death-haunted north. Together they shared an interlude in the between, apart from the grim parabola of history (the armada's future ambush by the superior navies of Japan). They became refugees, shared a moment's vulnerable love "at the edge of the flat sorrowful little town" in a lean-to shack built of "saplings and packing crates" (409). They learned only a few words to communicate, joined solely by the intensity of their passion. They learned the words "afraid, happy, sleep, love"—the very sequence from fear to love pointing out the rich possibility of their momentary embrace. Although the Russian sailor eventually returned to the Baltic Fleet, he left behind a legacy of his moment's refuge—a son, conceived during his moment's resistance to history; conceived, Pynchon underscores, during the Christmas season.

The Christmas imagery persists in Enzian's earliest experiences: his mother lives under the cruel oppression of an imperial colonial government (Germany), suffering through familiar acts that include a government census and a Herod-like slaughter of tribal children. Hounded by history from birth, Enzian emerges as a survivor, one of the *Mbakayere,* meaning "I am passed over" (421). He is the product of his father's heroic impetuousness to flee Their death sentence and a soft, African woman—whiteness (death) and blackness (life). As a black man in the white north, Enzian leads a race-in-exile recovering still two generations later from near extermination. In the mountains around Nordhausen, they live underground in abandoned mining shafts. What they recall, however, is their life before exile in the wilds of the open veldts of their native Africa. Such longing aligns the Hereros with the Argentinian anarchists and their nostalgic yearning for the anarchic openness of the pampas. Indeed, Pynchon echoes such sympathies between the African Südwest and the Argentinian pampas by his recurring references to the single continental landmass Gondwanaland, where "before the continents drifted apart...Argentina lay snuggled up to Südwest" (373).

Existing underground, the Hereros suggest two possibilities: burial or planting—endings or awakenings. There is the folk tale of the Herero woman "planted up to her shoulders" in an aardvark's hole. The woman, who has suffered multiple stillbirths, seeks in her interment—in the "incredible pressure...against her belly"—a rejuvenation of her birthing system, to be in touch "with Earth's gift for genesis" (367). It is just this rejuvenation that Enzian must oversee in the frozen ground of the north: a campaign to bring back to life a people threatened with racial extermination who now live in uncertain exile in the very locus of death—the rocket-launching sites at Nordhausen. What sustains Enzian in the Zone is the memory of his adolescent affair with the "young, lean" Weissmann as his protege during the German campaigns in Africa. Twenty years later, Enzian is still moved by memories of Weissmann's passion, his "nervous, imperial staff" (377). The loss of Weissmann to the rocket has left Enzian cold, "not so much a fire dying away as a positive coming on of cold, a bitter taste growing across the palate of love's first hopes" (377). Weissmann gives in to his fascination with the rocket—the "lifting and the scream that peaks past fear," the "love of the last explosion" (376). But Weissmann adopts the bastard youth and christens him Enzian; the rich foreignness of the name (from Rilke) creates about him a magic that is in keeping with his resistance against the plodding course of history. And Enzian falls completely into a powerful love thwarted by Weissmann's growing erotic attraction to the awesome possibilities of technology as a vehicle for transcedence beyond the cycle of waste and death (suggested to Weissmann by the sterility of homosexual love—sperm squirted over shit). Not content to find the between, Weissmann launches toward the beyond. It is a hopeless gesture of triumphing over gravity by moving beyond the organic, to life in artificial environments on the moon, where gravity is diminished. Had Enzian not separated himself from Weissmann before Weissmann mutated into the Zone's Kurtz figure, his fate would have been corroded to servile slavery, much like Gottfried, who wears a studded dog collar as Weissmann's lover-astronaut. It is up to Enzian to counter Gottfried's sacrificial act by espousing a now, an infinite moment of living under the pointed tip of the rocket.

The exquisite experience of Weissmann's love exacts a heavy price from Enzian. In return for the saving epiphanic moment in which he determines to shift his focus from the rocket to the ruins—a moment in which he understands war as mere distribution of power and an exercise of technology rather than the new religion of genesis and apocalypse—Enzian must place himself at a detached position, elevated and forever disconnected. Although he finds the ruins "in perfect working order simply waiting the moment of reconnection with that energy," Enzian himself cannot reconnect, cannot rediscover the powerful love that first carried him through the shock waves of history. In his encounter with Katje, another soul hopelessly infected by Weissmann, Enzian assures her of the things to hold on to. He recalls his "slender white adventurer" (769) that has since metamorphosed into a "fabulous monster" (770) and admits to growing cold, elevated, forever left alone. "There is no heart, anywhere now, where I exist. Do you know what that feels like?. . . that must be about as empty as things get" (769). Yet that memory of reciprocal passion sustains Enzian. At last glimpse, he stands over the final assembly of the Herero rocket—the assembly of which Pynchon juxtaposes against Slothrop's disassembly. He resists the varieties of "heresies" about the rocket, resists any as necessarily true. He rejects the vacuum concept of the universe to posit instead "the nostalgia of Aether," that rarified element believed by Victorian astronomers to fill the outer regions of space, a cosmic soup holding everything together. He finds Ludwig, who has been scouring the Zone for his pet lemming, Ursula. He has indeed found her—she has resisted her tribal march toward obliteration in the sea. And the message that Enzian culls from the rocket could serve as Pynchon's gospel for those who move away from the curve of history, away from the illusions of descent and cataclysm to confront life in the vulnerable openness:

> The Rocket comes as the Revealer. Showing that no society can protect, never could—they are as foolish as shields of paper. . . . They have lied to us. They can't keep us from dying, so They lie to us about death. A cooperative structure of lies. What have they ever given us in return for the trust, the love. . . we're supposed to owe Them? Can They keep us from even catching cold?. . . Before the Rocket we went on believing, because we wanted to. But the Rocket can penetrate, from the sky, at any given point. Nowhere is safe. We can't believe Them anymore. Not if we are still sane, and love the truth. (849)

Joined by Ursula, Enzian is poised to relieve Ombindi's men of their duties as safeguards over the rocket. And as he kneels in prayer in the Zone, he prays for the "vast Humility, sleepless, dying in pain tonight across the Zone, the preterite he loves" (853).

Gravity's Rainbow moves from London—its bombed streets cluttered with debris, towered over by labyrinthine buildings and crisscrossed underneath by mazes of tunnels and shelters made surreal by the flickering shadows of the gaslight—to the open anarchy of the Zone; still, characters there create private labyrinths out of fear of vulnerability. From Slothrop's insane and drug-soaked missions for the black market to Weissmann's frenzied apocalyptic hopes for a manned rocket, the list of labyrinth builders is finally as encyclopedic as the novel itself. Yet, Pynchon's characters live in a world governed by Gödel's theorem, the reassurance that no system can ever be theoretically complete (320). The cataclysm is forever countered, because, in Gödel's universe, ending implies completeness. It is this slim faith that compels Pynchon to open up the moment, that slice of time forever approaching but never reaching the zero.

The capitalization of the *t* in Technology has engendered a generation of enervated assimilators; cowards who sing in the chains of their own history; cataclysmics who simply cry beneath the relentless curve of the rainbow, who (like the cataclysmics in Vonnegut, Coover, and Percy) reduce history to the simplest terms, like a cartoon unwinding. In a magnificent aside about water bugs, Pynchon ruminates on the marvelous power of the resilient roaches to gnaw through containers. They cannot be sustained by anything less than the brittle edges of barriers. They are "agents of unification." Pynchon imbues his description of the roaches with elements of his resistance—they emerge from woodwork like "elves," suggesting a magic quality; they are swelled with pregnancy. Pynchon calls them "Christmas bugs" and writes of their restlessly chewing through the grasses scattered about the stable within halo light of the infant Christ, who would Himself gnaw through the labyrinths of history, break through to the authentic event. Seduced by passivity and justifying it by exalting helplessness as inevitable, educated only by the extermination camp ovens and by the decimation of atomic weaponry, numbed by the feeling of power slipping away and being siphoned to some shadowy bureau, we sit in dark movie theaters of our own making, boxed in, unaware, and strangely indifferent to the apocalyptic tremors in the street. It is only the aware who can conduct Pynchon's precarious resistance: the children of the twentieth century who have stared into the oven but have come away resolved to rediscover the life that such awesome endings threaten. They do not resolve to transcend the cycle of life and death as Weissmann madly contrives; they do not succumb to the odor and corruption of death as Katje does; they do not submit to the created fictions of history as Slothrop does; they do not take heart in the heartless calculations of mathematics and ballistics as Roger Mexico does.

It is a difficult resistance, a faith in magic in an age when miracles are programmable special effects; a faith in humanity in a century that has done little to encourage such investment. But that, traditionally, has been the stuff of the apocalyptic temper. Pynchon counsels a willingness to step clear from the narcotic illusion of the rainbow, of a locked history; to step free of gravity and recognize it as the eerie force of determinism that Lyle Bland does shortly before he moves forever free of it. Pynchon discounts those who are certain that history has gone ballistic and tenders his own hope in a civilization wrenching free of the rainbow. The literature examined here, however, indicates that such a wrenching does not come easily. Vonnegut's John/Jonah, after all, stands there angrily beneath the rainbow, muttering a fierce hatred, dreaming of cataclysm, and waiting, waiting; Coover's Justin Miller studiously plays at games of his own invention there, delighted not only by the elegance of his random moves, but occasionally drawn by the intricate play of color in the parabola locked overhead; like Pynchon's Londoners, the Brunists stand, robed and eyeless, beneath the arc, different only in that their approaching end is dropped from God's own steady hand; and Tom More dawdles for too long beneath the rainbow, lost in whiskey and immured in dreams, leaning against its stout leg like a drunk wrapped about a lamp post.

To step free in Pynchon's vision means forsaking the diversions of plot that so obsess his characters, the sense of quest that really plays into Their hands because it sacrifices authentic living for the pursuit of an illusion. The only journey successfully completed in the course of the book is by Geli Tripping (gaily tripping) who, with wonderful incantations and potent herbal potions, is finally reunited with her lover Tchitcherine. As they make passionate love under a bridge (under the arc as it were), Enzian's rocket convoy moves across the bridge, and Tchitcherine, under the spell of Geli's potent love, fails to recognize his hated half brother, thereby preventing a long-anticipated showdown that would most assuredly have meant the death of Pynchon's bravest resister.

Pynchon, of course, does not suggest that love is indeed the way of nature and that rediscovering its passionate whisper is all that people need do to forestall the cataclysmic stroke. But for Pynchon, it is the sole energy of redemption, the only alternative to silence. It is the energy of his apocalyptic temper, much as faith compelled the vision of John on Patmos. And those few who respond to such magic—like Oberst Enzian—are the reborn, the celebrants of private nativities. They are new babes, fragile and pink-skinned; yet, like Christ in the manger, they are able to shake free of a history curved by popular consent into gradual descent. Such a nativity, such a renewal, is the tonic force of Pynchon's offer of genuine passion. It is the pinprick of illuminating light far brighter than the shuddering stroke of the rocket, which is merely blinding and destructive. Like Pirate Prentice's sumptuous banana breakfast in the ruins of London under the very stripe of the rocket's trail, it is a celebration of the sacramental now under the cold, forbidding skies of this century, which have never been wholly clear, which have always been traced by the smudged white lines of technology's nightmarish weaponry.

Notes

1. The parabola as image/metaphor for descent and control is central to Molly Hite's chapter on *Gravity's Rainbow* (see especially pages 95–98), although her analysis concludes (much as Steven Weisenburger's) that the comedy of the novel comes from characters' assertions that history can have any definitive shape. Both Scott Sanders and Edward Mendelson (in the brief addendum to his essay on *The Crying of Lot 49*) also suggest that central to Pynchon is the choice between contingency and control, although neither essay addresses the question of the rainbow and the parabola.

2. For a careful analysis of Pynchon's emphatic uses of the now as an alternative moment to the grim past and the bleak future, see Marcus Smith and Khachig Toloyan, although their essay defines the now as a moment stolen futilely from a time sweep headed to "the imminent apocalypse of a rocket-borne atomic dawn" (176). This chapter argues the now as a moment elegantly created by characters in defiance of such a shaped history. See also Hite's introduction, which suggests that Pynchon stakes out the ground between alternatives and finds his richest comedy in those characters who choose extremes.

3. Although Miklos Thanatz, Greta Erdmann's husband, actually makes such a comparison between the Baby Jesus and the infant rocket (540), the confusion of the rocket with Christ is a recurring motif. Consider, for example, the story of Franz Pokler, a budding rocket engineer for the Reich who is enthralled with the potential power of the rocket to move humanity beyond the limits of earth. He is first attracted to the rocket when he witnesses an embryo rocket (the baby rocket) being assembled and tested in the outlying sections of Nordhausen, a spot to which he is drawn magi-like through a labyrinth of abandoned streets.

4. Even Ned Pointsman, the hard-bitten Pavlovian, is not immune to the Christmas moment, although he resolutely calls it "Xmas." He finds himself the stunned recipient of a blowjob during the office Christmas party at the White Visitation. In a closet scented with "surgical rubbers," Maudie Chilkes has her way with the shocked Pointsman right there among the "winter-pale clinical halls." It is, however, a moment of "perfect peace," when Pointsman feels suddenly the "tropics in the . . . English December" (196–97).

5. Pynchon refuses his contemporary world the actual celebration of Christmas—the novel moves from the Advent service to Boxing Day, the British post-Christmas holiday.

6. Much has been made of *Gravity's Rainbow*'s distracting sense of plotlessness, a criticism of it as being careless or self-indulgent. Stemming perhaps from Pynchon's remark quoted in Jules Siegel ("I was so fucked up while I was writing *Gravity's Rainbow* that I go back over some of those sequences and I can't figure out what I could have meant" [169]), such hard-line criticism misses the point of the deliberate thwarting of conventional plot. It allows Pynchon to resist that most conventional of plot devices—the climax. And in a novel that works to resist the drift to apocalypse, such avoidance is an article of faith. Here such connection is death, and plot is history itself.

7. See, for instance, Tanner, Frank D. McConnell, and Sanders.

8. See David Cowart's fine examination of the thorough use of the cinema in the novel, particularly pages 32–62.

9. No sentimental romantic, Pynchon is aware of the dangers of sloppy sentimentality. Indeed, one of the ongoing discussions among the inhabitants of the Zone is the merits of the music of Rossini against the music of Beethoven. Although Beethoven's music has sweep and grandeur, Rossini tunes can make a listener feel good, help lovers get together, help overcome isolation. Such sentimental music promises that *"love occurs,"* that the world can indeed be rushing together not moving apart. It argues in essence for "one great centripetal movement of the World" (513). Yet, a disputant points out that Rossini is good for snoring and farting, and better saved for good times. The argument of this chapter—that love is the passion Pynchon finds thriving in that vast open geography between the one and the zero—is not intended to propose Pynchon as an embroiderer of contemporary valentines. He is aware of the cost and the risks and the absence of modern love.

10. See, for instance, William M. Plater's sympathetic analysis on pages 182–85, and page 64 of Weisenburger.

11. At several points Roger confesses that the war is his mother, a disconcerting parentage for a resistance fighter, one that certainly implies a conflict of interest.

12. The phrase is echoed in a later remark by Enzian, who will emerge as Pynchon's resistance to this universe. He calls the postwar Continent a "red-shifting Zone" (605).

13. The phrase is borrowed from the song sung by the character who plays Gretel in the stage production of *Hansel and Gretel* that Roger and Jessica attend. The couplet reads, "And those voices you hear, Boy and Girl of the Year / Are of children who are learning to die" (205). The phrase suggests the condition that characterizes Pynchon's resistance fighters: the resiliency of the child merged with the awareness of the adult.

14. Katje is associated with paranoia in a strange tribal dance that she witnesses when she first enters the Zone (766). The Herero dance features a

Katje figure worshiped as Paranoia, which in the complicated grid of Pynchon's novel is strongly associated with gravity as a force that holds things together, the eerie energy of history.

15. Slothrop has been associated with Rabelais' Pantagruel (Hite); with Don Quixote (Cowart); and with Gulliver, Alice, and Everyman (Friedman and Puetz)—all characters who move through strange (and often hostile) lands with the grace and fluidity of innocence, naivete, and resiliency.

16. For a fine analysis of Slothrop's Puritanism as part of his death obsession, see John M. Krafft.

17. Douglas Fowler and Hite suggest that Enzian might be Pynchon's heroic element, although both deem such heroism as modest and doomed.

18. Much can be learned by juxtaposing Slothrop and Enzian, one as reader of the rocket, the other as reader of the ruins.

Chapter 5
The Eye Begins to See
The Apocalyptic Temper in the
1980s—William Gaddis
and Don DeLillo

When old Mother Pegg asked you for oil for her lamp and you told her to get out to hell, you knew what was happening then, no? You know what she died of, Mother Pegg? Of darkness.
Samuel Beckett, *Endgame*

In a dark time, the eye begins to see,
I meet my shadow in the deepening shade;
I hear my echo in the echoing wood—
A lord of nature weeping to a tree.
Theodore Roethke, "In a Dark Time"

Surely it is curious that in the 1980s—when the American voting public turned in such overwhelming numbers toward a political vision that emphasized security and promised strength, spoke hotly of military resuscitation with the iron commitment of a latter-day Crusade, and displayed the artifacts of Americanism with unapologetic sentiment— the literature of such a heady, confident time would sense the kind of anxious community-in-crisis open to the ministrations of the apocalyptic temper. The literary response to the emerging definition of Reagan's America registered not the furious pride of the new patriotism, but unsettling fears, fears indeed keener than any felt in the American experience of post-Hiroshima since the delicate brinkmanship of the Cuban missile crisis. Like seismographs tracking shifts in distant plates, these writers measured tremblings in the night. More than a clutch of shrill Cassandras or whining Chicken Littles, these writers spoke to a community uncertain of its own oddly cantankerous rhetoric, ill at ease with the chest-thumping arrogance and casual obstinacy of its own patriotic quasi religion that, a scant seven years after the publication of

Gravity's Rainbow, threatened to overwhelm Enzian's quiet prayer, to diminish it into an eerie silence.

In the 1980s writers grappled with a history grown suddenly belligerent and confrontational, one decidedly comfortable with the very Manichean simplicities Vonnegut had ridiculed twenty years earlier in *Cat's Cradle.* The world seemed to have been casually riven into good and evil; and writers, uncomfortable with such deliberate unambiguity, confronted the logical extension of the premise of Hiroshima—global incineration that would make the horrors of Hiroshima and Nagasaki mere metaphor. In ways unprecedented in the literature of the nuclear age, writers moved toward confronting the unforgiving stroke of the nuclear apocalypse itself. Paul Brians, in his exhaustive catalogue of nuclear holocaust fiction, cites 1984 as a watershed year for the publication of such fiction. Indeed, suddenly, it seemed the ideal moment for exercises in the cataclysmic imagination: that simple, naked glimpse of the detonating moment. Big-bang fiction—harsh, judgmental, claustrophobic, relentlessly end oriented—surged both in speculative-fiction markets and on best-seller lists. Exercises in thinking about the unthinkable not only lined bookstall shelves, but crowded network airtime, played in neighborhood movie theaters, surfaced on university syllabi, and generated reams of political rhetoric of every stripe and color. In ways suggestive of that first-generation Puritan settlement that stepped into the Massachusetts wilds largely to await the summary stroke of God's history, the conscience of this decade contemplated endtimes rigorously, thoroughly. But why? Surely the apocalyptic works of Vonnegut, Coover, Percy, and Pynchon all accepted the premise of nuclear endings; indeed, the soaring affirmations tendered by each are deliberate acts of faith against the evidence of their own history. Determined, they resist closure and offer to their characters (and to their anxious community of readers) avenues toward a hope iridescent against the backdrop of history's whirling *danse macabre.* But in the 1980s, the literary examination turned toward an unflinching realism that rendered Vonnegut's *ice-nine,* Coover's cult of the brain-damaged coal miner, Percy's heavy sodium reaction, and even Pynchon's screaming rocketry strangely metaphoric. The fictional voice adopted the studied cadence of the evening news and developed plot lines that could emerge as credible headlines. If the apocalyptic fiction examined thus far accepted the premise of nuclear apocalypse, this fiction examined the premise itself. Writers in remarkable concentration addressed within the decade's early years scenarios of a world reeling back to its beginnings, a world of ash. These writers—among them, Bernard Malamud (*God's Grace*), Russell Hoban (*Riddley Walker*), Paul Auster (*In the Country of Last Things*),

David Brin (*The Postman*), Tim O'Brien (*The Nuclear Age*), John Calvin Batchelor (*The Birth of the People's Republic of Antarctica*), Susan Morgan (*The Children of the Light*), and Denis Johnson (*Fiskadoro*)— addressed a community that sensed lights extinguishing, possibilities closing off. Clearly, the literary response to Reagan's America was dominated by the apocalyptic genre in each of its principal manifestations[1]— the strange, ugly grace of the cataclysmic imagination; the resilient optimism of the millennialist spirit; and the affirmation of the apocalyptic temper. But a review of this geopolitical terrain may help introduce such an argument. We begin with the question, Why did history seem to shade so quickly?

Surely, the shifting fortunes of world governments in the opening years of the decade contributed to an anxiety over global stability. The United States had not had a full two-term president in more than a generation. And it had undertaken a galvanic shift in philosophical direction with the conservative mandate of 1980 (and *that* directive was shaken by an assassination attempt against Reagan a scant two months after he entered office). The Soviet Union had undergone no fewer than four leadership changes in the early years of the decade before the emergence of Mikhail Gorbachev. In addition, international media invoked the rhetoric of the apocalypse to describe a variety of smaller, strategic nations judged to be sitting "on the brink," edging "toward catastrophe," as long-entrenched ruling institutions were threatened, toppled, or voted out—in Iran, Poland, South Africa, India, Lebanon, Nicaragua, South Korea, the Philippines, Haiti, Panama. Such perceptions of government instability were further reenforced by the steady pressure exerted during the decade by the invisible muscle of international terrorism, which would strike randomly and nervelessly from shadows in embassy compounds, on pleasure cruises, in airports packed with holiday crowds, on airplanes awaiting clearance for takeoff or already in midflight. Terrorism—political and religious—played to a horrified international audience in bold, dramatic strokes: the attempt on Pope John Paul II executed in the odd irony of a St. Peter's Square splashed in spring sunlight; the horrific carnage of the Anwar Sadat assassination, the gripping photograph of the government soldier emptying his machine gun into Sadat's reviewing stand suggesting the cold logic of the fanaticism that operated against the steadier hand of government; the flash of submachine-gun fire along the New Delhi streets that ended the enduring political strength of Indira Gandhi; the shattering early-morning explosion that killed more than two hundred American marines, most still sleeping, in the operations bunkhouse in Beirut. Inexplicable save by its own logic, determined to make political or religious arguments emphatic by the fury of bloodshed, such terrorism taught by its nearly unpreventable expression hard lessons in helplessness, paranoia, and uncertainty.

More disturbing, perhaps, was the American strategy to confront such global anxieties with the rhetorical excesses of a saber-rattling cold war assumed early on by the incoming administration. That rhetoric impelled the nation toward an urgent, confrontational belligerence and sanctioned reactive gestures: an incessant military rebuilding program; earnest talk of a winnable nuclear exchange; cavalier jokes about bombing the Soviet Union; the lightning-quick deployment of American troops in eccentric strategies in Beirut, Central America, Libya, and the Persian Gulf; and a steadfast intransigence toward Soviet leadership early on. The rhetoric not only sustained the caricature of Reagan as some nuclear cowboy yearning for high noon, but on a more fundamental level reflected Reagan's political education in the doctrine of rigid suspicion and tight containment nurtured in the early frost of the cold war. Surely Reagan's trademark reductive thought easily translated into a world divided between light and darkness (the "evil empire"). If such an unambiguous world view smacked of George Lucas's Hollywood pseudoepics, it sponsored a fury of defense spending that included the futuristic fantasy of the Strategic Defense Initiative, which promised that military technology might someday stake out a new battleground overhead.

Also under that Reagan mandate of 1980, a new credence was given to the religious/political expression one time dismissed as the far right. Of course, that wing had toned down its own flamethrowing rhetoric, considerably improved its selection of political bedfellows, drawn up a specific political agenda targeted to a voting public perceived to be more and more unimpressed with the exhausted energy of liberalism, and tapped with uncanny prescience the vast potential of telecommunications to emerge packaged more palatably as the new right. Yet this most practical conservatism seemed strangely comfortable with both the grim arithmetic of nuclear capability and the righteous rhetoric of Armageddon.[2] Assured that God cooperated with American military might, the new right could accept events as disparate as the megaton explosion of Mt. Saint Helen's and the inexorable spread of Acquired Immune Deficiency Syndrome into a matrix of approaching endtimes. In addition, the awesome assurance of fundamentalism counseled its followers to accept as impermanent any secular system, to nod in dispassionate agreement to fiery ministers who could hear the approaching hoofbeats, who could glimpse the glory of the approaching crack of light—whether the flash of God's descent or the noiseless flash of an American first strike. Enthralled by the patient job of decoding Revelation keyed to the evening news, such fundamentalism emerged in the decade not only with political legitimacy and real clout, but with a wider audience for its thumping assertions of this nuclear religion.

That audience, however, responded even more keenly to the fierce flag-waving of the insistent new patriotism. Taking its cue from the urgent, can-do optimism of Reagan's rolling shrug of the shoulders and reassuring thumbs-up, this compelling gospel embraced simplification, shook off the nuance of diplomacy and its associated efforts to creatively engage political and religious imperatives of cultures defined as "alien." This nationalism tapped so successfully by the Reagan conservative pledges of 1980 was birthed as much by the tortuous, decade-long coming to terms with the Vietnam experience as by the interminable frustration of the 444 days of Teheran. Surely in its finest expression, such patriotism encouraged respect long overdue to the Vietnam veterans and fueled massive relief projects targeted for African drought victims, the American farmer, and the American homeless. But it also encouraged a certain tunnel vision (witness the patriotic gore of the Soviet-less 1984 Summer Games in Los Angeles), as well as epic excesses (consider the Hollywood revue that overkilled the centennial of the Statue of Liberty). Far more distressing, the new patriotism revived a cold-war warrior figure, packaged for this decade as some grotesque mythic figure with the body of Rambo and the head of Bernhard Goetz, a creature suspicious, impatient, destroying what it will not tolerate, will not understand. Patriotism changed into an alarming gospel of justification, an explosive swinging of the big stick that counted among its military strikes a midnight raid of Libya and an invasion of the island communities on Grenada. Suddenly, might seemed a legitimate element of a foreign policy that appeared at critical moments to be fueled by fears of being perceived as weak or shaded with that most dreaded buzzword of the early Reagan years—*wimpy*. That confrontational mentality promised instinctive, reactive judgment and the mixed signals of a diplomacy of bullying and bluffing, all irresolvably out of place in the harsher realities of nuclear geopolitics.

In addition to harboring such emotional charges, the 1980s were also rocked by a stunning (if coincidental) concentration of catastrophes, unrelated until viewed through the unrelenting coverage of television, which imposed by its omniscience an eerie sort of pattern able to induce a bewildering helplessness, an awareness of sudden, swift, and—in most cases—massive death. Consider the decade's most riveting images: the uncomprehending looks in the faces of the children of Atlanta; the sudden menace of a bottle of Tylenol; the skeletal shapes haunched in the scorched dust of hundreds of African refugee camps; the half-empty washtub of purple fruit juice at the center of the eerie jungle quiet at the Jonestown compound; the gruesome pictures smuggled to the West of the killing fields of Cambodia; the desperate quiet in the eyes of AIDS patients lingering near death in hospices; the bits of floating debris—unmatched shoes and parts of suitcases—from the downed Korean jetliner scattered on the Sea of Japan; the stacked corpses in Bhopal, the survivors wandering about with dead, watery eyes, all gassed in their sleep by a Union Carbide plant gas leak; the blurred national television footage that framed the hopeless holy war of attrition that bled Iraq and Iran and measured its dead routinely in the thousands. Death on such grand scale stirred the American awareness, saturated its media. Not to argue, of course, that any one decade's natural disasters, repressive governments, or terrorist acts are measureable against another's: in 1985 alone a massive volcano in Colombia killed 25,000; an earthquake in Mexico City another 10,000; civil-aviation accidents claimed a record 1,900; acts of terrorism another 700. Even a soccer match claimed 38 lives. And a McDonald's restaurant, that most inviolable of America's clean, well-lighted places, played setting to the San Ysidro massacre, 21 dead and 19 wounded—the worst one-man rampage in the history of such records in the United States.

But apart from global political anxieties, the militant belligerence of the early Reagan White House, the emergence of the new right, the urgency of the new patriotism, or even these unsettling intimations of mortality, shaping such disparate energies was the legacy of tension that commenced with the nuclear power plant accident at Three Mile Island in March 1979, in many ways the birthdate of the decade. A nation suddenly acknowledged what it did not understand about an energy source that it had come uneasily to take for granted. It watched on national television as its defenders, its very builders, suddenly confessed their puzzlement. Robbed of its hesitant faith in the mystery of nuclear power, a people found disturbingly ominous photographs of nuclear power plant cooling towers looming darkly in the backgrounds of houses or schoolyards, images that would be reenforced in 1986 by the blurred black-and-white photos of the shattered cooling tower at Chernobyl. Fearful, a country found philosophical common ground with the more aggressive doctrinal antinuclearism already in place in continental Europe. Early in the decade, American deployment of Pershing II missiles in western Europe sparked months of angry debate and urgent rallying in the streets of European capitals. America heard the fervent rhetoric of a people certain that in a military strategy of a distant Washington they were the expendable, first-round victims of an ultimately winnable nuclear exchange. In this country, the antinuclear campaign found encouragement in the remnants of the peace movement of the sixties, in the vocal, militant branch of the Catholic church, and in the easy promulgation of popular music. Its greatest show of strength came during a rally in Central Park in 1982 that attracted nearly half a million demonstrators against nuclear weaponry.

Much additional soul searching was occasioned by the 1985 observance of the fortieth anniversary of the devastation of Hiroshima and Nagasaki. Hard questions were addressed to a younger generation, born too late to share an older generation's unshakable faith that atomic might had ended what would surely have collapsed into a grim land war for Japan. This nuclear generation had emerged under the complicated shadow of thermonuclear war, had watched the steady escalation of arms development, had wrestled with the convoluted logic of nuclear strategy—and it remained convinced that World War III would surely incinerate much of their world before they died. With powerful films (among them *The Day After, Threads, Testament, The Sacrifice*); important tracts by Jonathan Schell (*The Fate of the Earth*), Freeman Dyson (*Weapons and Hope*), Robert Jay Lifton and Richard Falk (*Indefensible Weapons*), Spencer Weart (*Nuclear Fear*); and urgent discussion in the scientific community of a nuclear winter that suggested the virtual unsurvivability of a limited nuclear exchange, the 1980s in its developmental moments moved toward a disturbing awareness of the terrifying mystery and awesome capability of a nuclear arsenal that had long waited silently out of mind in the underground silos of desert wastes.

In such a contradictory, trembling time—a time in which the overblown rhetoric of reassurance had ironically created a profound anxiety—the literary voice tested the cataclysmic imagination, the millennialist spirit, and the apocalyptic temper. The cataclysmic imagination, compelled by the approaching stroke itself or by its grim aftereffects, found expression in racks of urgent airport paperbacks that matched the globe to ashes, in the more studied paranoia of political and military white-knucklers, or in adventure stories that recycled age-old tales but played them against the unforgiving radioactive landscape of a postholocaust world.[3] It is on the whole a grim body of fiction: studies in the graphic details of radioactive effects; in the mutations possible of the human anatomy after a nuclear sweep; in the painful, day-to-day struggle to survive in a world lost. Much as with the traditional expressions of the cataclysmic imagination that leveled the world by alien interference, interplanetary goofs, natural phenomena gone wild, or even divine say-so, this fiction of nuclear cataclysm accepts a history gone critical and works only the thin hope of struggle and accommodation. In most cases, however, such a struggle to survive is secondary to the careful imagining of a world left to play stage for those trying to hold civilization together by its frayed ends. Such works defeat plot—the inevitability of the climactic stroke reduces the reading experience to something like watching water swirl down an open drain, obedient to laws of gravity. Whether the focus rests on living hopelessly with Its approach or on living desperately within Its reverberations, such fiction can only dish up stale cliches about the destructive capacity of nuclear weapons or battered Swiss Family Robinson cliches about humanity's ability to survive. Seeing global affairs collapse into the ugly anarchy of the mushroom cloud or watching the adjustment amid the rubble can offer little to the reader save the voyeuristic pleasure of watching such agony unfold harmlessly in the pages of fiction. Such fiction is testimony, however, to the failure of such writers to come to terms with the complication of living in the middest, in the sound and fury of nuclear America. They are rather like housekeepers content to switch off the lights in a messy room. Their fiction delights in our deepest fears, exploits our most profound concerns, and offers in turn only visions that seem products of night sweats. Such big-bang fiction is unnervingly disconnected from the urgency of its own history, the writers finally like corpulent people standing in a shark tank placidly staring at their own belly buttons.

If the pseudorealism of the cataclysmic imagination could not sustain a message of hope, other writers responding to the tremblings of the 1980s revived, in ways unlike any since the first hopeful years of the atomic age, the resilient and heady optimism of the millennialist spirit that accepted cataclysm as purgative and pointed the reader's vision beyond the special effects of detonation to a better world emerging steadily from radioactive ruins. Far from the odd mutated forms that struggle in the cataclysmic imagination, these are decidely human survivors who speak of a courage barely expressible in the present death-haunted, exhausted civilization. Although, of course, not working with the distinctions made here, Michael Dorris and Louise Erdrich dismiss such fictions—listing, among others, Malamud's *God's Grace*, Hoban's *Riddley Walker*, and Johnson's *Fiskadoro*—as "irrationally optimistic" (24). Yet the premise of such adjustment fiction (Brin's *The Postman*, Morgan's *The Children of Light*, and LeGuin's sprawling *Always Coming Home* could be added to the list) offers glimpses at a world possible after the feared nuclear trigger has been pulled. They are testimonials to endurance rather than simple animal survival.

Consider, for example, Carolyn See's *Golden Days* (1987), a graceful novel able to accommodate within its slender premise the unleashing of a nuclear attack along the southern California coast in 1990. At its center is Edith Langley, an enterprising woman who resiliently faces the actual nuclear moment and distills from such immense destructive power an even more impressive, constructive energy—her own determination to endure. At the beginning of the novel, Edith travels west, pioneerlike, to southern California, determined to ad-lib her way to financial security after being freed from a series of dead-end relationships with men too eager to define and dismiss her. Along the way, she takes her cue from a confidence-man at a weekend retreat at a posh hotel who peddles an upbeat message of can-do energy within an open universe where every fear can be wadded up and tossed away. And, against the claustrophobic backdrop of collapsing possibilities as political and military troubles in Central America escalate with eerie urgency, Edith sets about her own career and finds within the open complex that is southern California room enough to grow, to discover her own stamina and talent to excel.

Yet the world that opens up to her is crossed by the steel-gray shadows of the nuclear arsenal. It is never far from her awareness, or from her dreams. Very much a child of Hiroshima and the civil-defense drills of the 1950s, Edith soberly assesses her deepest fears—cancer, poverty, divorce—and sees that each is a metaphor for her most profound fear: the bomb itself. The bomb, Edith decides, is a decidedly male endeavor. Elements of her experience express a sense of outrage at what the male-dominated, military-political machinery has managed to create. Surely, Edith argues, men drive the train headed now for certain destruction; surely, she reasons, the dominant imagery of missile warfare and the language of nukespeak itself echo the phallic impulse. Indeed, in the dark days immediately after the initial sweep, Edith glimpses women castrating male corpses and hanging bloody penises on walls and smearing underneath them PEACEKEEPER.

But anger and blame are not what drive See's luminous parable of Edith Langley. In the time immediately following the moment, See offers opening rather than surrendering choices. When it happens, See makes few concessions to the cataclysmic imagination. It is a scant two-minute jolt "when the air begins to burn" (169). Afterward, Edith is still standing in a house that is still standing in a world otherwise dusted by ash. Certainly, See acknowledges the demands of the cataclysmic imagination, does dabble in the pseudorealism of graphic detailing: outbreaks of disease among corpses; fierce fires; poisonous rains; hideous burns; deaths by thirst. But these are dispensed in spare asides. Firmly within the millennialist spirit, See's interest here is in the miracle of survival, in the abundance of living. She dwells at length, for instance, on Edith's sucking down cool, rubbery snails that she finds in amazing numbers hugging the crumbled concrete of her driveway.

As noise returns, as skin begins to heal and to itch, a new world stirs. The novel moves swiftly from detonation to celebration; the dust jacket pictures a champagne bottle exploding, its spray of cold liquor shaping the mushroom cloud itself. Steadily, the narrative ushers the reader toward a climactic scene at the Pacific and offers nothing less than the sea itself, the immense cradle of all biological life that washes now on sand blasted into colored glass by the fierce heat of the nuclear exchange. That sand glints now, catching a most radiantly alive sun. What man destroyed, Edith proclaims, she has preserved. Ishmael-like, her *Pequod* run to its destruction by the angry madness of Ahabs that peopled a distant Pentagon, Edith lays claim in the closing pages to being supremely a storyteller. She evokes for willing audiences not merely her own golden days *before*, but (far more important) the golden days *since* as well. The security of her emerging identity, which defined itself even as the world inched toward the searing stroke, finally is secondary to the courageous description she offers of the colony of survivors who lived through the destroying light to a new time on a new golden coast. *Believe me*, Edith demands, pressing the reader. If Edith commences her southern California experience puzzled by the inexplicable acts of faith healing that she witnesses and assaulted by the hype of the New Age self-help cult with its trendy jargon of infinite possibilities, See blasts away such a charade with the noiseless flash itself; Edith finds her way certainly, with the unflappable determination of the mythos that shapes our endearing picture of the pioneer woman, to find in the awesome afterwash authentic promise, authentic healing, authentic possibility. The nuclear cataclysm is only briefly engaged; the worst shelter-fiction cliches are avoided. Edith does not merely survive and accommodate; Edith thrives. *Golden Days*, within the brave testimonial tradition of the millennialist spirit, returns a terminal world to beating vibrancy—much as Edith's considerably potent love helps to bring the terminal cancer of her older lover, Skip, into remission.

And therein lies the courage and cowardice of the millennialist spirit—its determination and its gospel of resiliency as well as its withdrawal from history and its impossible, demanding leap of faith into a realm that blurs into the nearly surreal. Well within the fiction of endtimes that emerged under the urgency of the 1980s, the novel here displays the radical commitment to a realistic scenario; a claustrophobic world of rapidly dwindling possibilities; a foreboding atmosphere of death that hangs about the narrative line like a stalled cold front. But, as with the other volumes of millennialist imaginings, its supreme optimism cannot reassure. Taken critically, indeed, it can succumb to the heartless overkill of irony. *Believe me*, Edith counsels. Surely for the reader, who is webbed within the tight confines of a community-in-crisis, erasing civilization cannot be taken so lightly, cannot be so cleanly done. As with other expressions within this tradition, reading through the exuberance of *Golden Days* can be like paging through the gospel text of a religion one does not profess. Where is the joy? Where is the reassurance? Where is the communion? See's novel is finally an artist's rendering in soft-pastel outline of a brave new paradise that, oddly, resists the most difficult struggle that engages its reader—living before the hammerstroke or under its very shadow. How is the reader of such an exercise, singing with confidence and intoxicated with its own possibilities, to confront the headlines tomorrow? With relief? With only casual concern? With arrogant confidence? Lost, finally, is that genuine gesture toward a community-in-crisis.

How, then, are writers in the 1980s to shape awareness into a philosophy of hope that manages to avoid the pyrotechnics of the cataclysmic imagination and the harmless fantasies of the millennialist spirit? This study will conclude with a discussion of two important books, both published in the mid-1980s, that work toward the consolation and strength of the apocalyptic temper. If humanity found itself indeed struggling between the hungry tiger and the chasm below in the 1980s, the tiger now seemed larger, hungrier; the chasm deeper, blacker. These novels, however, accept the heightened dilemma and refuse the simple arithmetic of subtraction typical of the cataclysmic imagination and the frenzied multiplication of possibilities typical of the millennialist spirit. They resist the simple antithesis of ashes and gold. And, supremely, both works—as examples of the affirmation possible in the sure confrontation with history—hark back to the determination of Vonnegut's Malachi Constant. They are indeed glad of the pain—for in such pain, they sift out the possibility of hope.

In Gaddis's *Carpenter's Gothic*, the world, trapped within the thick webbing of the intrigues of a curiously inept collection of plotters, feels in the novel's closing pages the first shudders of the coming cataclysm. As the novel rages against its own closing off, it points darkly to how easily the war of words can escalate into the war of the world. It is a fiercely sobering reading experience, made dramatically ironic by Gaddis's intentional parody of the Gothic formula that seems to allow the novel a comic effect. But Gaddis's anger is certain; his aim is true. In the end, the hope he can muster is as slim as a period left off the novel's closing sentence. In DeLillo's *White Noise*, however, the protagonist Jack Gladney, immured in language and overwhelmed by death, moves for all of us past both and discovers in such a perilous inner voyage a reconnection with the universe that lives and dies beyond the pale of nuclear egotism. DeLillo does not detonate the world, does not send it reeling back to ashes, does not shape his hope from pixie dust scattered amid the rubble. His is a most important response to the decade and more generally to the age that cannot shake its shadow death—still standing, puzzled, beneath the mushroom cloud, much like the citizenry of Hiroshima in Ibuse's *Black Rain*. In both Gaddis's and DeLillo's novels, writers (to different degrees) engage a most courageous challenge and in doing so perform that most traditional of imperatives accorded the apocalyptic temper—solace to a people in deep troubles.

I have read the Book of Revelation and, yes, I believe the world is going to end—by an act of God, I hope—but every day I think that time is running out.
Caspar W. Weinberger, Secretary of Defense

You know, I turn back to your ancient prophets in the Old Testament and the signs foretelling Armageddon, and I find myself wondering if—if we're the generation that's going to see that come true.
Ronald Reagan

Using the Gothic novel as model for a scenario of the long-feared nuclear apocalypse is fitting, though in disquieting ways. Given the premise that the approaching destruction will be so complete that it reaches beyond the imagination, such a scenario is perhaps best handled in a medium that has long delighted in heightened, extended, sensationalized realism. Gothicism delights in altering reality by complicating it into labyrinthine plots that unravel toward chaos amid the thick gloom that settles about once-noble mansions.[4] Nuclear apocalypses detonate, at least in fiction, amid tortuous government intrigues—explode amid the ruins of a once-noble Western civilization. Gothicism could as well convey much of the feeling that haunts contemporary nuclear apocalyptic fictions: a paranoiac sense of foreboding, of order threatened or giving way; the erotic fascination with death and destruction; the attraction to the power of evil, particularly the horror of science unbound by conscience; the rejection of reason in the face of approaching chaos. Gothic novels also move toward finales of conflagration, architectural collapse, familial downfall, indiscriminate murder, or passionate madness (internal collapse). If Gothicism at its peak moved romanticism toward a frightening (and therefore fascinating) brush with evil unbridled, if it threatened bourgeois reality by insisting that it is merely a tenuous element in a far vaster, more threatening cosmos, if its central impulse is terror and its driving force almost unbearable fear, certainly Gothicism can be numbered among the lineal ancestors of much contemporary nuclear apocalyptic literature. And given that Gothicism, like apocalypticism, flourishes during periods perceived to be undergoing sharp social upheavals, where the perception is widespread that reliable systems are giving way, it would certainly find in the post-Hiroshima landscape an appropriate setting.

Like the more baroque Gothic novels of the mid-nineteenth century, Gaddis's *Carpenter's Gothic* intentionally defies casual plot summary; and, like the more experimental Gothic novels of the mid-twentieth century, Gaddis uses such defiance to manipulate a distinct tension between the text and the reader—the reader is meant to feel as uneasy within the text as the characters themselves, who wander about a bizarre, contradictory landscape.[5] The basic narrative expands, halts, accelerates, stalls, and then in the closing handful of pages destroys itself—in a nuclear explosion off the mineral-rich coast of East Africa that foretells World War III and then, more startlingly, in the slaying of the heroine, Elizabeth Booth.

The book begins, however, calmly enough. Elizabeth and her husband, Paul, rent a furnished house—a rambling High Victorian carpenter's Gothic overlooking the Hudson River—from a mysterious geologist named McCandless.[6] Paul, a burned-out Vietnam veteran wounded by the men under his command and now a dangerously unsteady alcoholic, is desperate to put behind him an embarrassing past that is a succession of failed enterprises, including a bungled job as a bagman in several shady business deals for his father-in-law, the head of a vast mining consortium. When the father-in-law commits suicide a few scant steps ahead of a swarm of government investigating committees, Paul is brusquely moved out of the company and, feeling betrayed, resolves to set up a business on his own as a media consultant, a public relations man. His chief, and perhaps only, client is the Reverend Elton Ude, a passionate, messianic African preacher bent on establishing a worldwide communications operation for his "Voice of Salvation" radio show as part of his campaign against the Antichrist—the Big Brother government eager to thwart his radio program in America and the Marxist cartel slowly devouring Africa. Paul commits his energies to Ude's fanatical fundamentalist revival, developing a high profile for Ude in order to insure government licensing. Like a poor parody of the New Testament Paul, the first and most effective PR man for Christianity, Paul works to spread Ude's mission by keeping him in the newspapers.

Initial critical response to Gaddis's novel tried to reassemble the shattered narrative line,[7] one delivered in dialogue (speakers are only loosely identified and change without indication), in one-sided telephone conversations (the telephone ring interrupts nearly every scene in the novel), and in angry reactions by Liz and Paul to the mail—unpaid bills, insurance notices, VA letters, attorneys' notices, and glitzy postcards. The novel's tangled web of financial intrigues, government investigations, lawsuits and countersuits—as well as the confusion over each character's own history—intentionally resists easy retelling. Like Liz and Paul, who inhabit someone else's house and are forever bumping into someone else's furniture and receiving someone else's mail, the reader is not meant to feel at home here. In fine Gothic tradition, the narrative movement is somewhat ultrarealistic, even comic—from Paul's craven efforts to promote the Reverend Ude, the novel moves to the unleashing of the American nuclear arsenal after the deliberate shooting down of a passenger plane carrying an American senator, the same senator who was largely responsible for securing Ude's broadcast license. Rather than a crumbling castle collapsing into ruin or a family line lurching into madness, what explodes at the end of this Gothic novel is the world itself. Yet, the sense of games playing prevails. Gaddis unleashes the apocalypse over Kenya's Great Rift, where anthropologists have discovered the oldest human fossil remains: it will end, in fine fictive fashion, where it all began.

But there is more. When a beleaguered America of the all-too-recognizable present finally draws the line (a "howling for blood" [223]) and summons its considerable nuclear might, it is in response to the murder of a less-than-heroic senator (the "best senator money can buy" [34]). The senator is in Africa, Gaddis darkly points out, as part of an insidious alliance of politicos and businessmen interested in securing landrights to a reported motherlode of valuable minerals near Kenya's Great Rift. America draws the line not out of indignation over the assassination of Senator Teakell, but for the minerals themselves—vanadium, platinum, manganese, chromium—which are crucial to defense systems. But the irony does not end there. According to McCandless, who as a geologist was hired to do a mineral scanning of the Great Rift area, that cache is nonexistent. For his own rather twisted reasons, McCandless wants the world incinerated and, so, destroys the evidence of his scannings. That the world will be destroyed over a fiction, a seven-mile ridge of thornbush, is the supreme grotesque comic twist in Gaddis's apocalyptic temper.

The grim comedy—and the apocalypse itself—occurs only when any individual perception is accepted as the whole with all unmistakable vehemence of a paranoid. Each perception, Gaddis insists, is a fragment, finally a fiction. McCandless, who angrily and tediously rails against

America as the dark continent where ignorance reigns—where evolution can be legislated against as pleasant plausibility—refuses to release his mineral findings, pleased that Western civilization will destroy itself over nothing; in his poisoned eyes, this is an appropriate fulfillment of all that Christianity has ever embraced—wholesale slaughter over a fiction. As he details geological data to support his case against the Creation, McCandless seems the very voice of Reason. And the Reverend Ude, who simplifies government attempts to destroy his radio ministry as machinations of the Evil One and reduces the complicated intergovernmental chaos of independent Africa as the long-prophesied showdown between Satan and Christ, seems to play Revelation. The underpinning of his campaign to save Christian America—the Christian Recovery of the American People (C.R.A.P.)—is rooted in his often dubious reading of scripture. Like McCandless, whose tirades feature some of the best setpieces in the novel, Ude sways his audiences with the hypnotic power of his rolling voice. Indeed, in a novel in which Gaddis records with devastating accuracy the banal conversations of his characters, Ude, who never actually appears in the novel, is a mysterious presence, a magnificent voice. Adamant, unyielding, each convinced that moral rectitude rests with his position, and willing to immolate the world rather than alter that position, both McCandless and Ude—ultimately shabby parodies of Reason and Revelation—maneuver the world toward Armageddon. For different reasons, they move toward an ending with which each is strangely comfortable.

The comedic effect here comes mostly from Gaddis's studied parody of the Gothic novel and of *Jane Eyre* in particular.[8] That a literary antiquarian as demonstrably eclectic as Gaddis should be pigeonholed as working only with one genre—and such a popular and accessible one at that—would, of course, be unfairly limiting. Yet, given the particularly literary sort of despair that characterizes Gaddis's apocalypticism, an approach that begins with literary parody would be instructive. The novel, hailed by the publisher's dust-jacket blurb and by a covey of appreciative reviewers as "accessible Gaddis," works with many of the trademark devices of marketplace Gothic novels. For instance, the novel (with certain important adjustments) develops the central plot situation of Gothics: the tense struggle for survival by a retiring heroine who has been abandoned (financially and emotionally) by family, placed at the mercies of a savage world, tested both by passion (with a dark, malevolent stranger) and by exposure to a suprareal world, and who finally emerges stronger and more capable. Liz Booth is such a heroine. Her mother lies in the "cold embrace" of a nursing home (64). Her father was a distant, often cruel presence whose suicide has virtually disinherited her by placing her vast inheritance in a trust fund that is wrapped in tangles of stout red tape while being slowly drained by an infestation of appointed legal guardians. Her brother is a good-natured parasite. And Paul, violent (a purplish bruise on Liz's upper arm is evidence of his rage) and insensitive to her needs (he smokes constantly despite her asthma, swears despite her objections, pursues his sexual satisfactions with her despite her obvious discomfort from injuries in a plane crash years before), is profoundly unresponsive to her more complicated dissatisfactions over their marriage. Indeed, that marriage invests Liz, a sensual and apparently striking redhead, with rich Gothic resonances. She is the trapped heroine, locked into a repressive marriage within a stiflingly overcrowded "museum of a house" (51) with its perpetually grimy windows and air choked by cigarette smoke and dust. As her asthmatic condition suggests, she quite literally cannot breathe. Indifferent to her husband's efforts to launch his career as a media consultant (she recalls similar attempts to be a novelist, a filmmaker, a business executive), terrified by his potential for violent paranoia, and finally disenchanted even with McCandless, the mysterious stranger whom she takes to bed on a passionate impulse, Liz is the Gothic woman imperiled, trying to survive a dangerous, male-dominated world.

There are, of course, other Gothic elements to Gaddis's novel. The crumbling Victorian house with its labyrinthine hallways, fake chimneys, and appropriately haphazard arrangement of rooms, is a metaphoric suggestion of the complicated internal workings of the characters as well as of the baroque plot itself. Gaddis, in addition, creates the usual brooding atmosphere of the Gothic landscape. Occasional narrative paragraphs inserted between the banal patter of the characters' interminable dialogues suggest a chill, autumnal landscape where a yellowing sun seems forever setting, casting in cold bronze the onset of winter-death. The house, itself falling apart, stands at the deadend of a one-way street. On Halloween, central to the plot as the day McCandless and Liz spend together, costumed children coast like spectral figures along the sidewalks, menacing gangs of older kids prowl, and toilet paper streamers hang from telephone wires like ghosts. A rage of black crows haunts the trees outside Liz's bedroom, the birds squatting on the "scabrous fingers" of tree limbs "twisted in fruitless torment" (36). It is a most forbidding landscape. Gaddis invests such a geography with the Gothic sense of impending doom, suggested not only by the taut situation in Africa ("all four horsemen riding across the hills of Africa with every damned kind of war you could ask for" [87]), but by the Vorakers clan itself. Haunted by a father's suicide, the family is childless, sterile. Liz can perform only oral sex comfortably. Paul not only refuses to recognize a child in a Thai refugee camp, apparently an offspring of his war years, but at several odd moments expresses a decided preference for infidelities rather than marriage. Liz's brother is unmarried and a comfortable drifter indifferently involved with a New Jersey convert to Buddhism, a religion disinclined toward physical gratifications. Given the family's considerable financial stake in the mineral site that McCandless has already judged worthless, the novel seems a ready-made "Fall of the House of Vorakers."

Gaddis adds some Gothic frills. At the heart of the book is the powerful secret—the geological scannings done by McCandless (for which government men are quite willing to pay handsomely or to murder indifferently) and kept in a mysterious, locked room in the center of the house Liz and Paul rent. The novel has the Gothic ambiance of paranoia, of characters caught lying to each other until no word is beyond question. There is the sense of fast-approaching disorder, the imminence of complete collapse. Things are always breaking down, leaking, shattering; messages get lost; mail is misplaced. The marriage of Liz and Paul is itself deeply fissioned. A thick webbing of alienation wraps about the characters, each talking yet never being heard in dialogue that is at best sustained, juxtaposed monologues. There are strong doubts over each character's sanity, typical suspicions in a Gothic novel. It is clear that Paul is wound tightly. McCandless has spent some time in a mental hospital and is subject to launching into bitter diatribes with only the barest assurances of an audience. Even Liz is subject to curious fantasies, many propagated by her late-night viewing of *Jane Eyre* on television. She imagines lightning splitting a chestnut tree (as it does in the movie), yet the tree is not mentioned before or after and is more than likely not there at all. She imagines Paul asleep in a bed on fire (much like Jane's discovery of Rochester's bed afire), and again there is no evidence of a fire at McCandless's house, although that same week a fire does sweep through one of the Vorakers's estates during a practice drill run by the local fire department (yet another conflagration by mistake). Finally, there is the cast of stock characters, a standard device in Gothic novels. Gaddis arrays the Vietnam burnout, the neurotic and erotic housewife, the eccentric professor, the crooked senator, the zealous minister, the black-sheep brother, the manipulative family attorney.

Gaddis plays more deliberately with *Jane Eyre*; however, in keeping with the secondhand motif of carpenter's Gothic, what initially moves Liz is not the novel, but the 1935 film. Like Rochester, McCandless is the elusive owner of the house/mansion where Liz/Jane takes up residence, the mysterious master of the house whose sudden arrival commences a torrid romance. Much as Jane finds herself immediately attracted to the dark, mysterious figure of Rochester, Liz is compelled from her first meeting with McCandless. Yet, Gaddis subtly mocks such association and mimics the memorable first meeting of Jane and Rochester (a scene Liz watches on the bedroom television with her skirt unfastened and her blouse opened). When McCandless first arrives at the front door, a misty rain falls (not quite the swirling fog of the moors); McCandless is draped in a frayed, heavy raincoat (not quite Rochester's flowing cloak); and like Rochester, McCandless is escorted by a huge black dog, but this dog's nails are painted a gaudy red. Like the typical Gothic "heavy," McCandless proves powerfully persuasive, disquietingly near insanity, strongly sexual. Like Jane (or perhaps because of Jane), Liz is powerfully drawn to these characteristics. When McCandless mysteriously shows up one morning to sort through the accumulated papers locked away in the house's secret room, Liz is obviously flustered. She retreats to the protection of her bedroom, there to write McCandless into the private (and rather casually erotic) fiction that she keeps hidden in her dresser. During the rainy afternoon they spend together in the house, Liz is compelled by McCandless's vast intelligence and by his endless tales culled from globe-trotting adventures as a geologist-for-hire. To her claustrophobic existence, McCandless brings open space, room to travel, room to breathe. Much later in the book, a chance meeting with McCandless's wife confirms what the reader suspects, that McCandless's tales are just that, enticing fictions gleaned from shelves of eccentric readings. (Indeed, far from Rochester's madwoman-in-the-attic, McCandless's wife is apparently the sane one in the marriage.) But for Liz the immediate effect is stirring. She takes him to bed that afternoon. This experience energizes the dormant Liz. After dozing in a postcoital haze, she awakes to radiant sunshine and the cooing of doves at her window.[9] She dresses in vibrant Kelly green. This experience, however, is somewhat less than special to McCandless. He quietly withdraws from the bedroom as soon as Liz falls asleep. He pauses to look at her sleeping figure and describes her as if she were simply a stranger and, more disturbingly, as if she were dead (the passage is similar to Gaddis's description of Liz's body after she has been bludgeoned to death). Here in this elaborate parody of *Jane Eyre,* a disturbing pathos lurks and suggests the cataclysmic imagination that operates in this fanciful Gothic mockery: Liz is far from the survivor Jane Eyre. She never stands up to her impossible husband. She is disillusioned finally by McCandless and his torrential rhetoric. And she ends up ingloriously killed by an intruder. Despite the parody, despite the comic inversions of the Gothic form, horror—the supreme element of Gothic fiction—is the novel's disturbing distillation.

Gaddis uses the Gothic formula—unstable minds loose in an unstable world—to unleash his apocalypse. Yet, give the elements of Gothicism at work and the obvious mocking of the genre (even the title printed on the binding is a hokey Gothic type), why does the apocalypse here remain a disturbing one? Gothicism, after all, is adamantly antirealistic, its terror contrived and confined to its own tortured landscape. The apocalypse itself is announced to the reader as Paul (on the phone establishing his claim to the Vorakers fortune after the deaths of his wife and her brother) indifferently watches a housefly saunter across a newpaper with headlines screaming the news from Africa. This surely indicates Gaddis's preeminent concern for the architecture of his car-penter's Gothic, the soundness of the parody itself, the tricky technique (so much a hallmark of his fiction) of character revelation and plot momentum generated solely from dialogue. Surely, given the constrict-ing web of the plot lines, the lies, the "misinformation," the streaks of insanity, and the penchant for fiction making among the characters, the apocalypse (when it finally comes) is little more than a firecracker going off harmlessly in a nest of Chinese boxes. With obviously maimed char-acters in an obviously maimed landscape and the plot buried in a con-fusion of dialogue, the Gothic terror ought to be distant, the fear counterfeit. Why, then, is the novel so disturbing? Despite its cast of feral characters and the deliberate din of their often unfocused ex-changes, the parable of Gaddis's apocalypse seethes with an anger—not biting like Swift's or Orwell's, but passionately aroused, akin to Old Testament prophets whose fiery exhortations damned an entire race for bringing itself to its own endtime. The indictment must move the reader beyond simple admiration for the novel's careful Gothic trim to Gaddis's emphatic target.

That target is the insanity of the decade's pursuit of Armageddon, that national passion fueled not only by the infantile rhetoric of a cu-riously hostile president, but also by a slough of Hollywood pseudoepics that reduce the world, even the cosmos, to simple struggles between good and evil and by the grossly disproportionate hunger for the big stick—lost in the sludgy wake of the Vietnam failure, the shabby antics of Watergate, and the tortuous stalemates in Iran and Beirut—a hunger highlighted by the garish hoopla that surrounded the conquest of Grena-da. This is Gaddis's foundation for the meticulous construction of his own carpenter's Gothic.[10] It is the outrage of the consummate wordsmith realizing that the current lurch toward the apocalypse is more a construct of conflicting fictions, each defended with dangerous intensity, that has reduced moral absolutes to a (quite unconvincing) good and a (quite simplistic) evil and has provided the rhetoric necessary to trigger doomsday weapons systems capable of sending civilization back to ashes. Worked into the very fabric of this deliberately comic novel are narrative threads that are alarmingly real.[11] Species-threatening world events seem to be part of the comedy itself—profound stupidity, part bush-league corruption and part hapless bumbling. The comedy climaxes in the shouted headlines announcing both the unwarranted murder of Liz (killed presumably by a Mormon missionary-turned-government-operative desperate to get at the room where he mistakenly assumes McCandless has filed the scannings from the rift) and the unnecessary launching of a nuclear demonstration likely to ignite a chain-reaction response. That a comic novel ends with meaningless death, both individual and global, caused by misinformation, warns the reader that to laugh here is to be in peril. It is as if during the bumbling antics of a hack vaudeville act, the comics on stage accidentally start a fire that traps the audience and destroys the theater.

At the heart of Gaddis's apocalyptic wrath is the conflict between purpose and purposelessness. At one point McCandless ruminates about a novel he wrote when he was much younger. He describes the crusade of that novel's hero, Frank Kinkead, to wrestle life from the simple anarchy of chance and to render the splendor of purpose to its unfolding. The crusade leaves Frank bitter and disenchanted. Indeed, so certain does he become of a sort of cosmic purposelessness that he suggests that every man at birth ought to be given a chess set so that he can fill the void of existence with marvelous invention, games playing to entertain the mind as time slowly unravels in its purposeless course. These are the disturbing antipodes of Gaddis's apocalyptic temper: purposelessness, the natural state of things; and purpose, elaborate, even desperate, fictions that resist the natural order and are therefore artificial and finally fragile. Yet these desperate fictions define a manageable universe by framing a section of the void that defeats McCandless's hero. We abhor purposelessness and, hence, create purpose. As McCandless insists in his interminable critiques of the Creationists—foremost among them the African Ude—these religious zealots cannot accept purposelessness; they embrace the Creation. The pleasant poetry of Genesis is to McCandless an insolent refusal to accept the evidence of data available in high-school biology texts (for which McCandless writes). He proudly opts for the ruthlessly empirical wisdom of science. But Gaddis indicts McCandless for *his* intolerance of another's fiction—indeed, McCandless merely chooses the rigorously scientific fiction of Darwinian evolution (''monkey mythology,'' as a fundamentalist southern judge whom McCandless quotes describes it). Both McCandless and Ude choose to frame the universe within a fiction.

Appropriately enough, Gaddis's novel teems with such fiction makers. Not only are several of them practicing writers, but the characters display an unnerving penchant for spontaneous lying concerning their pasts and even their immediate situations. Paul, an adopted Jew, casts himself as the last legatee of a fabulous southern aristocratic family ruined by the Civil War. When he is enrolled in a military academy, he carries about an engraved sword and treasures a small box of worthless rocks that he tells his classmates are bits of masonry from his family's plantation destroyed during the war. It is all what Billy dismisses as Paul's "southern officer bullshit" (17). But more to the point that Gaddis will develop, it is a dangerous fiction—it is Paul's pretense to southern pride that drives the enlisted men in his platoon in Vietnam, most of them urban blacks, to try to kill him by rolling a hand grenade under his bed as he sleeps.

Paul's inclination to fiction does not stop when he leaves the service. He tries to write a novel shortly after returning from Vietnam. As media consultant for Ude, he regularly tries to plant stories in the newspaper that are roundly sentimentalized or overly dramatic. These fictions backfire as well. For instance, a press release trumpeting Ude's missionary work in Africa is bumped in favor of coverage of a drowning during one of Ude's river baptisms; later, when Paul tries to use the drowning as a springboard for launching Ude's religious mission, a sentimental account of the boy's funeral is upstaged in the newspaper by a story detailing the deaths of three schoolchildren in an accident involving a bus from Ude's mission, a bus apparently in poor repair.

Others indulge fiction. Billy casually adopts the Buddhist vocabulary of his live-in girlfriend, which Paul terms Billy's Buddhist "crap." To make extra money, Billy runs a tidy little scam using his girlfriend's apartment: he advertises for renters and accepts first-month rent from several prospects and then clears out for a while. And Liz is forced by her abysmal marriage to pretend constantly. She keeps her actual fiction, a "sort of a novel" (35), in a manila folder in her bedroom dresser, a never-ending story of supposing her life had been different. At the time of McCandless's arrival at the front door, she is working out the implications of supposing her mother had not married her father. As McCandless's influence shakes her loneliness, she creates a mysterious man for her mother, a man like McCandless with a vague, exciting past and hard, thick hands.

These are the fiction makers in Gaddis's world: mercenary, deceiving, bored, posturing. They are indeed a sorry lot. Like Paul, who abandons his novel, Liz is a poor writer—she writes slowly, with great effort, anchored to a dictionary, uncertain about words, thumbing through to check meanings and constantly distracted by definitions of obscene words. McCandless's novel, which rests forgotten inside its sickly yellow cover in his crowded library, is nothing more than the excesses of a young man schooled in the cliches of decadent despair who searches for meaning in the fashionably bleak void. Gaddis assembles a collection of hack writers whose work is unfinished, unfinishable, or badly finished. The novel is sustained by the collision and often unintentional cooperation of these hack writers' ongoing fiction making. From the pettiness of the lies that Liz tells her best friend, Edie, over the phone about her "marvelous" marriage to Ude's messianic campaign to defeat the Antichrist, lies sustain the plot, create it, propel it. They are the chess games of these inventive minds. Yet Gaddis smirks at their attempts.

Paul struggles to get his media-consulting business started and sharply criticizes Liz for her stubborn refusal to see the "Big Picture," how things will soon fall into place for them. Exasperated, Paul sketches on scrap paper a "simplified" picture of his intrigue to insure Ude's move into global communications. The more Paul explains, the more tangled and indecipherable the sheet becomes, a hatchwork of arrows, crosses, *x*'s. McCandless later mistakes it for the doodling of a child.

Gaddis undercuts Ude—the preacher abuses biblical quotations, peddles hokey religious relics (including vials of rank river water from the stream where he baptizes), pursues generous contributions for his campaign to ignite Armageddon, rebounds with an unconscionable media blitz after the drownings during one of his baptisms, and finesses senators and reporters with casual concern for truth.

Gaddis exposes McCandless as a pathological liar who is heartlessly cruel to Liz. At one point when Liz feels closest to McCandless, she confides that she would like to go to a planet by the nearest star and look back toward earth, back to her own childhood, and to see what she recalls as one of the few happy moments in her life. McCandless, asked what he would like to see, launches into a fabrication of being lost in Africa on a gold-hunting expedition under a "broiling sun" with a broken-down jeep, forced to drink radiator water (168). McCandless regales Liz with such hokey tales of his adventures. He uses his fictions, exploiting their obvious appeal to the bored and frustrated Liz. Curiously, his lovemaking to Liz is rendered in geological terms; he explores her hillocks, her crests, her swells, and finally her rift. Such jargon not only suggests the indifference of McCandless to Liz, but points up the exploitative nature of his lust. To complete that exploitation, McCandless, preparing to leave the country, sells out to a CIA operative for $16,000 in return for the clutter left in his study. It is fair to assume that this agent first kills Liz before searching through the locked room for the geological scannings of the Great Rift that McCandless long ago discarded.

With such a cast, there is no relish for fiction making. Gaddis offers an ensemble of losers and bad liars, deliberately exploitative in their fictions. These characters, like Paul in Vietnam, are finally trapped (as is the world) by their inept fictions—much as when Frank Kinkead must spend a hellish night during a river crossing with his thumbs pinned in the hinges of a folded steamer chair, trapped, in a sense, by his own weight. (Curiously, McCandless's thumbnails are blackened. He, of course, has a variety of stories to account for it, but the injury does mark him as one pinned by his own weight.) In the metafictional mood (which Gaddis consistently humors), writers often delight in offering characters who, abroad in a landscape of bleak opportunities and the haphazard, drift into nothingness and thrive by elaborate fiction making—characters for whom the only thing worse than being lost in the fun house is to be lost *to* the fun house. In a cosmos of such invented fictions, the only proper fear (as Liz points out to her brother) is finishing, endings. As long as the fiction continues, blind contingency, hapless chance, the wrenching realization that on top of everything else this impossibly routine life has to end—all are kept at bay. Energy is directed toward sustaining the fiction, keeping it going. Like the dustman whose spectral figure haunts the sidewalks in front of the McCandless house, fiction sustains purpose by defying routine, chance, death. The dustman patiently sweeps up leaves and gathers them into the trash, executing such duties methodically "with ceremonial concern, balanc[ing] the broom upright like a crossier" (35). Carefully, in steady defiance of the overwhelming absurdity of a sweeper of leaves in an autumn landscape, he asserts purpose, justifies his existence, and scares the hell out of the characters in the novel.

One indication of what jeopardizes the world in the hands of such bad fiction makers is that this dustman, whose silent Sisyphean presence speaks eloquently of the human need to preserve dignity and to assert purpose in a death-ridden universe, comes off as such an ominous presence. The first time Liz glimpses the dustman, she runs off to the telephone to check the price of airline tickets to Jamaica. McCandless admits, balancing a drink and gazing out the window at the man, that the dustman was most responsible for his leaving the house. Too many of the too-elaborate fictions point only to endings. Purpose—fiction created to justify the heroic struggle to live—now is handmaiden to the apocalypse in the hands of hack writers such as Paul, Ude, and McCandless. At one point, Liz, unable to understand why McCandless will not release his findings about the mineral lode in Africa, blasts him:

> "You're the one who wants it.... And it's why you've done nothing....
> to see them all go up like that smoke in the furnace all the stupid, ignorant,
> blown up in the clouds and there's nobody there, there's no rapture no
> anything just to see them wiped away for good it's really you, isn't it. That
> you're the one who wants Apocalypse, Armageddon all the sun going out
> and the sea turned to blood you can't wait no, you're the one who can't
> wait!... because you despise their, not their stupidity no, their hopes be-
> cause you haven't any, because you haven't any left." (243–44)

The fear of finishing, the deliberate, elaborate impulse to keep the fiction going, has been replaced by this fascination for endings. It is as if the inventive chess games are wearily heading for a Beckettian endgame.

As Liz's diatribe against the indifferent McCandless indicates, she does embody to some degree what resists the movement toward cataclysm. As the embattled heroine of a Gothic fiction, she struggles to preserve the more traditional fiction making. Her far-flung fictions can go on without ending. Unlike the mercenary fiction makers who surround her, Liz will not prostitute the art—she coldly declines to write a letter for Paul pretending to be Ude's mother asking for contributions to her son's campaign. For Liz—trapped in a fractured marriage, disinherited from the wealth that could offer the best chance for escape, denied the com-fort of her only friend Edie by her husband's ruthless paranoia and insensitivity, used by McCandless, cut off by injury from the reinvigo-ration of the sexual act—her fictions simply make life liveable. The scattered pages, heavily marked and laboriously reworked, get Liz through cold rainy afternoons, through long nights, through the ener-vating boredom of her marriage. Shortly before she is killed—trapped in the fiction spun by the evil McCandless—she is still hard at work on her fictions up in her bedroom. Indeed, the description Gaddis offers of Liz's last desperate efforts to breathe as she is dying on the floor after the assault climaxes with the image of her tongue spilling from her mouth—language, in essence, silenced.

The novel is finally a seamless collection of end fictions. Gaddis em-beds paraphrases from biblical apocalypses—God's warning to the Pha-raoh in Genesis, Isaiah's thundering anger, Paul's compassionate warning in 1 Thessalonians. He chooses for his Gothic model *Jane Eyre,* which itself moves toward a scene of apocalyptic fury—the conflagration of Rochester's house. Paul reads from Ude's brochures, which package Reve-lation and the final consummation in easy-to-follow comic books. Add to these apocalyptic fictions headlines that trace the political chess moves that make nuclear confrontation inevitable, and Gaddis's own narrative line that ends with the sudden, violent murder of Liz, and the reader senses that what is disturbing here is that Gaddis's smirk as Gothic parodist is balanced by the sobering reminder from one of the early practitioners of inventive fiction that destruction as well as survival can be cased in so many elaborate fictions.

In Gaddis's other fictions, the inevitable collapse of invented worlds found its atonement and its hope in the resiliency of the fiction maker or in the fiction-making process itself.[12] At the close of *The Recognitions*, a mighty Gothic cathedral falls in on its own weight, while a soaring organ solo survives its composer. Even in *JR*, where the reader follows the complicated amassing of a paper fortune by a clever sixth grader only to watch it crumble in a confusion of government investigations, JR is set at the close of the novel to begin again building another empire. That the closing sentence here—Paul, ever the cad, cozening up to Edie in the backseat of a "dark limousine" (260), uses the identical come-on line he recalls earlier having used on Liz—is without a period, is Gaddis the fiction maker refusing to end his own fiction, a slender offering indeed. From the mesmerizing rhetoric of Isaiah to the chilling hysteria of tomorrow's newspaper headlines, all other fictions point to endings. That the world can be incinerated over a fiction, or more exactly by the contrived and conflicting fictions of those who intolerantly mistake perception for reality, is the disturbing source of the horror of Gaddis's apocalyptic temper. The golden world of See's abundance and resilience, healing and recommencing seems here pitched only toward ending. Encased, enclosed, webbed within such fictions, the world, like Liz, is doomed to sudden, violent ending, trapped within the fictions of losers and liars who have lost the energy to hope. Unlike Vonnegut, who a scant twenty years earlier had undercut riotously such cataclysmic intimations by satirizing its most earnest messengers, Gaddis offers portrait after portrait of politicians, scientists, religious leaders that are unnervingly realistic. Such characters, he warns, are now turning the planet. *Carpenter's Gothic* is clearly a novel of lights going out, a latter-day fulfillment of Melville's *Confidence-Man*, which played its own parody on biblical apocalypse but ended nevertheless with a claustrophobic sense of dead ends, of suns extinguishing. Gaddis offers—to paraphrase Beckett—a world dying of darkness. It is left to the reader, still alert and alive within the world, to recognize that in such end-driven fictions, which shade all too closely current events, lurks the angry hunger of the cataclysmic imagination. It is left for the reader to see the hapless, spiritless exhaustion and to turn finally toward a more effective response to such a threatened community. Gaddis does console the reader, but by indirection; he teaches, but obliquely. Like the man who learns to relish the heady sweetness of the air only after being trapped in a stalled elevator, suspended and helpless in a closed, dead world, the readers here learn hope by immersing themselves in the constricting world of its absence; by extension, they learn to value living by regarding the nerveless, the corrupt, the dead. The hope is finally slender, no more than fiction-deep: a sentence without end. Gaddis cannot sustain a believable counterforce character; there is no Vince Bonali, no Victor Charles, no Oberst Enzian. Rather, Gaddis fashions such a character out of the reader, who closes the book (emerges from the elevator) taught.

> "You said there was no past, present, or future."
> "Only in our verbs. That's the only place we find it."
> (**White Noise, 24**)

When times are bad, observes J. A. K. Gladney in DeLillo's *White Noise*, people feel "compelled to overeat." And Blacksmith, Gladney's town, is "full of obese adults and children, baggypanted, short-legged, waddling" (14). In Blacksmith, a town squatting in the industrial Northeast, times are indeed bad. The town routinely endures the effects of noxious clouds of queer-colored industrial seepage—watery eyes, fouled water, headaches, a metallic taste in the mouth. The local grade school must be evacuated because children complain of eye irritation and nausea. In the course of examining the school, a government agent, clad in a protective Mylex suit, collapses and dies on the second floor. And one January night, following a train derailment involving a tank car carrying the toxic Nyodene D, an ominous black cloud of the contaminant passes glacierlike over the town, endangering townspeople jammed on the highway seeking the refuge of Red Cross shelters. Gladney, exposed to the cloud while he stops to pump gas into the family car, learns from a battery of cadaverous specialists that his two-and-a-half-minute exposure could be sufficient to kill him—it is, however, a matter of time; Nyodene D can survive as long as thirty years.

Yet DeLillo's novel is hardly an angry environmentalist polemic. Indeed, science, technology, the corporate world—all likely villains in such a novel—do not come under any real critical scrutiny. Rather, what DeLillo has fashioned is supremely an apocalyptic tale in its most traditional function—delivering hope to a troubled time. Like Pynchon's novel, *White Noise* poses the disturbing question of how we will live within a world of technological unease, with the imminence of death—

both private and global. All characters in the novel, adults and children alike, share a profound awareness of death. They are all the children of this century: fearful, vulnerable, severed from living because of such profound anxieties.

White Noise works through a series of exposures, not merely Gladney's exposure to the poisonous contaminant. Gladney, an academic, must be educated; he must be pulled away from an isolation, a detachment from living and a fear of dying that borders on the obsessive even before that January night. The process of his exposure, his growing acceptance of his vulnerability from a position of false contentment and security (which recalls the worst self-delusions of Percy's Tom More), exposes in turn language—its artificiality, randomness, illusions, dangers. Gladney, from the start of the novel, is a creature of language. In his most contented moments as an academic, as a loving father and husband, he still senses something greater, something apart from the throb of human activity about him. He tunes at such moments of fear to an irritating noise—he calls it a white noise—that hums incessantly just out of the pale of the familiar, just beyond what can be contained within language. This omnipotent "thing" is for Gladney, and for the generation to which DeLillo speaks, death itself.

Yet, to understand DeLillo's reassuring message, one must first recall that in the study of acoustics, white noise is static, interference that jams the information trying to get through. Lost to living by immuring himself in the insulating protection of language, Gladney reduces dying to a most common noun and trembles before death. It is the message of DeLillo's apocalyptic tale that survival in such an age of technological unease comes from reconnecting with the elemental, sweeping energy of dying, the verb. DeLillo commands his reader to recognize that dying is far more compelling than any language. The movement for Gladney is from language to silence—he ends the novel reconnected with the immediate, gathered with his wife and his youngest son (whose vocabulary has stalled at twenty-five words) at the highway overpass to watch the brilliance of a setting sun. In a world teeming with language, words merely interfere, promise control and finally fail, leaving those who pledge allegiance to their power lost and defenseless. It is silence, the reverent hush that mingles awe, wonder, and dread, that DeLillo offers. The manipulators of language—from Hitler to Stalin to the scientists obtaining data from the rubble of Hiroshima—have made death generic. But dying, DeLillo counsels, is a magnificent power beyond words. To discover its energy, one must stand apart, vulnerable and exposed.

As the novel opens, Gladney is impregnable, protected, happily surrendered to any number of systems, any number of crowds. He relishes the affirmation of his existence confirmed by his bank card. As he inserts his card into the machine and the computer verifies his own computations about the total in his savings, he feels that the system has blessed his life, supported him, approved him. It is for him a "pleasing interaction" (46). He serenely wheels his shopping cart through the local supermarket reassured by the stocked shelves, their neat, orderly system so familiar to him. His academic office is cloistered safely within the halls of another department's building, which is, in turn, at the College-on-the-Hill—itself at the very edge of town. And, as a colleague marvels, Gladney has been able "to evolve an entire system" about his academic specialty, Adolf Hitler, a "structure with countless substructures and interrelated fields of study" (12). Safely immured within this system, Galdney virtually surrenders his self. On the advice of the college's chancellor, Gladney changes his name. A "Jack Gladney" could never be taken seriously as a "Hitler innovator" (16). He invents an extra initial and becomes J. A. K. Gladney. He gains weight, badly needed bulk to fill out his already formidable six-foot frame. He wears thick-framed, dark glasses on campus and grows fond of the academic robes he must wear as a department head. He becomes "the false character that follows the name around" (17). Immediately the reader is alerted to the discrepancy between words and things, between Gladney and his adopted name.

Obsessed with his own mortality, Gladney is strongly attracted to the Wagnerian figure of Hitler, who lived as if he commanded death, who used death on a scale far greater than anyone ever imagined. The crowds jammed into stadiums and into halls during prewar Germany (in scenes from Nazi propaganda films that serve as part of Gladney's introductory lecture in a seminar on fascism) gathered defiantly under mortuary wreaths and the death's-head insignia. En masse, they defied death, exuded strength under death's grimmest symbols. At fifty-one, Gladney can indeed lecture on the appeal of such fascist tyranny. Indeed, Nazism to Gladney is one of language's supreme accomplishments—the cadenced, hypnotic sway of the rally speeches; the chants of soccer-stadium crowds; the Reich's arias and anthems; Hitler's habit of endless monologues and free association; and the prolix, rambling autobiography *Mein Kampf* (which Gladney cradles in his arm like a talisman):

> Crowds came to hear him speak, crowds erotically charged, the masses he once called his only bride. He closed his eyes, clenched his fists as he spoke, twisted his sweat-drenched body, remade his voice as a thrilling weapon. . . . Crowds came to be hypnotized by the voice, the party anthems, the torchlight parades. . . . Many of these crowds were assembled in the name of death. . . . Crowds came to form a shield against their own dying.

> To become a crowd is to keep out death. To break off from the crowd is
> to risk death as an individual, to face dying alone. Crowds came for this
> reason above all others. They were there to be a crowd. (73)

Nazism offers to Gladney what he so desperately needs—a fiction that
pretends strength over death, a creation (and an illusion) sustained by
language.[13] Within a system, surrounded by a crowd, sheltered by language, commanding a role, Gladney exudes contentment. Each Septem-
ber he relishes the return of students to the campus, the parade of
station wagons burdened with things. Such clutter necessarily attracts
him; such a community of like-thinking people reassures him in his role.
After a particularly affective lecture on Hitler and death, Gladney finds
himself surrounded by admiring students and colleagues. Momentarily
safe, he feels invulnerable before death; death is "strictly a professional
matter" (74). At such moments Gladney puts his faith in language; death
becomes a mere noun, a shelter from the harsher reality of death as an
activity, a verb.[14]

Insulated from experience and from himself by language, Gladney can
never be wholly at ease: the thing itself keeps threatening him, reminding him that as long as he cowers behind the flimsy artifice of language
he will feel keenly vulnerable even as he masquerades as invulnerable.[15]
On campus, by day, Gladney successfully resists the fear—he finds identity, security, purpose. Death is within his academic expertise. At home,
he enjoys a measure of domestic bliss. He radiates security as he conducts
his family from the supermarket, his arms laden with full sacks. He
loves Babette, his wife, and talks endlessly of their contentment, their
honesty, their trust. He celebrates Babette as a life-force, a woman handsomely girthed, dependable. At home, by day, Gladney is certain he will
eventually die a small-town death, one that is nonviolent, quiet. DeLillo
marks Gladney early as a father who accepts the responsibility to protect
his loved ones from the truth, from the "something" that "lurked inside
the truth" (8). It is his nature to avoid the thing, to relish shelter. But
the thing will not leave him in peace. At night, Gladney lurches awake,
drenched in a "death sweat" and trembles as the minutes tick off his
electric clock. He reads obituary columns, comparing his age to those
listed. As he flips through the family photograph album, he wonders
whether he or Babette will die first. To be reassured by language is to
be removed, sheltered from authenticity and, consequently, to be convinced of its malevolence. It is to be disconnected, lost to the thing
itself, attached only to words. Absence is relished, codified into language—presence itself is feared. Early in the semester, Gladney accompanies Murray Siskind, a colleague, to a local tourist attraction, the Most

Photographed Barn in America. Murray reminds Gladney that in seeing the barn, positioned as they are from the angle of its photographed image, they are merely maintaining an image, reaffirming the picture of the barn from the same angle as its famous photograph. In essence they never see the barn, merely the image. This surrender to the collective, this distancing, is what DeLillo shatters. Gladney must be exposed directly to the thing, to the vastness. He must strike up an original relationship with a universe that includes living as well as dying. Until that time Gladney frets before death, a word that threatens all his security, all his constructed systems, his various fictions. It is the thing apart. Amid the throbbing bustle of the supermarket, Gladney senses a greater throbbing, a hum outside the supermarket, a noise with a life of its own. When the local school is evacuated, people guess the contamination could have come from ventilation systems, paint and varnish, foam insulation, even cafeteria food; but Gladney points out it may come from something vaster, something "deeper. . . woven into the basic state of things" (35). The thing will not let him go—for all his domestic happiness, he fears "something live[s] in the basement" (27).

DeLillo suggests that if language has provided Gladney some small measure of security, that security is an illusion, an interference, a dodge. Behind closed doors, disrobed, Gladney and Babette discuss at length how best to put themselves in the mood and decide to read pornography, and then discuss which century's pornography would be best. Gladney praises contemporary erotica, letters in skin magazines that detail readers' sexual encounters—the artificial stimulation of language rather than the act of making love. There is the incessant stream of useless information babbling from the television and radio. Television is a symbol for the distancing of language, the loss of immediacy. With its grid of colored dots, the waves and radiation of its signal, television protects its viewers by insulating them. The Gladney family huddles about the nightly news, stuffing themselves with Chinese takeout and wishing every disaster coded on the television could be grander, more cataclysmic. Twentieth-century people, immured within television's grid, suffer from what Alfonse "Fast Food" Stompananto, chairman of the Pop Culture Department, terms "brain fade" (66), so disconnected from experience, so inundated by information and so bombarded by waves and radiation that cataclysm is relished as a break in the monotony. DeLillo suggests that the age of the media has created a demand for language to make experience authentic. After a plane carrying one of Gladney's children plummets several thousand feet before righting itself, the daughter deplanes, petulantly whining that the plane's brush with death apparently did not merit television coverage. Wan and white-faced, other passengers gather about one who tells the story, reliving it, receiving their own experience secondhand.

Long before Gladney's exposure to the vast cloud of Nyodene begins to unsettle his faith in language, DeLillo offers two disturbing anecdotes about the vulnerable who suddenly confront the vastness, caught momentarily with their systems down. The Treadwells, an elderly brother and sister, are lost for four days in the vast, ten-story Village Mall. Confused by the sheer size, forced to scavenge food scraps from trash baskets, the Treadwells wander about the mall. They have lived such insulated lives (no one can believe they actually left their home to go to the mall) that they are defenseless. Indeed, Gladys Treadwell dies from "lingering dread" (99) shortly after the experience. In another example, Dimitrios Cotsakis, who as the college's resident Elvis expert shares similarities with Gladney (Cotsakis is an ex-bouncer who, like Gladney, is a "monolith of thick and wadded flesh" [69]), disappears in the surf off Malibu over the Christmas recess. Despite his bulk and his academic credentials, he is lost in the immensity—much like the Treadwells, who (despite their name) do not tread well in the vastness of the mall. DeLillo warns that those who live by language, those who live sheltered, are finally unprepared for exposure to what language *pretends* to control and contain. When the system collapses, when the pretense fails, they experience either a fear so pure that it is beyond words (as do the passengers on the plane) or succumb to death, to the noun itself.

The exposure of Gladney begins in the "deep interior" (82) of a huge hardware store in the very mall where the Treadwells disappeared. Gladney walks absently among shelves full of things, surrounded by the vibrant hum of language ("English, Hindi, Vietnamese, related tongues" [82]) quite secure. He runs into a colleague, "slim and pale," with a "dangerous grin" (82) who sees Gladney for the first time off campus, without his robes and glasses. Exposed, as it were, Gladney strikes him as being just a "big, harmless, aging, indistinct sort of guy" (83)—the antithesis of his Hitler persona—vulnerable, mortal, and (worse) only *sort* of a guy. Such exposure puts Gladney "in the mood to shop." He immerses himself in the mall, loses himself in the surging crowds of "happy and vivid transaction" (84). In store after store he buys without flinching. He encourages his bewildered children to spend with similar ruthless abandon. He even eats more than usual. Such recklessness merely measures Gladney's vulnerability. Exposed, he heads for a crowd, where (ironically) he feels most in command.

The "airborne toxic event" that moves, shapeless and terrifying, through the town completes Gladney's exposure, forcing him into a showdown with the "thing," raw and powerful, before which his vo-cabulary, his control, his roles prove powerless. He is immeasurably reduced to a vulnerable entity. In turn, each of his shelters collapses before the cloud. First, his self-appointed role as academic fails. During the initial scare, Gladney patiently resists evacuating his family even after the strange cloud is sighted. "I'm not just a college professor. I'm head of a department. I don't see myself fleeing an airborne toxic event. That's for people who live in mobile homes out in the scrubby parts of the county, where the fish hatcheries are" (117). Even though the air-raid siren squawks and police cars move down the street ordering evacuation, Gladney moves his family to the station wagon only after dinner is finished and the table cleared.

Then language fails before the cloud. Gladney's oldest son, Heinrich, stationed with binoculars at a window on the top floor of Gladney's house, listens to the radio as one description after another of the toxic mass fails (109–14). Heinrich quibbles with each radio broadcast. The cloud of vaporized chemicals clearly defies language to encompass it. It grows from "a lot of smoke" to a "feathery plume" to a "black billowing cloud" to a "dark black breathing *thing* of smoke" (italics mine) to a "shapeless growing *thing*" (italics mine). When language finally collapses, the radio resorts to the nerveless jargon of imprecision that will characterize much of the informational output surrounding the chemical cloud. It becomes an airborne toxic event. Language is finally as powerless as the army helicopters that hover about the cloud: urgent, perhaps, but impotent.

As language fails, so in turn does its by-product—information. In the stalled traffic, Gladney nervously punches the radio selector for infor-mation. Symptoms of exposure keep changing. No reliable information about the cloud is available, either from the Mylex-suited government men who try to direct traffic or from the teams supervising the evacua-tion area set up in the abandoned Boy Scout camp outside town. That the evacuation and the toxic event itself occur in January during a messy snowstorm underscores this mangled informational network. It is like watching a television blurred by "snow." The cloud resists. Not only does it grow exponentially, but sudden shifts in the winter winds send it moving without apparent pattern. It is the real, the "dark black breathing thing," vast, shapeless, impervious to any attempts to control it.

Desperate for gasoline, Gladney must leave the protection of his station wagon. (Itself a microcosm of his constructed world, the car is a packed enclosure abuzz with misinformation and disconnected conversation whose inhabitants are alarmed over a menace that hovers just outside and is far larger than the enclosure itself.) As he pumps the gas, he confronts the cloud itself, suddenly looming right before him:

> The enormous dark mass moved like some death ship in a Norse legend, escorted across the night by armored creatures with spiral wings. . . . It was a terrible thing to see, so close, so low, packed with chlorides, benzines, phenols, hydrocarbons, or whatever the precise toxic content. But it was also spectacular, part of the grandness of a sweeping event. . . . Our fear was accompanied by a sense of awe that bordered on the religious. It was surely possible to be awed by the thing that threatens your life, to see it as a cosmic force, so much larger than yourself, more powerful, created by elemental and willful rhythms. This was a death made in a laboratory, defined and measurable, but we thought of it at the time in a simple and primitive way . . . something not subject to control. (127)

For Gladney, the cloud will come to embody what he fears most—death itself. Exposure to the cloud poisons Gladney. Exposed, he begins to die. Death is no longer a fear, a common noun; it is instead a verb, part of a process vast and elemental. He stands there alone (despite his predictable appropriation of the collective "our"), exposed. And connected with something so powerful, Gladney does what he so seldom does in the course of the novel—he feels.

Yet the eerie silence of that encounter quickly dissipates into the babel of the evacuation camp. There language reigns. Heinrich, so surly and withdrawn at home, blossoms at the camp. Gladney hears him, "speaking in a new-found voice," the focal point of a cluster of people listening apprehensively to what Heinrich knows from high-school chemistry about Nyodene derivative (which he pronounces with "unseemly relish" [130]). A family of Jehovah's Witnesses calmly passes out tracts about the end of the world. The father tells Gladney that he can feel Armageddon in his bones (135). For them the chemical cloud is an omen. Safely within their language, encoded within their tracts, the event has no wonder, no dread, no awe, no feeling at all. Like Heinrich's deadpan recitation of the terrible potency of the Nyodene, there is no ambiguity to the event—the father talks about the end with "matter-of-fact" earnestness (137). Uncertain about his exposure to Nyodene, Gladney stands in line to talk with technicians who are taking data from people exposed to the cloud. Here language proves its most sinister. The gaunt young man—yet another menacing death's-head type—tapping the keys on the computer console (he blandly tells Gladney that any man is merely the sum of his data) offers only mystifying uninformation to the apprehensive Gladney:

> "I tapped into your history. I'm getting bracketed numbers with pulsing stars."

"What does that mean?"

"You'd rather not know . . . ."

"Am I going to die?"

"Not as such . . . . It's not a question of words. It's a question of years. We'll know more in fifteen years. In the meantime we definitely have a situation." (140)

Not surprisingly, Gladney desperately tries to humor this spectral figure, answering each question with forced informality and longing for his academic robes and his glasses.

Exposed, feeling that he is dying, his faith in language shaken, his academic superstructure tottering, Gladney searches anew for some control and begins his ruinous pursuit of Dylar, a bogus drug promoted in supermarket tabloids that is intended to treat the fear of death chemically.[16] It is another illusion, again prepared by language (the enticing advertisement), intended to shelter Gladney from the direct experience he so desperately needs, and designed to reenforce his Hitleresque illusion of control over what is indeed uncontrollable. His tutor during this critical period of adjustment to his exposure is Murray Siskind, who counsels him during looping walks around the tree-lined campus (hence, doubly insulated) on how to handle death. In the latter half of the book, Murray emerges as DeLillo's Mephistophelian figure, a master manipulator of language and argumentation, a supreme theoretician who talks glibly, effortlessly, with an easy cynicism and whose philosophy of death is at once cruel, treacherous, and supremely dangerous. It is a measure of Gladney's desperation that he comes to be so mesmerized by Murray's conversation.

Long before Gladney's exposure, Murray slinks about the scenery of the novel, suspiciously satanic. Murray takes Gladney to the "Most Photographed Barn in America," yet celebrates the spiritual surrender implied by the place and seems "immensely pleased" by the removal from experience implied by the ceaseless clicking of cameras, the postcards, the slides. Collective perception—being in a crowd celebrating the sign rather than the thing—is for Murray "a religious experience" (12). Murray is by trade a sportswriter, an occupation suggesting not only a livelihood based on language, but one particularly prone to stylization and torrential cliches. He is a visiting lecturer from New York City, a brutal place of heat and smoke ("Heat. That's what cities mean to me" [10]) from which he is glad to have escaped, suggesting a devil escaping hell. Like Vulcan, Murray insists he is quite happy and at home in Blacksmith.

Stoop-shouldered, with dense, menacing eyebrows and wisps of hair (hornlike) about his ears, a Jew who does not react at all to Gladney's academic calling (indeed, he praises Gladney for the imaginative effort of creating his own Hitler), Murray is unpleasantly sensual, attached to things. In the grocery store, he insists on sniffing what he buys. He leers at Babette, clutching an arm about her as he sidles up to her in the store. Forsaking the complications of love, he indulges instead carnal lust: at the evacuation camp, he arranges for services with a collection of stranded hookers. He is a consummate performer: Gladney remarks that Murray's stiff little beard seems pasted on; Murray puffs a pipe and wears corduroy jackets because they suggest teacher to him; he admits to working on his vulnerability, which he finds an effective pose with most women. He admires the innocence of television, celebrates car crashes as evidence of American can-do optimism. A master of language (his conversation is pithy, epigrammatic), Murray is finally the embodiment of white noise, offering to Gladney only death itself. Surrounded by the shelves of colorful packaging in the grocery store, Murray fills his cart with generic food, admiring the plain, white packaging.[17]

It is about death that Murray talks at length. He plays the role of tempter. Indeed, at one point he admits to favoring complicated women (Babette, who resists not only his wolfish leers, but eventually his advice to Gladney) and simple men (his disciple Gladney). Weeks after the exposure, walking about the fringes of campus (appropriately, near a condominium where birds keep flying helplessly into plate-glass windows), Murray succeeds finally in convincing Gladney of the soundness of his notions about death. The scene is rendered almost entirely in dialogue, in language. Murray argues emphatically that in a technological age, death is virtually omnipotent. Nothing is stronger, not even love. Moderns must fear it—those who deny it are lying to themselves. The knowledge of it robs life, renders it incomplete, and reduces love of life to a quivering anxiety. Humans must therefore repress the fear of death. Repression, then, becomes the natural language of the species. Murray continues to argue that until death, humanity deals with this repression by indulging gorgeous evasions and great escapes, fictions, constructs of language, lies, diversions. Civilization itself is just such a purposeless evasion. The eloquent, persuasive argument climaxes with his theory of a way to control death:

"I believe...there are two kinds of people in the world. Killers and diers. Most of us are diers.... We let death happen. We lie down and die. But think what it's like to be a killer. Think how exciting it is, in theory, to kill a person in direct confrontation. If he dies, you cannot. To kill him is to gain life-credit. The more people you kill, the more credit you store up." (290)

To kill is to live. The logical extension of Murray's theory accounts for the twentieth-century horrors of Verdun, Auschwitz, Dresden, Hiroshima, My Lai, and any one of hundreds of despotic, totalitarian regimes. Naturally, Murray distances himself from such moral accountability (it is, he reminds Gladney, only a theory exchanged between academics). He dangles such a theory before Gladney, who is desperate indeed to be fooled and decides to try another role—killer. At the same highway overpass where later Gladney will move toward his closing redemption, he and Murray watch not the sunset, but the cars shooting by, and there Murray completes the temptation:

> "Are you a killer or a dier, Jack?"
> "You know the answer to that. I've been a dier all my life."
> "What can you do about it?"
> "What can a dier do? Isn't it implicit in his makeup that he can't cross over?"
> "Let's think about that. . . ." (292)

By the time they part (appropriately, in front of the campus library) the temptation has succeeded. Gladney begins to carry a gun ("a little bitty thing but it shoots real bullets" [253]) left to him by his dying father-in-law during a visit to Gladney's house. Gladney keeps it in his desk on campus, relishing the power it gives him. He pities those about him, the unarmed.

Even as Gladney moves toward this illusion of control and dark embrace of death (he will decide to kill Willie Mink, the man who dispensed Dylar to Babette), DeLillo provides a countermovement— Babette's, away from her desperate faith in Dylar. As her running clothes and her painful workouts up and down the college-stadium steps testify, Babette lives certain (at the outset of the novel) that life must be fundamentally correctable, that the elemental conditions are conducive to analysis and control (hence, her class for the elderly on correct posture and her promise to teach another class on good eating and drinking habits). Approaching midlife, like her husband, she lives in constant anxiety. Death terrifies her to the point that she bargains her body to become part of the Dylar experimenting program. She is attracted by the tabloid ad for a way to control, even correct, death itself by treating not the fact, but the fear. Indeed, Babette pops a Dylar tablet during the evacuation, telling her husband it is a "Life Saver" (134).

Yet Babette comes to realize that Dylar cannot work. The irony is that Gladney, the consummate creature of language, abandons his naive faith in his "full-souled woman," his "lover of daylight," his "life-force," because he cannot forgive her fear of death. It is a betrayal, a lie, far worse than her adultery. He abandons Babette at the very moment she is moving past the lie of Dylar and could be the most good to him—the authentic life-force he needs. She tells him there is no medicine for what ails them both. Death is more than a neuron response that can be addressed with Dylar's speedy relief, more than a chemical imbalance, more, in short, than a noun. She tells him that Murray's theory—that repression of death is natural—is false, mechanical, outdated. Hers is a profoundly humanistic observation, one in harmony with the movement of the book itself toward the closing scene at the highway overpass. Yet, it is a message that Gladney rejects out of hand. Babette, calling Dylar "Fool's Gold" (209), forsakes the illusion of protection and moves toward a reconnection with the authentic. Willing, it would seem, to accept the fundamental uncorrectability of some things, she begins to live without the crushing burden of death that so distorts Gladney's perception. After her sobering experience with Dylar, she indulges two habits: listening to talk radio and spending time with her youngest child, Wilder. Talk radio suggests the uselessness of language, a saturation of meaningless babble, a recognition of its profound nonsense. But, supremely, there is Wilder, with his stalled vocabulary and almost mystical silence, who gives Babette the help she needs to accept the process of dying by allowing her the experience of living. Staying active helps, she tells Gladney, but "Wilder helps more" (263).[18] Educated to the lie of language, she even accepts Wilder's wordlessness: "I don't want him to talk. The less he talks, the better" (264).

For Gladney, however, the cure for his exposure must come from the determination to play killer, to become (by murdering Willie Mink) a small-scale Hitler, killing to live. His journey to Mink's seedy motel becomes a pathetic attempt to defy limits, laws, rules. To get to Germantown, he steals a neighbor's car (the keys, however, are in the ignition); he races through a red light (at a deserted intersection); he refuses to yield when merging onto the highway; he charges through a tollgate (the toll is a mere quarter). Yet, he feels himself lighter than air, defying even the laws of gravity. In his head he concocts one scenario after another about the showdown: he will demand the Dylar, then shoot Mink, then set up the shooting to look like a suicide. One elegant plot after another, one fiction after another.

He finds Willie Mink, a pathetic figure in Budweiser shorts, slouched before a television, ingesting fistfuls of Dylar, his eyes half-closed, his speech rambling and incoherent. Still Gladney feels power, "looming, dominant, gaining life-power, storing up life-credit" (312). He fancies himself Death; he can hear only "a noise, faint, monotonous, white" (306)—"White noise everywhere" (310). (Indeed, Willie Mink remarks on how pale Gladney looks by the light of the television screen.) All channels jammed, Gladney hears only death. And when he does shoot Mink, it is supremely an act of language, the reverberations of his revolver more an assault of nouns: "I fired the gun, the weapon, the pistol, the firearm, the automatic" (312).

As the novel has warned all along, even here Gladney's marvelous system—his scenario—must collapse. Hardly dead, the dazed Willie Mink manages to shoot Gladney in the wrist as Gladney positions his own gun in Mink's hand to set up the suicide. "The world collapsed inward, all those vivid textures and connections buried in mounds of ordinary stuff" (313). One system shot, so to speak, Gladney resorts to building another, a new lie, a new pretense, a new role. Feeling a rush of compassion and remorse, he abandons the role of killer to become humanitarian rescuer. He drags the wounded man to his car, administers a hasty mouth-to-mouth, and drives him to a shelter for medical attention—an act he fancies redemptive, something "large and grand and scenic" (314). He promotes himself as hero, feels his humanity soaring, revels in his virtue while all the time murmuring steadily to the dazed Willie that Willie had in fact shot first and had wounded both himself and Gladney. Like a good Hitler, he hides from his act behind the protective shield of language.

When the nun at the confinement center shows no interest in listening to his story, Gladney is puzzled. It is indeed ironic that this nun, an immigrant German named Sister Hermann Marie, will oversee Gladney's final exposure and destroy his persistent faith in language, leaving him to stand vulnerable before the thing itself. As the wounded Gladney looks about the clinic, he feels once again a warm sense of security—amused and reassured by "the merry sight" (316) of the ancient nuns in full, pre–Vatican II regalia moving slowly through the halls, rosaries swinging from their arthritic hands and dangling from their belts. He focuses particularly on a framed picture on the wall of a young, vigorous Jack Kennedy holding hands with John XXIII in heaven (a "partly cloudy place" [316]). Why not believe in such a wonderful place, he thinks, and he commits himself once again to a sign, once removed from the real. (The nun tosses the revolver Gladney hands to her into a drawer filled with knives and handguns, a suggestion of the surrounding neighborhood; Gladney prefers the illusion of finding a little haven, a little heaven.) It is another fiction, another deception. He feels relieved surrounded by nuns, angels of mercy, and these nuns particularly, running their haven of comfort surrounded by the urban blight of Germantown. He has found the refuge he has searched for all along.

As Sister Hermann Marie wordlessly tends to Gladney's wrist, he amuses himself by speaking German to her, counting and then naming objects in the emergency room—a cozy little language game. He playfully asks her questions about heaven and angels. At that point the nun forcefully blasts Gladney for his naive faith in such an idea—angels, clouds, heaven. "Do you think we are stupid?" (317). Gladney is rudely shaken. The nun, who speaks a harsh, broken English, is finally so annoyed at Gladney that she sprays him with her native German, telling him coldly that belief is for fools, the "dumb" (319). She tells Gladney that her belief is a role well played, that "to abandon such beliefs completely" would threaten the race (318). Someone, she says, "must appear to believe"; "we are your lunatics. . . . We are your fools" (319). That this nun can so readily separate what she believes from her role as nun stuns and angers Gladney. "You're a nun. Act like one" (320). Here, however, is a nun who quite resolutely will not be a nun, a thing that radically resists the constraint of the word for that thing. Sister Hermann Marie represents a radical dislocation of the word from the thing. Gladney, left alone and (appropriately) wounded, returns to his house stripped of language. Like Babette after her disillusionment over Dylar, Gladney turns for comfort to his children. Now in silence, he watches them sleep, "fumbling through their dreams," and comes to terms with the implications of Sister Hermann Marie. The wound has given him "heightened pulse" and a resolution to seek the sunset:

> I got into bed next to Babette, fully dressed except for my shoes, somehow knowing she wouldn't think it strange. But my mind kept racing. I couldn't sleep. After a while I went down to the kitchen to sit with a cup of coffee, feel the pain in my wrist, the heightened pulse.
> There was nothing to do but wait for the next sunset, when the sky would ring like bronze. (321)

In many ways, DeLillo's novel is a novel about children. Gladney's house teems with children from his and his wife's previous marriages. In an artificial world of illusory control through the manipulation of language, a world of adults finally cowering beneath flimsy shelters fearing the onslaught of the real, DeLillo offers children as a striking metaphor for that original, ever shifting, joyous experience of the immediate world. Unafraid, unhesitating, independent, marvelously free of the burdens and deceptions of language, children are bound only to the thing itself. They maneuver about their little worlds free of limits, certain that tomorrow will come. A most curious combination of tenacity, innate power, unflappable tranquility, and unquenchable curiosity, children even appear to revel in helplessness, squealing with delight, for instance, while being tickled or picked up and dangled above the ground. Lost to the significance of measured time, the child is everything. Unlike the adults who cluster about the most-photographed barn in America, children make original signs, ones they hang on telephone poles around Blacksmith announcing a search for lost dogs and cats (4).

Yet, in Gladney's house, there is something terribly amiss. Sadly, his children all talk like adults: they speak cleverly; they are well read; they are expert arguers. The children's voices are heard mouthing the terrifying facts about carcinogens; the dangers of caffeine; data on the average life expectancy, on radiation exposure, on toxic contamination, and on drug abuse. They are children inundated with the adult fears of the technological age. Fascinated by television, afflicted with terminal "brain fade," they rush to see the footage of a plane crash repeated in slow motion by the evening news. Educated to the jargon of the late-twentieth-century technology, they are strangely unchildlike. They know the dangers of sunlight, air, food, water, and sex. The natural world has been taken from them. And their awareness draws them toward the fears of their parents. Afraid of living, unaware of dying, taught only the grim reality of endings (both sudden and violent and drawn out and painful), these children simply know death.

Heinrich, for instance, seldom leaves his room, as insulated as his father at the College-on-the-Hill. He corresponds with a sniper on death row and defends the convict, understands his need to fire on people indiscriminately. (Babette fears that he will die in a "barricaded room, spraying hundreds of rounds of automatic fire across an empty mall before the SWAT teams come for him" [22]). His hairline is receding. At fourteen, he worries about it, pondering whether his classmates will think he is undergoing chemotherapy. He calmly explains to his family the cycle of exploding stars that will one day doom earth. He discounts emotions explaining them as complex responses in the neurological system, matters of "brain chemistry" (45). Perhaps most distressing— even more so than his strange elation over the possibility of widespread havoc wreaked by the cloud, which he tracks with his binoculars—is Heinrich's sober disavowal of his senses. At one point, while rain slides down the car windshield, Heinrich argues his father out of being able to prove that it is actually raining. Unlike the child who traditionally revels in the outdoors, Heinrich has been educated to doubt it, to comprehend its potential dangers, to protect himself from its poisons. He knows, for example, exposure to the sun as a bombardment of low-level radiation. He prefers his bedroom dark, save for the light of the television. Denise, a "hard-nosed kid of 11," watches with alarm her mother's habit of smoking and taking diet pills and warns her of the danger of cancer from both. Disturbed by Babette's Dylar, Denise lugs about a copy of the *Physicians' Desk Reference* to determine what her mother is taking, educated to assume that she is an addict. It is Denise who must alert Gladney that in pumping gas he has suffered some exposure. Like her father with his thick-framed glasses and Heinrich with his ever-present hooded sweatshirt, Denise sports a green visor while indoors or out, insulating and distancing herself. Even young Steffie, who loves the smell of burning toast and enjoys sitting for long periods in her own dirty bath water, watches evening-news footage of a volcano and an earthquake with total absorption.

These are the educated children, lost and afraid. Yet DeLillo does offer one child in this family who is still able to respond to the elemental world with the vulnerability, wonder, and even fear that marks an original relationship with the universe: the wordless Wilder, Babette's youngest (and hence not related at all to Gladney), who with his dopey face and "great round head" suggests "some primitive clay figurine or idol" (242). Wilder's very name suggests a movement beyond limits, beyond the constructs of language. In a novel that teems with people whose names are often devices or cheap dodges (Gladney saddles his first-born with the ponderous Teutonic name Heinrich because he believes such a grand name will shield and protect his son; Gladney adjusts his own name for professional reasons; Babette's name is shortened to the nonsensical "Baba"), Wilder is his name—unafraid, venturesome, and strongly independent. The thing is word exactly.

Even before he becomes a primary focus in the novel's closing chapter, Wilder is glimpsed occasionally, peripherally, at peace in the Gladney household maelstrom. During the chaos of a family lunch, for instance, Wilder sits still and serene as Buddha, surrounded by the rubble of strewn food and wrappers and the incessant din of the family conversations. During the airborne toxic event, Wilder sleeps in his mother's arms. Yet, despite his "dopey countenance," Wilder exhibits evidence of a "complex intelligence" (78), an awareness of a wider perspective, which sets him apart from the Gladney household. For instance, he stares steadily into the oven window—a grisly habit, given Gladney's academic interests. He stares quietly into pots of churning, boiling water. Unlike the other children educated already to prefer the word rather than the thing, Wilder is confused when the family watches Babette on a local cable-television program. Wilder sobs quietly, tracing his mother's features on the color screen, unable to separate the thing from its image. During a most disturbing afternoon, Wilder cries for nearly seven hours straight. His crying is not simple blubbering, Gladney says, but a mourning, a desolation that seems to come from a profound depth of sadness, a keening, a ululation.[19] Wilder communicates in a most basic unit of nonlanguage. The worried parents rush him off to a doctor who, helpless before such simple, raw emotion, prescribes a cliche—bed rest and aspirin. Gladney tries to distract Wilder by letting him sit in his lap and pretend to drive the station wagon. But Wilder does not stop crying. Unlike his father, who is quite content to pretend control, Wilder is not so easily duped. When Wilder finally stops, entirely on his own, Gladney remarks that it is as if he had returned from

> a period of wandering in some remote and holy place, in sand barrens or snowy ranges—a place where things are said, sights are seen, distances reached which we in our ordinary toil can only regard with the mingled reverence and wonder we hold in reserve for feats of the most sublime and difficult dimensions. (79)

It is the place, in fact, where Gladney will find himself finally: at the highway overpass, watching with reverent silence the bronze of the setting sun. Wordless Wilder had been there long before.

Such are the antipodes of DeLillo's apocalyptic temper: Gladney's insulation and consequent angst and death sweats, his keen sense of "deft acceleration" (18); and Wilder's naive celebration of each sensation, the "aimless drift of days" (18) with only an unarticulated sense of some deeper level to such happy existence. Of course, neither offers a solution; neither performs the most exacting function of apocalyptic literature—the extension of genuine hope to a troubled people. Gladney is certainly schooled to realize that systems built to protect are frail shelters, that every system changes, the people as consummate systems builders are forever vulnerable. Educated in the difficult lesson of dying, Gladney makes the journey to the overpass. Wilder, sadly, cannot remain the romantic icon, the untutored child, for naivete leaves him unprotected, reckless as well as aimless, drifting without realizing the immense bounty that surrounds him. The solution is carefully worked out in the closing chapter when Wilder sets off on his plastic tricycle to pedal furiously across a crowded highway that runs behind the Gladney house and Gladney is seen at the highway overpass at sunset. Gladney comes to terms with the thing that thrives beyond the claustrophobic limits of the systems he has lived within so carefully; and Wilder, who manages during a heart-stopping passage to cross the highway, ends up wailing helplessly, his tricycle upset in the highway embankment. As his father has moved to a hesitating knowledge of what lies beyond rules and control, the infant Wilder must be moved to his first knowledge of limits. It is, indeed, the running away from the very knowledge that has so distorted Gladney's fifty-one years of anxiety and death sweats.

Gladney is a rejuvenated man in the closing chapter. Fear of death has been replaced with an emotional knowledge that dying and living are merely different words for the identical elemental universal process. Only death can be harnessed by language, caged within systems, used by people. Dying cannot be embraced with the codes of language any more than living. Gladney sheds his insulating robes and stands at the overpass (appropriately with Babette and the newly indoctrinated Wilder) systemless, wordless. The vignette at the highway overpass is a marvelous artifact of hope offered to DeLillo's reader. Indeed, the sunset watchers are reminiscent of the water gazers in the opening chapter of *Moby-Dick*—those who, in uncertain secular times, are hungry for that religious experience, that connection with the vast and elemental, that sacramental exhilaration that mingles wonder and fear.[20]

The congregation gathers at the overpass rain or shine to look westward, to be a part of the anticipation that "tends toward silence" (324). DeLillo deliberately plays on images of the religious converging on a healing shrine, the middle-aged, the elderly, the "handicapped and the helpless," "twisted by disease" (325). Here no one speaks; no radios blare. They go to the overpass to watch the sunsets. Gladney admits to a confusing, ambiguous response—a fear and an elation compounded with joy and anticipation. It is in sharp contrast indeed to Gladney's previous religious experience, as he watched the black cloud move past him like a Norse death ship. He has moved from that cloud now to the sunset, one that is burning off with marvelous energy the residue of the chemical cloud. "The spirit of those evenings [spent watching the sunsets]" is "hard to describe" (324). It is finally beyond the banal categorizations of language.

Gladney stands finally exposed, watching as "something golden falls," even as Mylex-suited men still monitor the town and his own doctor waits to read for him the results of tests, "eager to see the progress of his death" (325). Gladney connects, communes in a silence DeLillo offers as the closest that those in the technological age can come to authentic prayer. Like traditional prayer, this silence is a measure of human connection with something greater, a recognition of something vaster. In the technological age where even nuns deride with vehement disgust talk about heaven and saints, at the overpass one achieves that necessary communion with the elemental. In his own modest way, DeLillo offers a valiant secular peroration on a par with the energy and vision of John the Divine.

That reassurance is finally the highest achievement of the apocalyptic tradition. *White Noise* addresses a people in difficult times, a people enervated by helplessness, a people so death-ridden as to question the very premise of their own survival. It addresses, in short, a hopeless age. It is a reminder that any apocalypse—ecological catastrophe, nuclear holocaust, even the private and painful process of individual death—can devolve into a manipulation of language, an illusion of ordering an energy far stronger than any vocabulary. As Gaddis despairingly notes, the apocalypse, enclosed and ultimately finite, is self-serving artificiality, self-important rhetoric, and, most dangerous of all, self-generated doom.

To such a death-ridden people, DeLillo offers a tough lesson, a tough avenue to hope. He performs, perhaps unknowingly, the healing most particular to traditional apocalyptic literature.[21] He reminds a people, anchored in time, of a scale far beyond the measure of minutes, days, years (which so profoundly frightens Gladney). He reconnects that people with the elemental, in which endings are simply a phase of living itself. It is a difficult lesson, one easily mistaken for passivity, one out of sync with the contemporary urgency toward control. Without a traditional God able to intervene and to right history, DeLillo takes his characters to the overpass, to bathe them in the bronze light of something universal, to remind them of the finite, deceptive nature of human systems. He can offer living, or more precisely a reconnecting with the magnificent energy of a living cosmos, one barely tinged by "mighty" technology. In a novel throbbing with noise and tense with anxieties that are themselves endlessly debated, the crowd at the overpass is calm, strong, and silent.

In uncanny ways, the rejuvenation of Gladney, his journey to that "sublime and difficult dimension," summarizes the frustrations and the triumphs of characters in the novels discussed in this study. Unlike Vonnegut's pseudoapocalyptics John/Jonah and Billy Pilgrim, both of whom are defeated by history and measured time, Gladney finds his way out of that simple dimension. There, history is a lighted fuse, and every person's life a grim, cadenced shuffle toward death. At the overpass, Gladney reconciles himself to a dimension that defies the simple yardstick of minutes, hours, and days. In discovering dying, Gladney marvels at the miracle of living. Trapped within the web of history, John/Jonah and Billy Pilgrim (and, more recently, Vonnegut himself) merely reenforce what Gladney can overcome—the banal certainty of death.

Not only does Gladney point a way out of the defeatism of Vonnegut's angry pseudoapocalypticism, but in Gladney's awakening to the cosmos suggested by his hushed response to the sunset, he opens himself to the same sort of energy, of vastness, that Tom More in *Love in the Ruins* denies himself. Like Percy the prophet, who offers the acknowledgment of God as remedy for humanity's self-generated apocalyptic dilemma, DeLillo reconciles his character with the eternal. Although DeLillo cannot make the exacting theological leap to faith that Percy prescribes and finally moves More toward in *The Thanatos Syndrome,* his character does respond to a vastness beyond the pale of human control. In this respect, Gladney is on a par with Percy's Victor Charles, whose steadfast belief in Jesus provides his life direction despite the apocalyptic landscape. DeLillo acknowledges what Percy underscores—hope in the apocalyptic age of technological anxiety begins just beyond the limit of human pretense to omnipotence. For both Percy and DeLillo, survival begins with surrender.

Finally, Gladney moves away from the protection of his assorted refuges—his role playing, his academic posturings, his paranoid pleasure in the accumulation of things, his escapes into language—to stand at the overpass acknowledging vulnerability before the awesome reminder that dying is as glorious a process as the sunset that shatters the sky into bronze. Unlike Coover's Justin Miller, who denies authentic experience and opts for the pleasant inanity of role playing, Gladney moves beyond the absurd costuming of his academic robes and his role as a poor-man's Hitler. Unlike Pynchon's Slothrop, a paranoid who shares Gladney's marked obsession with death but concedes the vastness of the Zone and refuses its invitation to forsake the labyrinth, Gladney comes to terms with a universe far beyond the petty pretense of even his consummate skill at language. Much like Gaddis who warns of the danger of staying within the labyrinth to the point where insulation becomes trap, where life itself (from private to global) is threatened, DeLillo has his character, Gladney, break free. Gladney joins Coover's Vince Bonali and Pynchon's Oberst Enzian in the movement toward authentic experience, and in doing so, refutes the destruction so grimly accepted by Coover's and Pynchon's failures and stands at the overpass much like Vince Bonali under the spring sky studded with stars, or like Enzian bowed in modest prayer. These characters, Gladney supremely, offer the resilient message of hope delivered in the manner of the most sublime artifacts in the traditional apocalyptic genre.

This may seem an awesome burden to place on a novel that deals at times so comically with the dilemma of adjusting to death in the latter days of the twentieth century. But DeLillo addresses a world in fear, a world driven either to a numbed, studied apathy or to a desperate faith in the very people—technocrats, scientists, and politicians—responsible for the apocalyptic anxiety. He addresses a people certain that death will finally win, a people demoralized by a century that first created death on a scale that stunned the imagination and then proceeded to render it both omnipotent and meaningless by an insanity of genocides. This is the legacy of the twentieth century.

To such a world, DeLillo refuses to resist closures, to tremble before the implications of ending—to do so would place him servile to death. To a world as compulsively schizoid as Gladney's day/night personae— a world of consummate organization, technological marvels, and computer miracles undergirded nevertheless by weapons of species extermination and the queer nonlanguage that can (and will) justify their use—DeLillo, with a compassion in keeping with the most eloquent apocalyptics, ushers his perhaps resisting reader to the overpass. He encourages the reader to journey, like Wilder, to a vast and holy place and there to stand without flinching before the magnificent evidence of limitations, the unnerving, awesome beauty of mortality and vulnerability that from the Bronze Age to the nuclear age has been humanity's perplexing yet finally reassuring position within the cosmos.

Notes

1. It is nearly impossible to underestimate the impact of apocalyptic thinking that shaped the literary response to the Reagan era. The literature of endtimes found expression in novels, short stories, nonfiction, periodical press, film, and stage. Works far too numerous to catalogue here treated the themes of nuclear anxiety and apocalyptic certainty and, in many cases, worked such awareness into a gospel of faith typical of the apocalyptic temper. A selection of titles may help.

Many novels directly confronted the possibility of a world silvered into nuclear ash: *Time Capsule* (1987) by Mitch Berman; *This is the Way the World Ends* (1986) by James Morrow; *Waiting for the End of the World* (1985) by Madison Smartt Bell. Other works examined the legacy of Hiroshima generally and of Los Alamos specifically, including *Countrymen of Bones* (1983) by Robert Olen Butler; *Shelter* (1986) by Marty Asher; *The Accident* (1955, reprinted by Penguin in 1985) by Dexter Masters; *Stallion Gate* (1986) by Martin Cruz Smith; *The Organ Builder* (1988) by Robert Cohen. In addition, commemorative reprints of critical works appeared in the decade: Hersey's *Hiroshima,* Miller's *Canticle for Leibowitz.* And Ibuse's *Black Rain* appeared in translation in 1985 to coincide with the American observance of the fortieth anniversary of Hiroshima. Three collections of short stories, many of them crude experiments in the cataclysmic imagination, appeared in 1985 alone: *Countdown to Midnight* (edited by H. Bruce Franklin); *Beyond Armageddon: Twenty-One Sermons to the Dead* (edited by Walter Miller, Martin Greenberg, and Donald I. Fine); and *Afterwar* (edited by Janet Morris). *The Northwest Review* and the *New England Review and Bread Loaf Quarterly* devoted special issues to confronting the nuclear age. An anthology of thoughtful essays edited by Valerie Andrews, Robert Bosnak, and Karen Walter Goodwin (*Facing Apocalypse,* 1987) explored this country's coming-to-terms with nuclear weaponry and its nearly incomprehensible threat. Two extensive historical studies traced the development of the bomb itself: Peter Wyden's *Day One* (1984) and Richard Rhodes's encyclopedic *The Making of the Atomic Bomb* (1986). Otto Friedrich offered important historic continuities in which to examine this nuclear response in *The End of the World* (1982). Popular periodicals contributed as well: *Atlantic* ("Waiting for the End," June 1982); *Vogue* ("Nuclear Visions," March 1984); *Psychology Today* ("Psychology and Armageddon," May 1982); as well as special issues by both *Time* and *Newsweek* examining the bomb on the fortieth anniversary of Hiroshima. Films—apart from those listed in the chapter—included Marshall Brickman's *The Manhattan Project,* John Badham's *Wargames,* and Mike Newell's *Amazing Grace and Chuck.* And dramatic expressions, most prominently Arthur Kopit's *The End of the World* (1986) and Lee Blessing's *A Walk in the Woods* (1988), contributed as well to the decade's dialogue. Even Billy Graham published his own response to the times—*Approaching Hoofbeats* (1983).

2. The connections that link the new right conservative political machine with the rhetoric of traditional fundamentalist religion are examined most revealingly by A. G. Mojtabai's 1986 study *Blessed Assurance: At Home with the Bomb in Amarillo, Texas.* By examining the lives of people who work at Amarillo's Pantex plant, where (deep in the Bible Belt) all nuclear weapons in the United States are assembled, that study works on the double meaning implied by the title—the "blessed assurance" of God's elect at the end of the world and the "blessed assurance" that God will deliver America from its foes.

3. Listing these works of the cataclysmic imagination by title would merely duplicate the impressive cataloguing accomplished by Brians in his 1987 bibliography. Mention might be made of *Warday,* which was a more thoughtful contribution to this genre and topped best-seller lists during 1985. That work, by Whitney Streiber and James Kunetka, takes as its premise the authors' journey across a nation left in disarray by nuclear exchange. The writing is gripping and the command of nuclear capabilities impressive enough to render the portrait unnervingly real.

4. The following lengthy analysis of the elements of Gothic fiction is culled at least in part from the work of Linda Bayer-Berenbaum and David Punter. The reader is directed to their fine works for a more complete documentation of these Gothic elements.

5. Punter uses John Hawkes as the exemplary twentieth-century Gothicist intent on alienating the reader from the text.

6. The carpenter's Gothic style is crucial to Gaddis's novel. The style, a sort of domesticated Gothic, came into popularity in the mid- and late-nineteenth century in America, where the invention of the jigsaw and other handy tools led to a Gothic realized in the relative ease of woodworking rather than the laborious process of stonecutting (Pierson, 419–20). The carpenter's Gothic style was noted for its inventiveness; each cottage or house exhibited a certain individuality, as fanciful and as sinuous as the designer wanted it to be. The style is marked by a decided tendency toward decoration (hence, the assumption that Gaddis here is involved with the intricacies of construction and the pleasure of the edifice). It is a style designed from the outside, with a view to how it looks rather than with a concern for the inside arrangement of rooms. Gaddis works the idea with his use of dialogue to reveal characters who are known only through the facade of what they say. That each character here fashions his or her own carpenter's Gothic (decorative fiction) is part of the plan. That such Gothic work was scorned as a poor-man's Gothic, a cheap reductionist use of Gothic itself, also works, since Gaddis goes about undercutting the efforts of his "artists." And, of course, there is the carpenter's Gothic aspect of the novel's parody of *Jane Eyre*. Indeed, the image of a carpenter's Gothic architect working in wood to copy an edifice originally built in stone suggests something of Gaddis's intention in parodying the classic Gothic novel.

7. To her credit, Cynthia Ozick, in her review published in the *New York Times Book Review,* accurately defines "plot" here as prey to Gaddis's larger intention. "Plot is what Mr. Gaddis travesties and teases and two-times and swindles" (18).

8. In keeping with the motif of carpenter's Gothic, however, Liz is moved not by the novel, but by the film (secondhand Gothic, as it were)—the 1935 version that heightened the Gothicism of Charlotte Brontë's original, highly moral novel.

9. To understand something of this rejuvenation, one should note that earlier in the novel, Liz watched as a gang of boys played a gruesome version of baseball using a stick and a mottled dead dove as a ball.

10. Although Gaddis is not given to frequent interviews, a suggestion of his political awareness can be heard in two sources. In remarks included in the Peter Prescott review of *Carpenter's Gothic* in *Newsweek,* Gaddis mentions the danger of the current patriotic fervor. He labels Reagan a "president who uses dumb, nine-year old phrases like, 'We're going to make them say Uncle'." Further, he indicates that although Vietnam is more central to the plot and Africa more involved in the novel's geography, the novel itself is "really partly about Central America. Stupidity and sentimental values are guiding us in Central America right now." A more extensive articulation of Gaddis's anger can be studied in his 1981 *Harper's* essay "The Rush for Second Place," in which he decries the American loss of courage and foresight and closes by reminding readers that monumental stupidity could leave humanity left to sing "Yes, We Have No Mananas" (39).

11. Among other topical references in Gaddis's novel: the shooting down of Senator Teakell's plane suggests the downing of the KAL flight 007 carrying congressman Larry McDonald; Paul shoots to death a would-be mugger, Bernhard Goetz style; the American interest in African relief; the emerging telecommunications ministries of the new right; the Creation/evolution showdowns in southern courts; and Reagan's reference to the Soviet Union as "the evil empire," which is quoted in one of the headlines announcing the decision to commence a nuclear strike.

12. See the fine analysis by Joseph S. Salemi, "To Soar in Atonement: Art as Expiation in Gaddis's *The Recognitions*."

13. DeLillo works deliberately to make an association between the German language and death. Because of the legacy of Nazism, German seems a proper language of death in the twentieth century. It is appropriate that at the opening of the novel, Gladney is deciding to learn the German language, as a protective device (again, not surprising) for when he must chair a gathering of Hitler scholars in the spring. Teaching the language warps the otherwise undistinguished face of the German instructor into a "grimacing humanoid" (71). The language cannot be spoken, it must be croaked, spewed, spurted. It is the very "language of strangulation" (74); as the instructor begins to speak German, it is as if a cord has been twisted about his larynx. Murray Siskind remarks that the instructor, who lives in the same boarding house, strikes him as someone who would find a corpse erotically attractive.

DeLillo carries on this German/death association. The gun left to Gladney by his father-in-law is a German-made Zumwalt. The district of Iron City where Willie Mink lives is called Germantown. And the nun who finally destroys Gladney's faith in language is a German immigrant.

14. To underscore Gladney's faith in the random patterns of language, constructs that are only as sturdy as the faith invested in them, Gladney interrupts the narrative at odd moments to list randomly three related proper nouns— nouns that have nothing to do with the narrrative in progress. For instance, the moment when the Gladney family is fleeing the toxic cloud, Gladney inserts "Krylon, Rust-oleum, Red Devil" (159), each a brand of spray paint. This sort of interruption happens eight times in the novel. More to the point, Gladney seems generally attracted to items of three; he usually groups answers in trios of nouns. Further, the novel itself is a series of three sections.

The unprepared reader could spend inventive time attempting to create a pattern, a reason for the patterns of threes, for the interruptions of the series; but the point is that such an investment of faith in something completely haphazard and random is exactly what Gladney busies himself doing—inventing patterns and then believing in them. Perhaps the reader, like Gladney, prefers to squeeze from the nouns some obscure reference to the action, thus allowing the reader to believe in pattern, in constructs. They indicate more the pathology of Gladney's character—from the chaos, assemble a manageable reality, a pattern.

15. DeLillo carefully works this difference between the thing and mere things. First confronted with the evidence of his exposure, Gladney, who has always been solaced by immuring himself in things (for instance, the shelves at the store), begins a tedious process of ridding his house of its accumulated junk—old, useless items catalogued by Gladney with a Whitmanesque relish. Yet, he can lose only his attachment to such things: the thing itself, that which defies and escapes the manipulation of his language system, that thing must still be faced. DeLillo uses variations on the word *thing* to reenforce Gladney's immersion in language, his refuge from the real.

16. Dylar, as chemically analyzed by a colleague of Gladney's, is a "wonderful little system" (188) and "a super piece of engineering" (229), yet another system for Gladney.

17. The association DeLillo makes between Murray and the white coloring of the generic food he always buys can be added to the association in American literature made between whiteness and death, from Melville's monstrous whale to Pynchon's monstrous Blicero. Here, DeLillo will go on to connect Murray with white noise, the message of death that Gladney must first reject before he can go to the overpass.

18. Interestingly, when Babette first tries to tell Gladney about her attraction to Wilder ("I think it's being with Wilder that picks me up"), Gladney without hesitation launches into a lengthy paragraph in which he analyzes the pleasures of the naive child. Such an analysis keeps Gladney within the boundaries of trying to capture something elusive within the clumsy web of language. Babette, herself already beyond belief in such trickery, corrects Gladney: "That may be true but there's something else about him that gives me a lift. Something bigger, grander, that I can't quite put my finger on." Characteristically, Gladney remarks, "Remind me to ask Murray," deciding without hesitation that Murray can code the attraction of Wilder into language (209). Indeed, Murray is clearly a menace to the children in Gladney's house—in one scene, as the children sit about the television reacting variously to what they see, Murray is with them furiously writing down what they say, encoding their reactions within the confines of language. It is Wilder, however, who particularly attracts Murray, and he voices a most unnerving preference for being near the child. During the evacuation, Wilder is missing momentarily, and Babette panics when Gladney jokes that Murray "stole him" (114).

19. Not surprisingly, these are just a few of the words Gladney desperately uses to try to define what sadness is compelling Wilder to sob. Confronted with something beyond his understanding, Gladney ropes it clumsily within an assault of nouns. It is as pointless as the doctor's advice. Gladney tries to define Wilder's crying by trying to get a hold on it through language.

20. DeLillo does use one minor character, the campus neurochemist Winnie Richards, as an early sunset watcher. Indeed, as Gladney follows her across campus in an effort to talk with her about the analysis she has done on the Dylar, she is simply standing, watching the sunset, where "the edge of the earth trembled in a darkish haze." Gladney, intent on finding out information, merely rates the sunset as inferior to other recent ones. Winnie Richards, compelled by the sight, remarks, "What can you think about in the face of this kind of beauty. I get scared, I know that" (227). That mixture of reaction, that movement beyond language, will mark the crowd of sunset watchers. Not surprisingly, Winnie Richards advises Gladney not to pursue Dylar, not to lose his awareness of endings; that knowledge, she tells him, helps humanity to define itself (228–29).

21. DeLillo, in a brief interview that accompanies Jayne Anne Philips's review of the novel in the *New York Times Book Review*, acknowledges the book's apocalyptic message: "I never set out to write an apocalyptic novel" (31). Yet, it is likely, given the context of the remark, that DeLillo was talking less about the traditional literary genre than about his novel's obsessive focus on death.

Epilogue

Next time what I'd do is look at
the earth before saying anything. I'd stop
just before going into a house
and be an emperor for a minute
and listen better to the wind
or to the air being still.

When anyone talked to me, whether
blame or praise or just passing time,
I'd watch the face, how the mouth
had to work, and see any strain, any
sign of what lifted the voice.

And for all, I'd know more—the earth
bracing itself and soaring, the air
finding every leaf and feather over
forest and water, and for every person
the body glowing inside the clothes
like a light.

William Stafford, "Next Time"

Epilogue

The Surer Grip, the Sweeter Berry

I have set before you life and death,
the blessing and the curse;
therefore choose life,
that both you and your descendants may live.
                                    Deuteronomy

On display in the Peace Museum in the heart of rebuilt Hiroshima are pocket watches, scorched and blackened, with tiny iron hands stopped exactly at 8:16—forever marking the ferocious stroke of a shattering moment when a city disappeared and with it a way of thinking, a way of perceiving the world, a way of perceiving ourselves. They mark as well the moment when the apocalypse itself reentered our history with alarming immediacy, so long relegated to dry-as-chalk tomes on historical curiosities, so long a part of the tragicomic excesses of fundamentalist religions, so long the amusing metaphor for world-weary artistes attracted to the challenge of rendering carefully and absurdly the death of metaphoric worlds. Now we no longer needed to imagine the end of the world: indeed, newspapers carefully debated it; scientists dispassionately described it; military strategists calmly planned it; politicians hotly pledged to avoid it. In its own way, apocalypse became the buzzword of the atomic age. And the boiling mushroom cloud that broke urgently toward the August skies over Hiroshima became a generation's most striking image: unrelentingly evil; undefinably powerful; and most ferociously, darkly attractive. As such, it resists the easy simplification into yet another emphatic moment in a grim, century-long act of witnessing the horrors humanity can visit upon its own species, a history that speaks in the cold, spare eloquence of grainy, black-and-white photographs of stacked, skeletal corpses; of open, mass graves in countrysides; of proud cities incinerated, their buildings stark shells; of children playing games among the rubble of the ruins. Such a history challenges centuries-old traditions that speak of the inherent dignity of life; but the mushroom cloud, with its simple symmetry, threatened finally what we cherish most—tomorrow.

The literature that has been driven to find its voice within the resonating thunder of that initial shudder has struggled to resist for nearly half a century the simple endgames of paranoia or powerlessness, waiting or ignorance. Such resistance has not been easy. Indeed, at times, our literary voice has spoken with the bored eagerness of a theater critic during a bad play: passionate in the anticipation of the end. Encouraged by an impressive arsenal of nuclear weaponry that expanded with casual exponential ferocity and promised a cataclysmic stroke measured in the sobering arithmetic of megatonnage, writers long after Hiroshima have propped up fictional worlds only to level them and then deliver odd lessons about humanity's stupidity or arrogance or ambitiousness.

But, commencing most emphatically with the startling immediacy of the Cuban missile crisis in 1962, that voice has argued passionately that its literature cannot afford to indulge such a flair for dramatic endings. These writers found in the cataclysmic imagination graceless images of a civilization reclining with the desperate hopelessness of a cartoon character at ease on a keg of powder within sound of the fierce hiss of a lighted fuse. The early works of Vonnegut and Coover and the works of Percy, Pynchon, Gaddis, and DeLillo argue that such a community cannot afford the simple exhaustion that marks the concession to the unforgiving dogmatics of cataclysm and speaks in a wearied voice bristling only with irritation and contempt untempered by hope or compassion. This literary voice would reject passivity—we cannot afford not to think about the unthinkable, cannot pretend to turn back the watches melted dead at Hiroshima. It would reject protest—such a threat cannot be batted away with the easy swing of protest signs. Slogans and chants cannot remedy a threat arsenaled in reenforced concrete silos.

What the twentieth century has so unnervingly fashioned and what these writers have finally faced is death on so large a scale that it discounts humanity. As its first step toward revival, this literature recognizes just such a death. It is death that snarls at the center of John/ Jonah's fantasy; it blows about the glowing embers of the Dresden moonscape in which Billy Pilgrim wanders; it calls the Brunists, sirenlike, to the hill; it gelds Tom More into the laughable cavalier; it splinters Tyrone Slothrop; it strangles the world of Liz Booth; and it breathes, steady and strong, in Jack Gladney's basement on unendurable nights when sleep will not come. Characters as different as Victor Charles and Oberst Enzian, Vince Bonali and Jack Gladney, begin by accepting the vulnerability that must come with any steady engagement of this century's history. Unwilling to temper such a look back with greeting-card simplicities or with the gee-whiz naivete that so quickly withers into ignorance and twists so damningly into rude postures suggesting ostriches with heads stuck into protective sands, these writers move characters from such recognition to resolution, the defiance of simply accepting that such a civilization is marked with ashes on its forehead. Where they have turned is toward the heart. When Vonnegut lovingly dances his comic arabesques on the thin ledge of today; when Coover challenges West Condon to accept the vulnerability of living in a century fractured and uncertain; when Percy finds the persuasive reassurance of eyes turned upward, full of sunlight; when Pynchon coaxes souls most thoroughly singed by history to pray nevertheless for humanity; when Gaddis teaches hope by suspending its delicate energy; when DeLillo leads Gladney to the overpass—then these writers defy the newer laws of historical gravity first written by the initial crack of light at Trinity Test Site.

It is the energy of that resistance that marks this literature's bravest affirmation, its commitment to its community, its ministering to a critical moment in history, a moment when we stand about our own history, the sun shadowed black by stacks of corpses piled like cordwood—that is the history of this century. Goliath-like, it glowers above; David-like, these writers have moved toward revival in most untraditional expressions, all within the tradition of the apocalyptic temper: the overwhelming caricature of the defeated John/Jonah; the hesitating moment under the spring sky in *Origins*; Tom More's humble ministerings in the AIDS hospice; Oberst Enzian's whispered prayer for the preterite; Gaddis's suspended period; DeLillo's service at the overpass.

Of course, fiction cannot resolve the anxieties of the nuclear age, cannot calm the generation living under the premise of Hiroshima. That generation is a tense and anxious one, as measured by the exaggerated sigh of relief that greeted the relatively low-impact INF agreement in late 1988. Hungry for good news, a people cheered the diplomatic stroke of that agreement, a pact urged more by the pragmatism of domestic concerns in the Soviet Union than by any reliable drive toward real arms reduction. And so we wait in a world we did not ask for. Surely, the apocalyptic temper has moved considerably from the image in *The Day of the Locust*: the quail, trapped and helpless, singing its sweet, hopeless song. That image was described a scant handful of years before the startled thrust of the mushroom cloud would create a generation in crisis with its own history, a generation straining for something finer than a sweet, helpless song.

The literature surveyed by this study offers not a chorus of giggling Pollyannas, but a family of Ishmaels, schooled in madness and determined to reclaim, nevertheless, the hope that is the birthright of any generation. From Vonnegut's early determination to survive the insanity into which he had been plunged to DeLillo's Gladney, who must accept vulnerability before he can begin the miracle of living, the stances assumed by these writers are struck precariously but nevertheless defiantly against the whirlwind of their own history. They are gestures that speak of consolation, a literature that reminds its moment in history of what John spoke so steadily from his rock prison on the Island of Patmos—that only in a dark time will the eye begin to see. Resisting as counterfeit gestures the shelter fictions that promise heroism in the ashes; resisting as snake oil the attractive promise of civilizations re-emerging, phoenixlike, from the nuclear cinder piles, this literature counsels that hope commences not in acquiescence or retreat, but in accommodation: the demanding gesture of Vonnegut's Malachi Constant, that backward look at this century's legacy, a troubled chronicle that seems nothing if not a fuse lit. That gesture, moved by a compassion for humanity, begins with acknowledgment and ends with resuscitation.

Confronting such a dilemma, when gestures of passivity or paranoia or helplessness come too easily, requires a literature of enormous energy, a vision that moves unashamedly toward a scale long diminished as the novel grew smaller and smaller, pulled more and more into itself, into the games playing of aesthetic exercises. It, the mystique and wonder of such an imminent stroke uncontained even within the powerful ambiguity and strange omnipotence of that appallingly simple pronoun, demanded a literature of a community—spirited, resistant, alive, vehement in its affirmation. It demanded us. Against the wailing of civil-defense alarms, against the nerveless assembling of nuclear warheads, against the heated rhetoric that called into existence the sundered world of nuclear politics, these writers cannot afford to whisper. And it is to them we turn. We cast suspicions on politicos, for they deal in the irrational jargon of nukespeak; we withhold faith from scientists, for they fashioned the Frankenstein that pounds at the door; we cast troubled eyes on the military, for it too often seems hungry; and we cannot move into the simple vernal embrace of a natural world, for that itself seems dwindling and threatened.

Clearly, the literature of this age cannot embrace nuclear annihilation itself within the logic of plot, but surely that literature has confronted the premise of Hiroshima. It opts for hope in a world where the geography of ground zero seems limitless and immediate, where the basic promise of a next generation seems casually tenuous; where we step into each decade tentatively, like children out too far on a frozen country pond. What these writers have confronted is not the simple stroke of nuclear fury, but the far more critical accommodation to death that marks this century's emerging history of exhausted possibilities and dead ends. If the watches stopped at Hiroshima, our hearts did not. The melted watch is a fitting suggestion of the new age, timed on a different watch that commenced its tremulous movement even before the lingering fires finally died out in Hiroshima. Hiroshima has proven a most demanding teacher. It has taught to the literature of this age the lesson of those webbed within the middest that has been the stuff of the apocalyptic temper since John addressed his community-in-crisis. If that explosion of roiling light revealed that humanity was indeed to be suspended much as that man dangling over the cliff, hanging precariously above the chasm and below the jaws of that hungry tiger, Hiroshima recalled with ferocity the lesson of that parable and the lesson of the apocalyptic temper: it is the tiger alone that makes the grip surer, the berry sweeter.

Works Cited
Primary Sources

Coover, Robert. *The Origin of the Brunists*. 1966. Reprint. New York: Seaver-Viking, 1978.

DeLillo, Don. *White Noise*. New York: Sifton-Viking, 1985.

Edwards, Jonathan. *Apocalyptic Writings*. Edited by Stephen J. Stein. Vol. 5 of *The Works of Jonathan Edwards*. 5 vols. New Haven, Conn.: Yale University Press, 1977.

————. *History of the Work of Redemption*. Vol. 2 of *The Works of President Edwards*, 9–395. 8 vols. Worcester, Mass.: Isaiah Thomas, 1808.

Gaddis, William. *Carpenter's Gothic*. New York: Sifton-Viking, 1985.

Melville, Herman. *The Confidence-Man: His Masquerade*. 1857. Reprint, edited by Hershel Parker. New York: Norton, 1971.

————. *Moby-Dick, or The Whale*. 1851. Reprint, edited by Charles Feidelson, Jr. Indianapolis, Ind.: Bobbs, 1964.

Percy, Walker. *Love in the Ruins: The Adventures of a Bad Catholic at a Time near the End of the World*. 1971. Reprint. New York: Avon, 1981.

————. *The Thanatos Syndrome*. New York: Farrar, 1987.

Pynchon, Thomas. *Gravity's Rainbow*. 1973. Reprint. New York: Bantam, 1974.

Vonnegut, Kurt, Jr. *Cat's Cradle*. 1963. Reprint. New York: Dell, 1981.

————. *Slaughterhouse-Five or The Children's Crusade: A Duty-Dance with Death*. 1969. Reprint. New York: Dell, 1984.

West, Nathanael. *Miss Lonelyhearts and The Day of the Locust*. New York: New Directions, 1962.

Secondary Sources

Agosta, Lucien L. "Ah-Whoom!: Egotism and Apocalypse in Kurt Vonnegut's *Cat's Cradle*." *Kansas Quarterly* 14.2 (1982): 127–34.

Alter, Robert. "The Apocalyptic Temper." *Commentary* 41 (June 1966): 61–66.

Andersen, Richard. *Robert Coover*. Twayne's United States Authors Series 400. Boston, Mass.: Hall, 1981.

Works Cited

Aron, Raymond. *The Century of Total War*. Garden City, N.Y.: Doubleday, 1954.

Auden, W. H. *For the Time Being: A Christmas Oratorio*. London: Faber, 1953.

Banta, Martha. *Failure and Success in America: A Literary Debate*. Princeton, N.J.: Princeton University Press, 1978.

Bass, Thomas Alden. "An Encounter with Robert Coover." *Antioch Review* 40 (1982): 287–302.

Bayer-Berenbaum, Linda. *The Gothic Imagination: Expansion in Gothic Literature and Art*. Rutherford, N.J.: Fairleigh Dickinson University Press, 1982.

Bercovitch, Sacvan. *The American Jeremiad*. Madison: University of Wisconsin Press, 1978.

Boyer, Paul. *By the Bomb's Early Light: American Thought and Culture at the Dawn of the Atomic Age*. New York: Pantheon-Random, 1985.

Branculli, David. "Vonnegut: New Book, New Mood." *Philadelphia Inquirer*, 6 May 1985, section F, 1 and 5.

Brians, Paul. *Nuclear Holocausts: Atomic War in Fiction, 1895–1984*. Kent, Ohio: Kent State University Press, 1987.

Brodtkorb, Paul, Jr. "*The Confidence-Man*: The Con-Man as Hero." *Studies in the Novel* 1 (1969): 421–35.

Browne, Corinne, and Robert Munro. *Time Bomb: Understanding the Threat of Nuclear Power*. New York: Morrow, 1981.

Brueggemann, Walter. *Genesis: A Biblical Commentary for Teaching and Preaching*, 73–97, Atlanta, Ga.: Knox, 1982.

———. *Tradition for Crisis: A Study in Hosea*. Atlanta, Ga.: Knox, 1968.

Buber, Martin. "Prophecy, Apocalyptic, and the Historical Hour." In his *Pointing the Way: Collected Essays*, translated and edited by Maurice Friedman, 192–207. New York: Harper, 1957.

Buck, Lynn. "Vonnegut's World of Comic Futility." *Studies in American Fiction* 3 (1975): 181–98.

Capouya, Emile. "Real Life in an Unreal World." Review of *The Origin of the Brunists*, by Robert Coover. *Saturday Review*, 15 Oct. 1966, 38–40.

Chesnick, Eugene. "Novel's Ending and World's End: The Fiction of Walker Percy." *Hollins Critic* 10.5 (1973): 1–11.

Coles, Robert. *Walker Percy: An American Search*. Boston, Mass.: Little, 1978.

Collins, Adela Yarbro. *Crisis and Catharsis: The Power of the Apocalypse.* Philadelphia, Pa.: Westminster, 1984.

Comerchero, Victor. *Nathanael West: The Ironic Prophet*, 1–50, 120–51. Syracuse, N.Y.: Syracuse University Press, 1964.

Cooper, James Fenimore. *The Crater, or Vulcan's Peak.* 1847. Reprinted in vol. 20 of *The Works of Fenimore Cooper.* 32 vols. New York: Collier, 1893.

Coover, Robert. "The Brother." In *Pricksongs and Descants: Fictions*, 92–98. New York: Dutton, 1969.

———. "The Last Quixote." *New American Review* 11 (1971): 132–43.

Cope, Jackson I. "Robert Coover's Fictions." *Iowa Review* 2.4 (1971): 94–110.

Cotton, John. "The Powring Out of the Seven Vialls: or an Exposition of the 16. Chapter of the Revelation; with an Application of it to our Times." London, 1642.

Cowart, David. *Thomas Pynchon: The Art of Allusion.* Carbondale: Southern Illinois University Press, 1980.

Davidson, James West. *The Logic of Millennial Thought: Eighteenth-Century New England.* New Haven, Conn.: Yale University Press, 1977.

———. "Searching for the Millennium: Problems for the 1790s and 1970s." *New England Quarterly* 45 (1972): 241–61.

Dewey, Bradley. "Walker Percy Talks about Kierkegaard: An Annotated Interview." *Journal of Religion* 54 (1974): 273–98.

Dillard, R. H. W. "The Wisdom of the Beast: The Fiction of Robert Coover." *Hollins Critic* 7.2 (1970): 1–11.

Donnelly, Ignatius. *Caesar's Column: A Story of the Twentieth Century.* 1891. Reprint. Cambridge, Mass.: Harvard University Press, Belknap Press, 1960.

Dorris, Michael, and Louise Erdrich. "Bangs and Whimpers: Novelists at Armageddon." *New York Times Book Review*, 3 Mar. 1988, 1, 24–25.

Dowie, William. "Walker Percy: Sensualist-Thinker." *Novel* 6 (1972): 52–65.

Dylan, Bob. "Day of the Locusts." *Lyrics 1962–1985.* New York: Knopf, 1985. 286.

Ellul, Jacques. *Apocalypse: The Book of Revelation.* New York: Seabury, 1977.

Eubanks, Cecil L. "Walker Percy: Eschatology and the Politics of Grace." *Southern Quarterly* 18 (1980): 121–35.

Festinger, Leon, Henry W. Riecken, and Stanley Schlachter. *When Prophecy Fails*. Minneapolis: University of Minnesota Press, 1956.

Fiedler, Leslie A. "The Divine Stupidity of Kurt Vonnegut." *Esquire*, Sept. 1970, 195–97ff.

Foster, Elizabeth S. Introduction to *The Confidence-Man: His Masquerade*, xiii–xcv. New York: Hendricks House, 1954.

Fowler, Douglas. *A Reader's Guide to "Gravity's Rainbow."* Ann Arbor, Mich.: Ardis, 1980.

Friedman, Alan J., and Manfred Puetz. "Science as Metaphor: Thomas Pynchon and *Gravity's Rainbow.*" *Contemporary Literature* 15 (1974): 345–59.

Friedrich, Otto. *The End of the World: A History*. New York: Coward, 1982.

Gaddis, William. "The Rush for Second Place." *Harper's*, Apr. 1981, 31–39.

Gado, Frank. "Interview with Robert Coover." *First Person: Conversations on Writers and Writing*, 142–59. New York: Union College Press, 1973.

Giannone, Richard. *Vonnegut: A Preface to His Novels*. Port Washington, N.Y.: Kennikat, 1977.

Giegerich, Wolfgang. "Saving the Nuclear Bomb." In *Facing Apocalypse*, edited by Valerie Andrews, Robert Bosnak, and Karen Walter Goodwin, 96–108. Dallas: Spring, 1987.

Giraudoux, Jean. *Sodome et Gomorrhe*. 1943. Reprinted in *Théâtre Complet*. Paris: Gallimard, 1982.

Godshalk, William Leigh. "*Love in the Ruins:* Thomas More's Distorted Vision." In *The Art of Walker Percy: Strategems for Being*, edited by Panthea Reid Broughton, 137–56. Baton Rouge: Louisiana State University Press, 1979.

Goen, C.C. "Jonathan Edwards and a New Departure in Eschatology." *Church History* 28 (1959): 25–40.

Goldsmith, David H. *Kurt Vonnegut, Fantasist of Fire and Ice*. Popular Writers Series 2. Bowling Green, Ohio: Bowling Green State University Popular Press, 1972.

Gordon, Lois. *Robert Coover: The Universal Fictionmaking Process*. Carbondale: Southern Illinois University Press, 1983.

Greiner, Donald J. "Vonnegut's Science Fiction and the Fiction of Atrocity." *Critique* 14.3 (1973): 38–51.

Hansen, Arlen J. "The Dice of God: Einstein, Heisenberg, and Robert Coover." *Novel* 10 (1976): 49–58.

Hanson, Paul D. *The Dawn of Apocalyptic*. Philadelphia, Pa.: Fortress Press, 1975.

Hardy, John Edward. "Percy and Place: Some Beginnings and Endings." *Southern Quarterly* 18.3 (1980): 1–25.

Haroutunian, Joseph. *Piety Versus Moralism: The Passing of the New England Theology.* New York: Holt, 1932.

Harris, Charles B. *Contemporary American Novelists of the Absurd*. New Haven, Conn.: College and University Press, 1971.

Harrison, J. F. C. *The Second Coming: Popular Millenarianism 1780–1850*. New Brunswick, N.J.: Rutgers University Press, 1979.

Hawthorne, Nathaniel. "Earth's Holocaust." 1843. Reprinted in *Tales and Sketches,* 887–906. Library of America Series. New York: Viking, 1982.

Hearron, William Thomas. "New Approaches in the Post-Modern American Novel: Joseph Heller, Kurt Vonnegut, and Richard Brautigan." Ph.D. diss., State University of New York at Buffalo, 1973.

Heckard, Margaret. "Robert Coover, Metafiction, and Freedom." *Twentieth Century Fiction* 22 (1976): 210–27.

Heimert, Alan. *Religion and the American Mind*. Cambridge, Mass.: Harvard University Press, 1966.

Hertzel, Leo J. "An Interview with Robert Coover." *Critique* 11.3 (1969): 25–29.

————. "What's Wrong with the Christians?" *Critique* 11.3 (1969): 11–22.

Hite, Molly. *Ideas of Order in the Novels of Thomas Pynchon*. Columbus: Ohio State University Press, 1983.

Holbert, John C. "'Deliverance Belongs to Yahweh!': Satire in the Book of Jonah." *Journal for the Study of the Old Testament* 21 (1981): 59–81.

Hume, Kathryn. "Robert Coover's Fiction: The Naked and the Mythic." *Novel* 12 (1979): 127–48.

Humphrey, Nicholas. "Four Minutes to Midnight." *Consciousness Regained: Chapters in the Development of Mind*, 194–209. New York: Oxford University Press, 1983.

Ibuse, Masuji. *Black Rain*. 1969. Translated by John Bester. New York: Bantam, 1985.

Jaher, Frederic Cople. *Doubters and Dissenters. Cataclysmic Thought in America, 1885–1918*. New York: Free Press of Glencoe, 1964.

Jaspers, Karl. *The Future of Mankind.* 1958. Translated by E. B. Ashton. Chicago, Ill.: University of Chicago Press, 1961.

Karl, Frederick R. *American Fictions, 1940–1980.* New York: Harper, 1983.

Kennedy, J. Gerald. "The Sundered Self and the Riven World: *Love in the Ruins.*" In *The Art of Walker Percy: Strategems for Being,* edited by Panthea Reid Broughton, 115–36. Baton Rouge: Louisiana State University Press, 1979.

Kermode, Frank. *The Sense of an Ending.* New York: Oxford University Press, 1967.

Ketterer, David. *New Worlds for Old: The Apocalyptic Imagination, Science Fiction, and American Literature.* Bloomington: Indiana University Press, 1974.

Klinkowitz, Jerome. *Kurt Vonnegut.* Contemporary Writers Series. London: Methuen, 1982.

Krafft, John M. " 'And How Far Fallen': Puritan Themes in *Gravity's Rainbow.*" *Critique* 18.3 (1977): 55–73.

Lacocque, Andre, and Pierre-Emmanuel Lacocque. *The Jonah Complex.* Atlanta, Ga.: Knox, 1981.

Langer, Lawrence L. *The Age of Anxiety: Death in Modern Literature.* Boston, Mass.: Beacon, 1978.

Lawrence, D. H. *Apocalypse.* 1931. Reprint. New York: Penguin, 1981.

LeClair, Thomas. "Robert Coover, *The Public Burning,* and the Art of Excess." *Critique* 23.3 (1982): 5–28.

———. "Walker Percy's Devil." *Southern Literary Journal* 10.1 (1977): 3–13.

Lewicki, Zbigniew. *The Bang and the Whimper: Apocalypse and Entropy in American Literature.* Contributions in American Studies 71. Westport, Conn.: Greenwood, 1984.

Lewis, R. W. B. "Days of Wrath and Laughter." In *Trials of the Word: Essays in American Literature and the Humanistic Tradition,* 184–235. New Haven, Conn.: Yale University Press, 1965.

Lifton, Robert Jay. *Death in Life: Survivors of Hiroshima.* New York: Basic Books, 1967.

Light, James F. *Nathanael West: An Interpretative Study.* 1961. Reprint. Evanston, Ill.: Northwestern University Press, 1971.

Lowell, Robert. "Fall 1961." In *For the Union Dead.* New York: Farrar, 1964.

Lundquist, James. *Kurt Vonnegut.* New York: Ungar, 1977.

Luschei, Martin. *The Sovereign Wayfarer: Walker Percy's Diagnosis of the Malaise.* Baton Rouge: Louisiana State University Press, 1972.

McCaffery, Larry. "An Interview with Robert Coover." In *Anything Can Happen: Interviews with Contemporary American Novelists,* edited by Thomas LeClair and Larry McCaffery, 63–78. Urbana: University of Illinois Press, 1983.

McConnell, Frank D. *Four Postwar American Novelists: Bellow, Mailer, Barth, and Pynchon.* Chicago, Ill.: University of Chicago Press, 1977.

McGinn, Bernard. *Visions of the End: Apocalyptic Traditions in the Middle Ages,* 1–36. New York: Columbia University Press, 1979.

McGuane, Thomas. "This Is the Way the World Will End." Review of *Love in the Ruins,* by Walker Percy. *New York Times Book Review,* 23 May 1971, 7, 37.

McKeating, Henry, ed. *The Books of Amos, Hosea, and Micah,* 71–154. The Cambridge Bible Commentary Series. Cambridge, England: Cambridge University Press, 1971.

MacLear, J. F. "New England and the Fifth Monarchy: The Quest for the Millennium in Early American Puritanism." *William and Mary Quarterly* 3d ser. 32 (1975): 223–60.

Mani, Lakshmi. *The Apocalyptic Vision in Nineteenth Century American Fiction: A Study of Cooper, Hawthorne, and Melville.* Washington, D.C.: University Press of America, 1981.

Martin, Jay. *Nathanael West: The Art of His Life.* New York: Hayden, 1970.

Mauchline, John, ed. Introduction to *The Book of Hosea,* 553–725. Vol. 6 of *The Interpreter's Bible.* 12 vols. New York: Abington, 1956.

May, John R. *Toward a New Earth: Apocalypse in the American Novel.* Notre Dame, Ind.: University of Notre Dame Press, 1972.

———. "Vonnegut's Humor and the Limits of Hope." *Twentieth Century Literature* 18 (1972): 25–36.

Mellard, James. "The Modes of Vonnegut's Fiction: Or, *Player Piano Ousts Mechanical Bride* and *The Sirens of Titan* Invade *The Gutenberg Galaxy.*" In *The Vonnegut Statement,* edited by Jerome Klinkowitz and John Somer, 178–203. New York: Lawrence-Delacort, 1973.

Mendelson, Edward. "The Sacred, the Profane, and *The Crying of Lot 49.*" In *Individual and Community: Variations on a Theme in American Fiction,* edited by Kenneth H. Baldwin and David Kirby. Durham, N.C.: Duke University Press, 1975. Reprinted in *Pynchon: A Collection of Critical Essays,* edited by Edward Mendelson, 112–46. Englewood Cliffs, N.J.: Prentice, 1978.

Middlekauff, Robert. *The Mathers: Three Generations of Puritan Intellectuals.* New York: Oxford University Press, 1971.

Miller, Perry. "The End of the World." *William and Mary Quarterly.* 3d ser. 8 (1951): 171–91.

Mojtabai, A. G. *Blessed Assurance: At Home with the Bomb in Amarillo, Texas.* Boston, Mass.: Houghton, 1986.

Mumford, Lewis. "Mirrors of a Violent Half-Century." In *In the Name of Sanity,* 100–110. New York: Harcourt, 1954.

New American Bible. New York: P. J. Kenedy, 1970.

Nowell, Irene. "The Book of *Jonah*: Repentance of Conversion." *The Bible Today* 21 (1983): 363–68.

Oakes, Urian. *New England Pleaded With.* Cambridge, Mass., 1673.

Olderman, Raymond M. *Beyond the Waste Land: The American Novel in the 1960's.* New Haven, Conn.: Yale University Press, 1972.

Ozick, Cynthia. "Fakery and Stoney Truths." Review of *Carpenter's Gothic,* by William Gaddis. *New York Times Book Review,* 7 July 1985, 1, 18–19.

Percy, Walker. *The Message in the Bottle: How Queer Man Is, How Queer Language Is, and What One Has to Do with the Other.* 1975. Reprint. New York: Farrar, 1983.

———. "Notes for a Novel about the End of the World." *Katallagete* 3 (1970): 5–12.

———. "Questions They Never Ask Me." *Esquire,* Dec. 1977, 170ff.

———. *The Second Coming.* New York: Farrar, 1980.

———. "The State of the Novel: Dying Art or New Science." *Michigan Quarterly Review* 16 (1977): 359–73.

Philips, Jayne Anne. "Crowding out Death." Review of *White Noise,* by Don DeLillo. *New York Times Book Review,* 13 Jan. 1985, 1, 30–31.

Pierson, William Harvey, Jr. *Technology and the Picturesque.* Vol. 2 of *American Buildings and Their Architects.* 4 vols. Garden City, N.Y.: Anchor, 1976–80.

Plater, William M. *The Grim Phoenix: Reconstructing Thomas Pynchon.* Bloomington: Indiana University Press, 1978.

Prescott, Peter S. "Slouching toward Bethlehem." Review of *Carpenter's Gothic,* by William Gaddis. *Newsweek,* 15 July 1985, 64.

Punter, David. *The Literature of Terror: A History of Gothic Fictions from 1765 to the Present Day.* London: Longman, 1980.

Reid, Randall. *The Fiction of Nathanael West: No Redeemer, No Promised Land,* 1–12, 116–63. Chicago, Ill.: University of Chicago Press, 1967.

Robinson, Douglas. *American Apocalypses: The Image of the End of the World in American Literature.* Baltimore, Md.: Johns Hopkins University Press, 1985.

Roemer, Kenneth M. *The Obsolete Necessity: America in Utopian Writings, 1888–1900.* Kent, Ohio: Kent State Univeristy Press, 1976.

Roethke, Theodore. "In a Dark Time." In *Collected Poems.* 1966. Reprint. Seattle: University of Washington Press, 1982. 239.

Rovit, Earl. "On the Contemporary Apocalyptic Imagination." *American Scholar* 37 (1968): 453–68.

Russell, D. S. *Apocalyptic: Ancient and Modern.* Philadelphia, Pa.: Fortress, 1978.

———. *The Method and Message of Jewish Apocalyptic: 200 BC–AD 100.* 1964. Reprint. Philadelphia, Pa.: Westminster, 1976.

Salemi, Joseph S. "'To Soar in Atonement': Art as Expiation in Gaddis's *The Recognitions.*" *Novel* 10 (1971): 127–36.

Sanders, Scott. "Pynchon's Paranoid History." *Twentieth Century Literature* 21 (1975): 177–92.

Scarlett, William, ed. *The Book of Jonah,* 871–94. Vol. 6 of *The Interpreter's Bible.* 12 vols. New York: Abington, 1956.

Schatt, Stanley. *Kurt Vonnegut, Jr.* Twayne's United States Authors Series 276. Boston, Mass.: Hall, 1976.

Schieck, William J. "The Grand Design: Jonathan Edwards' *History of the Work of Redemption.*" *Eighteenth-Century Studies* 8 (1975): 300–314.

Schley, James, ed. *Writers in the Nuclear Age. New England Review and Bread Loaf Quarterly* 5 (1983).

Schmithals, Walter. *The Apocalyptic Movement: Introduction and Interpretation.* 1973. Translated by John E. Seely. Nashville, Tenn.: Abington, 1975.

Schmitz, Neil. "Robert Coover and the Hazards of Metafiction." *Novel* 7 (1974): 210–19.

Schott, Webster. "All the Hidden Nuts Cracked Open." Review of *The Origin of the Brunists,* by Robert Coover. *New York Times Book Review,* 25 Sept. 1966, 4.

Schulz, Max F. *Black Humor Fiction of the Sixties: A Pluralistic Definition of Man and His World.* Athens: Ohio University Press, 1973.

Scott, Nathan. *The Broken Center: Studies in the Theological Horizon of Modern Literature.* New Haven, Conn.: Yale University Press, 1966.

Scott, Nathan. " 'New Heav'ns, New Earth': The Landscape of Contemporary Apocalypse." *Journal of Religion* 53 (1973): 1–35.

See, Carolyn. *Golden Days.* New York: McGraw, 1987.

Shroeder, John W. "Sources and Symbols for Melville's *Confidence-Man.*" *PMLA* 66 (1951): 364–80.

Siegel, Jules. "Who Is Thomas Pynchon and Why Did He Take Off with My Wife?" *Playboy,* Mar. 1977, 97ff.

Smith, Marcus, and Khachig Toloyan. "The New Jeremiah: *Gravity's Rainbow.*" In *Critical Essays on Thomas Pynchon,* edited by Richard Pearce, 169–86. Boston, Mass.: Hall, 1981.

Stafford, William. "Next Time." *New England Review and Bread Loaf Quarterly* 5 (1983): 616.

Stein, Gertrude. "Reflections on the Atomic Bomb." *Yale Poetry Review* 7 (1947): 3–4.

Stein, Stephen J. "An Apocalyptic Rationale for the American Revolution." *Early American Literature* 9 (1975): 211–25.

———. "A Notebook on the Apocalypse by Jonathan Edwards." *William and Mary Quarterly.* 3d ser. 29 (1972): 623–34.

Sutton, Walter. "Apocalyptic History and the American Epic: Cotton Mather and Joel Barlow." In *Toward a New American Literary History,* edited by Louis J. Budd, Edwin H. Cady, and Carl L. Anderson, 69–83. Durham, N.C.: Duke University Press, 1980.

Tanner, Tony. *City of Words.* New York: Harper, 1971.

Telotte, J. P. "A Symbolic Structure for Walker Percy's Fiction." *Modern Fiction Studies* 26 (1980): 227–40.

Thompson, Lawrence. *Melville's Quarrel with God.* Princeton, N.J.: Princeton University Press, 1952.

Tichi, Cecelia. "The American Revolution and the New Earth." *Early American Literature* 11 (1976): 202–10.

Tilton, John W. "*Slaughterhouse-Five*: Life against Death-In-Life." In *Cosmic Satire in the Contemporary Novel,* 69–103. Lewisburg, Pa.: Bucknell University Press, 1977.

Tuveson, Ernest Lee. *Millennium and Utopia: A Study in the Background of the Idea of Progress.* Berkeley and Los Angeles: University of California Press, 1949.

———. *Redeemer Nation: The Idea of America's Millennial Role.* 1968. Reprint. Chicago, Ill.: University of Chicago Press, 1980.

Vonnegut, Kurt, Jr. "Address to Graduating Class at Bennington College, 1970." In *Wampeters, Foma, and Granfalloons,* 159–68. New York: Lawrence-Delacorte, 1974.

———. *Breakfast of Champions.* 1973. Reprint. New York: Dell, 1975.

———. *Galápagos.* New York: Delacorte, 1985.

———. *Palm Sunday: An Autobiographical Collage.* New York: Dell, 1981.

———. *The Sirens of Titan.* 1959. Reprint. New York: Dell, 1977.

———. *Slapstick; or Lonesome No More!* New York: Delacorte, 1976.

Wagar, Warren W. *Terminal Visions: The Literature of Last Things.* Bloomington: Indiana University Press, 1982.

Weisenburger, Steven. "The End of History?: Thomas Pynchon and the Uses of the Past." *Twentieth Century Literature* 25 (1979): 54–72.

White, E. B. *The Wild Flag: Editorials from "The New Yorker" on Federal World Government and Other Matters,* 105–10. Boston, Mass.: Houghton, 1946.

Widmer, Kingsley. "The Last Masquerade." In *Nathanael West: The Cheaters and the Cheated,* edited by David Madden, 179–93. DeLand, Fla.: Everett/Edwards, 1973.

Wigglesworth, Michael. "The Day of Doom, or A Poetical Description of the Great and Last Judgement." 1662. In *The Puritans,* edited by Perry Miller and Thomas H. Johnson, 2:587–606. Rev. ed. 2 vols. New York: Harper, 1963.

Wilder, Amos N. "The Rhetoric of Ancient and Modern Apocalyptic." *Interpretation* 25 (1971): 436–53.

Wood, Michael. "Dancing in the Dark." Review of *Breakfast of Champions,* by Kurt Vonnegut, Jr. *New York Review of Books,* 31 May 1973, 23–25.

Wright, Nathalia. *Melville's Use of the Bible.* 1949. Reprint. New York: Octagon, 1969.

Wyden, Peter. *Day One: Before Hiroshima and After.* New York: Schuster, 1984.

Yates, Francis. "Giordano Bruno," 405–8. Vol. 1 of *The Encyclopedia of Philosophy.* Reprint. 16 vols. in 8. New York: MacMillan, 1972.

Zuckerman, Edward. *The Day after World War III.* New York: Viking, 1984.

Index